Seeing Symphonically

THE SUNY SERIES

HORIZONS OF CINEMA

MURRAY POMERANCE | EDITOR

Seeing Symphonically

Avant-Garde Film, Urban Planning, and the Utopian Image of New York

Erica Stein

Cover image: The final shot of *Bridges-Go-Round* parodies and critiques the touristic views of the city used by Circle Line and other engines of possessive speculation. (Shirley Clarke, Dir. *Bridges-Go-Round*. 1958; New York: Milestone Films, 2016. DVD. Courtesy of the Wisconsin Center for Theater and Film Research.)

Published by State University of New York Press, Albany

For information, contact State University of New York Press, Albany, NY
www.sunypress.edu

Library of Congress Cataloging-in-Publication Data

Name: Stein, Erica, author.
Title: Seeing symphonically : avant-garde film, urban planning, and the
    utopian image of New York / Erica Stein.
Description: Albany : State University of New York, [2021] | Includes
    bibliographical references and index.
Identifiers: LCCN 2021016729 (print) | LCCN 2021016730 (ebook) | ISBN
    9781438486635 (hardcover : alk. paper) | ISBN 9781438486628 (pbk. : alk.
    paper) | ISBN 9781438486642 (ebook)
Subjects: LCSH: City symphonies (Motion pictures)—United States—History
    and criticism. | City and town life in motion pictures. | Rhythm in
    motion pictures | Utopias in motion pictures. | Independent films—United
    States—History—20th century. | City planning—New York (State)—New
    York—History—20th century. | Urban renewal—New York (State)—
    New York—History—20th century. | New York (N.Y.)—In motion
    pictures. | New York (N.Y.)—History—1898–1951. | New York
    (N.Y.)—History—1951–
Classification: LCC PN1995.9.N49 S74 2021 (print) | LCC PN1995.9.N49
    (ebook) | DDC 791.43/627471—dc23
LC record available at https://lccn.loc.gov/2021016729
LC ebook record available at https://lccn.loc.gov/2021016730

10 9 8 7 6 5 4 3 2 1

For my mother, who drew my first maps of New York,
and for my father, who taught me to walk in it

Contents

Illustrations ix

Acknowledgments xiii

Introduction: Carving Out an Island 1

1 Tomorrow Has No Smell: *The City*, Regional Planning,
and the National Day 33

2 City/Text: *Weegee's New York*, Urban Renewal, and the
Miniature-Gigantic 73

3 Secret Passages: Symphonies of the Margins, Slum Clearance,
and Blight 113

4 Spectacle in Progress: Symphonies of the Center and
Advocacy Planning 153

5 Image/City/Fracture: *The Cool World*, the Urban Crisis,
and Nostalgia for Modernity 193

Coda: Repair 231

Notes 239

Bibliography 263

Index 273

Illustrations

I.1 The attenuated graduation ceremony in *Go! Go! Go!*   2

I.2 Lobby cards for *Little Fugitive* exemplify the relative
popular exposure and success independent cinema could
achieve in late modern New York.   21

1.1 An artist's rendering of *Democracity* at the 1939–1940
World's Fair emphasized viewers' elevated vantage point.   38

1.2 A point of view shot provides a survey of the town of
Shirley, Massachusetts in the opening section of *The City*.   55

1.3 A Black miner, wearing a prosthetic leg, enters a shack
in *The City*'s Pittsburgh section.   59

1.4 The second shot of *The City*'s New York section, which
composes an internal, embedded viewpoint.   62

1.5 A school from the Greenbelt section of *The City*. It
closely resembles the other municipal and office buildings
in the section.   69

2.1 A "bright hot light" shines on a midtown crowd in the
"New York Fantasy" section of *Weegee's New York*.   76

2.2 Det. Halloran ponders the case from an elevated vantage
point that mimics an urban planner's position and
miniaturizes New York in *Naked City*.   86

2.3 Optical effects diffract light around the lion sculptures that
guard the New York Public Library in "New York Fantasy."   98

2.4   The opening shot of "Coney Island" asserts the normality
      of the huge crowd it features.   103

2.5   One of the casual threesomes that populate the middle
      section of "Coney Island."   108

3.1   Black children playing in a vacant lot at the end of
      In the Street appropriate the camera as a toy.   129

3.2   The first shot of the bridge in *Under Brooklyn Bridge*
      defamiliarizes this iconic structure.   134

3.3   Ray and other indigent Bowery residents are seen through
      the prison-like bars at the local mission.   141

3.4   Joey goes on a quest for Pepsi bottles to turn into nickels
      and pony rides in *Little Fugitive*.   148

4.1   The first shot of Penn Station in *N.Y., N.Y.* eschews the
      optical effects for which the film is otherwise known.   154

4.2   The performance artist and composer Moondog plays the
      role of a modern-day Times Square saint in *Jazz of Lights*.   167

4.3   Floating capital in *N.Y., N.Y.*   178

4.4   Clarke depicts a series of caring, communal gestures that
      contest the empty movements of the spectacle in
      Melting Pot.   183

4.5   The final shot of *Bridges-Go-Round* parodies and critiques
      the touristic views of the city used by the Circle Line and
      other engines of possessive speculation.   186

4.6   St. Patrick's Cathedral glimpsed through the unfinished
      floor of the Tishman Building, linking past and future in a
      single image in *Skyscraper*.   189

5.1   The Fair Corporation published many promotional images
      like this one—a photograph of the diorama exhibited in
      the American Express pavilion—that erased the city and
      its environs.   196

5.2   The Panorama of the City of New York was one of several
      exhibits that appropriated aspects of the city symphony to
      communicate a nostalgia for modernity.   201

5.3 The artists' rendering of the exterior of the Johnson Wax
     Pavilion, in which *To Be Alive!* was screened for more than
     8,000 people a day.   204

5.4 The white police officers in *The Cool World* challenge
     the camera and the African American boys whose perspective
     it embodies.   213

5.5 *The Cool World* evokes the utopian aspects of liminality
     in its Coney Island scenes, particularly in Duke and
     Luanne's conversation by the ocean.   221

Acknowledgments

This project began at the University of Iowa, where Lauren Rabinovitz showed me new ways of thinking about the city and inspired my study of American independent film. As my dissertation chair, Lauren generously shared her own research notes from earlier projects on Shirley Clarke and World's Fairs, made me rewrite chapter 4 twice (it needed it), and line-edited the entire manuscript. I am indebted to her beyond measure for her guidance, infectious enthusiasm, and high standards in all things. I am also grateful to many other Iowa faculty: Rick Altman, Paula Amad, Corey Creekmur, David Wittenberg, Louis-Georges Schwartz, and Rosalind Galt. In the years since we both left Iowa, Rosalind has offered endless advice and support. I am so fortunate to have her as a teacher and a friend.

At Iowa I was exceptionally lucky to be part of an expansive and caring community of peers, including Peter Schaefer and Margaret Schwartz, Kevin MacDonald and Gina Giotta, Gerald Sim, Claudia Pummer, Jennifer Fleeger, Anastasia Saverino, Allison McGuffie, Leslie Delassus, Kyle Stine, Mike Hetra, Michael Slowik, David Oscar Harvey, and Alison Wielgus. Sushmita Banerji offered insight and commentary that invigorated every class we took together and sharpened my thinking about the politics of cinematic space. Her conversation, tough-mindedness, and encouragement have been highlights of the last fifteen years. Ofer Eliaz read each draft of this book and shaped my thinking and writing, while reminding me that they are the same thing, at every turn. At Iowa, the highlight of my week was walking over to Nilo Couret's apartment on Sunday afternoons for takeout and TV. Over a conference breakfast years later, he not only untangled a major structural problem that led to the current organization of this book but also shared his beignets. Each time I see him, in Ann Arbor or Seattle or Rio, he introduces me to something new, extraordinary, or just plain fun.

As this project evolved from dissertation to book, my thoughts on media and urbanism have been profoundly influenced and improved by discussions with colleagues like Brendan Kredell, Paula Massood, Mark Shiel, Shannon Mattern, Stan Corkin, Germaine Halegoua, Malini Guha, Merrill Scheleir, Josh Gleich, Lawrence Webb, Anna Viola Sborgi, S. Topiary Landberg, Josh Glick, Liz Patton, Nathan Holmes, Ling Zhang, Floris Paalman, Anthony Kinik, and Noelle Griffis. Noelle, Ling, Nathan, and Kathrine Model also helped revise the introduction and chapter 1 in our local writing group. A brilliant writer and an endlessly supportive mentor, Sabine Haenni first introduced me to many of the concepts central to this book. I am also grateful to the members of the 2019 SCMS Expanding and Reconsidering the City Symphony Seminar.

I was and am supported by the scholarly community at Vassar College. Mia Mask, Sophia Harvey, Shane Slattery-Quintanilla, Denise Iris, Alex Kupfer, and our staff make the Film Department a great place to work and teach. My research assistants, Lucy Rosenthal, Dylan Lynch, and Lena Stevens, contributed to every part of this project. Tahirih Motazedian, Osman Nemli, Krystle McLaughlin, Anne Brancky, Jasmine Syedullah, and Lori Newman have created a wonderful community of junior faculty, while Kenisha Kelly, Erin McCloskey, Lisa Brawley, and Katie Hite have generously used their experience to help me find my place at the College. This project benefited immensely from the Manuscript Review workshop that Katie introduced to Vassar. My session with Sophia, Lisa (who reminded me about several extremely useful urban planning resources), and Pamela Robertson-Wojcik, who generously came to campus as an external participant, was instrumental in articulating the central goals of this book.

Archival research for this book was conducted at the Wisconsin Center for Film and Theater Research and the Research Study Rooms at the New York Public Library (NYPL). At Wisconsin, I am especially grateful to Mary Huelsbeck and at NYPL to Melanie Locay. Funding from the Vassar Research Committee made possible the inclusion of many of the images I found there. At SUNY, I benefited from Murray Pomerance's lively conversation and careful editorial eye. Rafael Chaiken and James Pelz shepherded the project through the acquisition process, while Catherine Blackwell, Laura Glenn, and Ryan Morris walked me through the ins and outs of image rights, copy edits, and production. I also appreciate the comments made by three anonymous peer reviewers, which improved the manuscript in its late stages. An excerpt of an early version of chapter 1 appeared in *Media Fields Journal* 1, no. 3 (2011) as

"The Road to Heaven Twists: *The City*, Urban Planning, and Experiential Space," http://mediafieldsjournal.org/the-road-to-heaven-twists. An early version of the second half of chapter 5 appeared in *Studies in the Humanities* 42, no. 1–2 (2015): 223–58 as "Mapping the Blind City: The Urban Crisis and False Narrative in Shirley Clarke's *The Cool World*."

Finally, my friends and family have sustained me throughout the long gestation of this book. Nate and Thea Brown, Andy Guess, Freda Ready, Elise Corey, Becca Farber, Lauren Kurtz and Dave Dopson, Kelly Bonner and Jens Wegener, Erin Greenwell, Dan Hunt, Jenny Dixon, Kate Bowers, Katie Montgomery, Alycen Ashburn and Josh Knapp: thank you for hosting me on research trips to Madison, answering questions about 1950s Supreme Court cases, schlepping out to Flushing Meadows, and making sure I occasionally did things that weren't related to city symphonies. Rachael and Nick Hilliard have been constants in my life since the start of college, and whether hanging out in our neighborhood in the city, stargazing upstate, or getting very lost on the Isle of Skye, being with them has been a delight. Noelle Griffis appears in two places in these acknowledgments, only appropriate for a brilliant colleague and dear friend, who, more than anyone else, has been part of my daily experience of New York as I worked and talked through this book in coffee shops, theaters, and bars, and who has dragged me to the far reaches of the five boroughs in search of music and history.

My mom and dad, Paula and Bob Stein, have always been my biggest fans. Holding my hands so I could look up at the ceiling as we walked through Grand Central or sitting down to watch *The Wizard of Oz* again and again, they sparked my love for New York and for film. They have supported me in every way possible, from dutifully attending exhibits and screenings to sharing their memories of the 1964 World's Fair. My siblings and their husbands, Joanna Stein-Weiner and Scott Weiner, and Alex Stein and Tyler Ray, inspire me with their spirit of adventure and ability to make anyplace they live a welcoming home. Thank you for offering me a quiet place to work, evenings out, and an endless tolerance for weird movies. My nephews, Andy and Lucas Weiner, offered absolutely no help but did let me jump on their trampoline. Last and always, Andrew Kosenko's love is a joy and a gift, and I am endlessly glad to be his person.

Introduction

Carving Out an Island

Reality includes that which is not yet.

—Ruth Levitas

W ITH ITS FIRST SHOT, Marie Menken's city symphony *Go! Go! Go!* (1962–1964) declares its intention to remake and reimagine New York. As Menken's hand waves in front of the Brooklyn Bridge, her simple human gesture momentarily blots out the huge structure. The rest of the eleven-minute film realizes this intention and the inversions of scale that accompany it by depicting a day in New York through a combination of rapid time lapse and stop-motion photography, all edited together with dazzling montage. *Go! Go! Go!* uses a fixed, often low, vantage point to elide the differences of mass and building materials that determine the relative importance of various locations in the city. When a car traverses the Brooklyn Bridge early in the film, its bulk is largely held offscreen by tight framing and an extreme low angle that focuses on individual cables, lampposts, and the interplay of stone and steel, while denying a panoramic view of the bridge's iconic frame. The same treatment that removes the bridge's landmark nature grants it to the residential neighborhoods of Two Bridges, Chinatown, and the Lower East Side, which have more screen time than the bridge and are approached from the same camera height with a straight frame

1

line. Menken's use of a low vantage point and medium camera distance defamiliarizes the bridge, shrinking it to a more human size and emphasizing its tactile qualities. Applied to Chinatown, these same tactics make monuments of modest apartment buildings and sidewalk stands. With one exception, Menken never offers a complete view of a given site or action, always arriving in the middle of a boat's crossing of the Hudson River or cutting away from a garden party in progress. The exception is a college graduation ceremony, which is depicted from beginning to end over the course of two minutes (figure I.1). The length of the sequence is a mystery—why does it take up so much time?

Go! Go! Go! uses the rhythms of quotidian New York and a dense, syncopated montage aesthetic to pose and answer this question, which is part of its redefinition and critique of the urban environment. These qualities establish the film as a city symphony. Beginning with Sheeler and Strand's *Manhatta* (1921) and continuing with astonishing frequency through Tan Pin Pin's *In Time to Come* (2017), city symphonies have com-

Figure I.1. The attenuated graduation ceremony in *Go! Go! Go!* (Marie Menken, Dir. *Go! Go! Go!* 1962–1964; New York: Anthology Film Archives, 2010, 16 mm.)

bined documentary, experimental, and narrative techniques to produce a typical day in the life of a given urban environment. The films marry the classical unities of time, space, and theme to highly complex montage to depict the city as a cross-section of people, phenomena, and architecture. Historically, city symphonies appear in cycles. They emerge in periods and locations in which the definition and function of the city is being renegotiated through intensive urban redevelopment.[1] These cycles cohere around avant-garde movements, which provide an industrial and institutional context that facilitates the production and consumption of city symphonies. Such movements also generate a set of aesthetic practices that associate city symphonies with larger trends across contemporary visual media.

Whatever cycle they belong to, and no matter what kind of redevelopment they negotiate, city symphonies foreground the rhythms of urban existence. Rhythm is, like narrative, a matter of pattern recognition. It is a series of weak and strong stresses that, through repetition, achieve the status of rules and thereby make meaning. Rhythm, in the realm of the urban, is the law of how and in what ways the movements of bodies and the built environment reoccur. Rhythms contain and construct the *regulation* of urban existence.[2] They generate and interpret the increasingly complex movements in, and imaginings of, the city in modernity. When a city symphony like *Go! Go! Go!* builds its own rhythm out of everyday New York and then breaks it with something like the graduation scene, it is asking why the ceremony justifies this rupture. For what does this elaborate ritual prepare its adherents?

Menken answers the question by juxtaposing the graduation sequence with a depiction of an office plaza. The final shot of the graduation sequence features the students moving across and down a stage from left to right. The next sequence begins with an endless stream of white-collar workers flowing left to right along a Midtown Manhattan street, then entering the revolving doors of an office building in the style of Mies van der Rohe. This transition answers the question posed by the prior sequence. The graduation, a celebratory metonym for the entire capital investment in higher education and its promised access to self-improvement, social maturity, and economic success, prepares its initiates only for a never-ending series of identical movements throughout their working life. The questions that city symphonies like *Go! Go! Go!* ask through rhythm problematize and make visible the relations of production that produce the urban everyday.

In this book I argue that the New York city symphony cycle of 1939–1964 produced a Marxist critique of the patterns and regulation of everyday life as urban redevelopment transformed it on an unprecedented scale. During the mid-century, New York became a world capital, a cultural center, and a core of the American workforce. It also began to lose its middle-income population base to the surrounding suburbs and new Sun Belt cities, and demolished much of the housing and neighborhood structures its poor residents relied on. These changes are encapsulated by urban planning projects like the United Nations Headquarters, federally subsidized suburban developments like Long Island's Levittown, and the destruction of poor neighborhoods in the urban core like East Harlem. These projects followed different currents of urban planning, some of which had progressive goals or positive effects. Yet they all assumed and reaffirmed that capital had the ultimate right to shape the city and the lives within it. Each film of the New York city symphony cycle challenged this assumption. The tactics the films used varied with the specific kind of urban planning they addressed. They therefore display significant formal heterogeneity, ranging from abstract studies of architecture throughout the city's center, like Francis Thompson's *N.Y., N.Y.: A Day in New York* (1957), to emphatic portraits of a single peripheral neighborhood's residents, like Rudy Burckhardt's *Under the Brooklyn Bridge* (1953). Despite these diverse aesthetics, all of the films in this city symphony cycle produce a dialectic critique of a particular form of urban planning at the level of rhythm.

The New York city symphonies articulate their critique less through an analysis *of* rhythm than an analysis *with* rhythm. The Marxist sociologist Henri Lefebvre calls such a method "rhythmanalysis." Rhythmanalysis inscribes itself within the socio-spatial relations being studied, a "struggle against time within time itself."[3] Like other forms of dialectic, it uncovers the contradictions within a single idea, policy, or set of relations. It also surfaces the temporary resolution of those contradictions in subsequent ideas, policies, and relations. Rhythmanalysis has the power to take our perception elsewhere, to take us away from the society the relations under analysis produce to a place where we can "think that which is not thought."[4] This mode of analysis proceeds from a body—including a filmic one—that has become hypochondriac. The body is now conscious of processes, like breathing, that are usually automatic. Rhythmanalysis disarticulates and "unwraps the bundle" of the body's internal, intimate rhythms before extending outward to encompass the external patterns in which that body is enmeshed and "unbundle" those patterns as well.[5]

Rhythmanalysis estranges the current production of space. It allows an analyst to investigate and isolate rhythms while remaining

conscious of themselves as subject to them, rather than artificially erasing themselves as the point from which the analysis proceeds. This
visual intercession enables us to perceive the structuring absences that
organize our reality as well as the alternative to that reality circulat-
ing within it as otherwise excluded content.[6] Rhythmanalysis encompasses three structures of lived experience. The first is eurthymia, the
induced harmony of everyday life. The second is arrhythmia, a pause
in or other interruption of this harmony. The third is polyrhythmia, a
many-faceted, self-analyzing diagnosis of the everyday. Rhythmanalysis's
hypochondriac nature inserts a break in the eurthymia of a daily activity
or motion, such as the pattern of traffic lights at a crosswalk. In the
arrhythmic stutter of that break, the analyst pulls apart the enmeshed
strands of housing prices, federally subsidized automotive manufacture,
cycling lobbyists, environmental regulations, police surveillance, and
neighborhood advocacy groups that collectively determine how long
a red light lasts, and whether there is a crosswalk at all. Once these
multiple strands are visible, the flows of capital and state power that
inhere within them emerge in their contradictions: we can see the rules
behind the pattern.[7]

The New York city symphonies evoke the structure of the working
day via formal structures—including camera movement, editing, and optical effects—that articulate rhythm. Through these structures, the films
lay bare the delimiting of daily life under capital as shaped by urban
redevelopment. These formal techniques also surface an alternative social
order, another world, present in the same images. In this world, bodies take their own, nonproductive time. The New York city symphonies
organize what Lefebvre describes as an extraordinary sight not otherwise
possible.

> But look harder and longer. This simultaneity, up to a cer-
> tain point, is only apparent: a surface, a spectacle. Go deeper,
> dig beneath the surface, listen attentively instead of simply
> looking, of reflecting the effects in a mirror. You thus per-
> ceive that each plant, each tree, has its rhythm, made up of
> several: the trees, the flowers, the seeds and fruits, each have
> their time . . . Continue and you will see this garden and the
> *objects* (which are in no way things) *polyrhythmically*, or if you
> prefer *symphonically*. In place of a collection of fixed things,
> you will follow each being, each body, as having above all its
> time [emphasis in the original].[8]

Developing this symphonic sight allows for a knowledge of lived reality that, "without claiming to change life, but by fully reinstating the sensible in consciousness and in thought, enables the analyst to accomplish a tiny part of the revolutionary transformation of this world."[9] City symphonies like *Go! Go! Go!* develop a sight through montage and other aesthetics that looks at quotidian phenomena like a graduation ceremony and separates out the various rhythms, individual and collective, short and long term, bodily and mental, caught up in them. They trace these rhythms back to the regulations that produce them but, in separating them out, they also point to a set of alternate regulations that might change these rhythms and the lives they organize.

City symphonies have historically been called "symphonies" for three reasons. First, after Walter Ruttmann's *Berlin: Symphony of a Great City* (1928), which influenced many other films, even lending its name to Brazilian and Dutch symphonies made in the late 1920s and early 1930s. Second, because many early city symphonies were directly linked to various experiments in the cinematic image's ability to reproduce or do without qualities associated with sound. In these films, editing in particular took on the work of producing rhythms more commonly associated with musicality. Third, they are called symphonies because of the films' structure, in which the polysemic representation that results from their divergent themes, sights, and locations is rendered univocal once more through a triumphant resolution at their end.[10] Lefebvre's description of rhythmanalysis as symphonic sight provides another way of understanding the city symphony, one that ties its political critique to the kind of sight it engenders. By seeing symphonically, the New York city symphonies estrange and contest urban planning and capital's seizure of urban space. Their tiny revolutionary transformations teach us to desire the reconstitution of society around inhabitants' right to remake their city's physical and social spaces—and thereby its relations of production—as they see fit.[11] Through rhythmanalysis, the New York city symphonies "prevent the erasure of the past and the foreclosure of the future" and turn back "the assault by the present on the rest of time" by transforming the present into a series of presences that cannot be valued through exchange.[12] The New York city symphonies ask: what would a city constituted around something other than capital be like? What would determine its rhythms? What would New York look like if all its inhabitants got to make decisions about how it looked?

These are utopian questions, which have always sought answers in New York, particularly during the middle of the twentieth century.

Utopia is commonly understood as the representation of a place whose perfection is also the condition of its impossibility. When the term is attached to New York, it is as often used to describe the idealized view of early cinematic panoramas like Edwin Porter's *Coney Island at Night* (1905) as it is the urban planning that utterly remade the mid-century city. In these instances, utopia connotes an unrealistic, top-down project characterized by naive enthusiasm detached from extant social reality and the damaging failures that such unmoored dreams invariably generate. Yet for Marxist scholars like Louis Marin, Fredric Jameson, and Ruth Levitas, utopia is not so much a perfect place, or an impossible place, as it is the other of place. This other of place can, in fact, be generated by depictions of the everyday. For these scholars, utopia is a diagnostic procedure through which we can "imagine the reconstitution of society," as Levitas puts it.[13] These scholars define utopia as a figuration of the infinite and the bounded, a constant negotiation between unending freedom and perfect order. Utopia uncovers the structuring absences on which contemporary social relations are founded. It asks what must be left out, what must be made impossible even to think, in order for a society to exist. By locating such an absence, utopia exposes a society's constitutive contradictions. This allows utopia, simultaneously, to indicate other ways of living, societies founded on the very relations our own makes impossible.

Utopia in this sense, as neither one place nor its opposite, but rather a location suspended between them that helps us imagine the nature of both, has a particularly close association with New York. For example, in Jonathan Demme's *Swimming to Cambodia* (1987), the humorist and actor Spalding Gray explains his arrival in New York City in this way: "I knew I couldn't live in America and I wasn't ready to live in Europe, so I moved to an island off the coast of America." In this instance, New York is not utopian in the sense of being a perfect place, but utopian in that it clarifies the contradictions and commonalities shared by America and Europe. Gray's comments, where space stands in for larger sociocultural concerns, recall Michel de Certeau's description of Manhattan from his famous "Walking in the City" chapter in *The Practice of Everyday Life*. De Certeau calls the island a "stage of concrete, steel, and glass, cut out between two oceans (the Atlantic and the American) by a frigid body of water."[14] Gray and de Certeau use these islanding descriptions to construct New York, especially Manhattan, as a liminal space suspended between the United States and its Other(s). Though rendered especially poetic by these authors, the idea of New York as exceptional with regard to the rest of the nation, or even as opposed to it, is commonplace enough to inhere in advertising campaigns, critiques of infrastructure funding, and half-serious advocacy for the five boroughs' succession from the United States.[15] In every case, the city's island nature is articulated to a more abstract sense of absolute borders and irreducible differences.[16] These constructions resonate with Jameson's reminder that islanding is the first step toward the figuration of utopia; it is necessary that all utopias should be islands.[17] Marin argues the first formal literary utopia—Thomas More's 1516 book of the same name—is a reaction to Europe's newly discovered continent, the very large island, of America itself.[18] Gray's anecdote, and the discourse it typifies, suggests New York as America's own utopia.

That utopian status intensified between 1939 and 1964, a moment in American history when the federal government invested heavily in urban development while federal legislation shaped urban infrastructure and public housing. This period was atypical in its social relations and relations of production. It was notable for exceptional prosperity and social mobility, the unprecedented success and stability of labor, and an extraordinary degree of federal intervention in economics, social control, and urban planning.[19] This same quarter century brought New York into an unusual alignment with the national imaginary. One of the reasons the federal government invested so heavily in the planning and remaking of New York was that it privileged the city as the face the United States showed the world as a new global capital—one that offered proof of capital's success during the Cold War. Yet cold warriors and mainstream popular publications alike also named New York as the embodiment of un-American social policies, modes of governance, and racial and ethnic identities. In a 1961 article for the *New York Times Magazine*, Jacob Javits, New York state's widely respected, moderate Republican senator, summarized this paradox. Javits stated that, although New York City "occupies a unique role as America's showcase" as "the nation's largest port of entry and the home of the United Nations," its inhabitants had to understand that to many Americans, these very qualities "simply confirm the suspicion that New York City is somehow the center of what they consider foreign or radical thinking."[20]

The urban historian Samuel Zipp argues that, in this period, New York was both America's way forward to a globally dominant future and a deviant socio-spatial assemblage threatening the rest of the nation.[21] New York's utopian function was evident even in the language of mid-century planning debates, which repeatedly used island imagery to describe parts of the city. Proponents of public housing developments described them as "islands of hope" in otherwise derelict areas, while opponents claimed that these same structures destroyed the local social fabric by "islanding" themselves from the surrounding neighborhood.[22] During the mid-century, New York pioneered a mode of production and a mode of vision that consistently reinscribed this island identity and utopian function through urban planning and popular culture.

The New York city symphony cycle occurred in a city engaged in a frenzy of creative destruction and struggles over its own identity, struggles bound up in debates about the function and future of the urban as a global phenomenon. In 1939 and again in 1964, New York hosted World's Fairs, both of which were held on the outskirts of Queens, and both of which imagined a better future for urban forms and city living. Between—and in part inspired by—these "worlds of tomorrow," New York undertook an extensive remaking of its built environment and social structures through slum clearance, the erection of high-rise public housing, and infrastructure expansion, all of which were underwritten by federal policy and dollars. Such programs resulted in the erection of segregated, middle-income housing like Stuyvesant Town as well as civic landmarks like the United Nations, which plowed over the working-class Slaughterhouse District.

Urban redevelopment was only one-half of the federal government's policy during the middle of the twentieth century. The complement to urban redevelopment was suburbanization, which historians following Kenneth Jackson's pathbreaking *The Crabgrass Frontier* (1985) have called "the other subsidized housing." At the beginning of this period, federal agencies and policies subsidized the movement of the white middle class to newly built spaces outside the city. Moving a key segment of the labor pool outside the city required the construction of new infrastructure such as highways, a new quotidian rhythm built around cars and commuting, and new sites where capital could accumulate.[23] By the end of this period, the city began to deindustrialize as manufacturing concerns, factories, and other companies moved to the suburbs, also drawn there by state and federal subsidies, accelerating the withdrawal of federal and state funding from the city. That funding followed the white middle class to the suburbs, helping to develop the accumulation of capital on the spot outside the city center. These policies, urban redevelopment and suburbanization, reshaped the city's built environment while displacing large swaths of its population and redistributing their wealth upward, dispossessing poor people, especially people of color, in the name of the public good. Over the quarter-century between the World's Fairs, urban redevelopment was responsible for unprecedented partnerships of public and private capital, the privatization of previously public space, intensified economic stratification, and increased racial segregation.

This redevelopment especially focused on mobility, both the literal movement of the workforce and the figurative movement of capital through the built environment. Signature urban redevelopment undertakings—including infrastructure projects like the Brooklyn–Battery Tunnel and the Cross Bronx Expressway, subsidized suburbanization, the modernization of workers' housing in the urban core, and the increase of green spaces in the city—all promote movement. Yet this movement was paradoxically tied to a discourse, including in popular culture, that imagined this newly freed, highly mobile, productive, and perfected city as a unified, coherent, transparent, and static image. For example, prewar planners turned to aerial photography to instantly capture the true flaws of the extant city and disclose exactly what would need to change to fix it. Postwar popular film like Jules Dassin's *Naked City* (1948) alternated elevated shots with street scenes to generate an X-ray of criminal activity for its detectives to set right. Later, even intellectuals who contested the way urban planning was destroying the city's social fabric advocated understanding and negotiating the city through an immobile mental map.[24] One way to understand these images is as an induced or false eurhythmia that turns the varied patterns generated by urban bodies, both human and architectural, into artificial harmony. Stilling the city's rhythms in an image abrogates the need for a truly transformed city that is valued for things other than productivity and whose rhythms are generated by the needs of its inhabitants. Mid-century planning and popular culture produced New York as a place that inhabitants always already master and control because they can visually decode and consume it.

To critique mid-century New York, to unpack the relations of production it makes possible, to indicate its structuring absences, requires setting this image into motion and examining the rhythms that constitute it. Thus, a city symphony like *Go! Go! Go!* proceeds by teasing out the tangle of spatial practices that the dominant production of space congeals into an image. It identifies the false harmony on which their unification in/as the present depends and induces a pause or fracture by reversing the relative spatial and temporal primacy of a monument like the Brooklyn Bridge and a marginal neighborhood like the Lower East Side. It subjects the forces that compel bodies through the revolving doors of white-collar industry to an analysis that makes their contradictions and exclusions, and therefore the future and the past they deny, palpable.

As New York was redeveloped between 1939 and 1964, city symphonies proliferated within New York's experimental, documentary, and independent film communities. These communities initially emerged around Amos Vogel's Cinema 16, the country's first subscription film society, and later through the New American Cinema movement. These institutions assembled a critical density of independent filmmakers like Lionel Rogosin, Marie Menken, and Shirley Clarke. They enabled the collective, direct distribution of their work. As Lauren Rabinovitz has shown, members of the New American Cinema sought to generate a New York–based production, distribution, and exhibition network that offered an alternative to Hollywood, garnering larger audiences and popular exposure for independent cinema.[25] In part because of this goal, filmmakers and gatekeepers in the community understood not only the short experimental subject but also the documentary and the independently financed and distributed fiction film as key aspects of the New York avant-garde. This openness to mixed and multiple film forms suggests why the city symphony, which has always been a hybrid mode, was a core component of the New York avant-garde during this period.

The New York city symphonies formed an intensive cycle of films between 1948 and 1964, with progenitors released earlier in the decade and at the 1939 World's Fair itself. City symphonies were some of the most popular films screened at Cinema 16 and found a surprisingly broad audience beyond it. Films like *N.Y., N.Y.* were extensively reviewed in the *New York Times* and played to sold-out audiences at the Museum of Modern Art. Others, like Shirley Clarke and Willard Van Dyke's *Skyscraper* (1959), represented the United States at festivals and world's fairs. The makers of the New York city symphonies defined themselves and their films against Hollywood, and against America as a set of standard visual iconographies attached to purportedly shared values as depicted in Hollywood's product.

The New York city symphonies thereby contributed to the utopian nature of the relationship between New York and America during the mid-century. Their use of rhythmanalysis, however, raises them to the level of utopian critique. They think, they criticize, they do, in the way that Gilles Deleuze understands cinema itself—rather than its creative personnel or its audiences—as capable of directly theorizing social reality.[26] In his study of montage in politically engaged postmodern and postcolonial cinema, Christopher Pavsek makes a similar claim, that such utopian films think or hypothesize through their aesthetics, with the inherent contradiction of "thinking in images" granting them the power of a negative dialectic.[27] Pavsek argues that cinema and utopia's privileged relationship extends into a mutual project: "the promises of cinema will be realized only when the promises of emancipation that slumber uneasily in the history of humankind have also been met."[28] Like the films Pavsek studies, the thought process of the New York city symphonies occurs in their aesthetics; they theorize social reality through their development of rhythmanalysis. Their symphonic sight picks apart the quotidian rhythms and epochal trends that make up mid-century New York and diagnose what that city must render impossible in order to exist. The films make intelligible what the current production of space otherwise forbids from thought: a city to which capital has no right. The New York city symphonies illuminate the structuring absences and constitutive contradictions of the mid-century production of American urban space. They surface this epoch's organization around the rescaling of capital to the national level, the channeling of property and capital into the hands of white elites, and the reinscription of the urban center as a space of exchange. They also indicate the rules and patterns that would coalesce an alternative to this space, one planned around urban inhabitants' right to their city.

The term *right to the city* is used by contemporary Marxist urbanists like the critical geographer David Harvey, and was originated by Lefebvre in the 1960s.[29] For Lefebvre, to have "the right to the city" is to have the ability and the power to determine what urban space is for, to direct the processes and policies of urbanization and development, and to have unfettered access to the places that result. Since the Enlightenment, capital has reserved this right for itself. As a result, the purpose of the city is to increase the exchange value of the urban ensemble, both individually and collectively. This means that the maximization of exchange value shapes urban development and determines the circumstances under which public and private spaces may be accessed. This rule generates the patterns of everyday life, including the terms under which inhabitants of the city interact with the state, with capital, and with one another, as police and citizens, landlords and tenants, and competitors for jobs, homes, and education.

What could a city be if its spaces were constructed as something other than real estate? If ownership of a place meant more than title to its maximum possible ground rent? For Lefebvre, this alternative city would be organized around encounter. For "the masses [to] have the right to the city" they require the right to encounter one another outside the demands of exchange value—demands so central to the rhythms of daily life in the city that it is difficult to imagine interactions that do not depend on them. A city organized around the right to encounter one another would not always consist of encounters that were friction-less, or kind, or peaceful. They would include theater and riots, people's markets and public comment sessions alike. Lefebvre's point is that the rules and rhythms that coalesced the relations of production, as well as social relations, would be fundamentally different from what they are now. A city based on the right to encounter one another would be a collective work of art always in progress, what Lefebvre calls an *oeuvre*. This masterwork is produced through formal and informal festivals and public performance as well as the various rhythms engendered as we go about our quotidian activities with one another; the work of art is our artful urban living.[30] The New York city symphonies indicate what this work of art might look like through the gaps left by the rhythms of the current city, the one structured by exchange. They identify the ways in which this extant city depends on the exclusion, the structuring absence, of the rights of inhabitants to shape their city, and the contradictions that arise from this.

Constructing the City Symphony

Cycles of city symphonies arise during historical moments in which the definition of the city is being renegotiated, often due to new forms of urbanization and their impact on daily life. These cycles are linked insti-tutionally and aesthetically to avant-garde groups, as well as to the film forms and languages developed by those groups. In the 1920s and early 1930s, city symphonies were produced across many countries, including the United States, The Netherlands, Brazil, and Japan. They coalesced as a distinct cycle in continental Europe, where countries like France and Germany not only produced their own films but also popularized those of others.[31] This cycle includes the best-known examples of the form as a whole: Ruttmann's *Berlin* and Dziga Vertov's *Man with a Movie Camera* (1929). Films in this cycle display a classically "symphonic" logic, com-bining experimental and documentary techniques with footage of mon-uments and marginal areas alike to produce a "multipartite but unified and coherent performance."[32] These films are aligned with diverse avant-garde movements and styles, including Constructivism, Surrealism, and Impressionism, and espouse politics as divergent. However, from William Ulricchio's 1982 account to Steven Jacobs, Anthony Kinik, and Eva Hielscher's 2018 study, scholars agree that the films in this cycle "all insist that they be understood as one day-in-the-life of the city in question."[33]

The city symphonies of the first cycle—including New York–set films like *Manhatta* and Jay Leyda's *A Bronx Morning* (1931)—established the genre's core semantic and syntactic properties. These films include: poetic or observational documentary style; experimental montage, super-imposition, and stop-motion effects; interpolated and often allegorical fiction content; twenty-four hour, day-in-the-life structure; concentration on the working day and typical forms of labor; a section focusing on lei-sure activities; a kaleidoscopic visual logic that evokes the overwhelming sensorium of modernity and articulates its characteristic fragmentation to the films' own montage aesthetic.[34] The first cycle films use these tactics to establish themselves as the proper cinematic form of urban modernity, capable of parsing this new epoch and offering its audience compre-hension, or even control, of it. They foreground many of the "shocks," from the assembly line to a newly electrified landscape, which assaulted the modern urbanite, and teach the audience how to negotiate these jolts.[35] Laura Marcus associates the 1920s city symphonies with a larger tradition in modernist culture of using rhythm to access, articulate, and celebrate aspects of bodily and "savage" existence that otherwise resist rational discussion or figuration.[36] This can include a problematic but still often sympathetic ethnographic gaze that penetrates and celebrates subcultural and minority spaces. However, the primary function of the first city symphonies was ultimately tutelary, instructing the audience on how to negotiate the physical reality of the modern city through the visual reality of film.[37]

This function, and its stakes, are especially evident in *Berlin: Sym-phony of a Great City*. Ruttmann's film begins with a predawn sequence set in the natural world. A train then departs this rural area for the city. The train encounters increasing signs of urban modernity along the way. The pace and complexity of editing accelerates until the train arrives in a cathedral-like station in the urban center. The opening simultaneously suggests the primordial landscape along the Spree before the city and its environs were built, a heavily telescoped history of urbanization, and the rhythms of the daily commute. The day that follows is organized around the mechanization and gendered division of industrial labor and domestic space, privileging the pace set by men who labor outside the home and the consumption by women this enables. *Berlin's* five acts depict preparations to leave the house, morning shift, lunch break, afternoon labor and consumption, and the nighttime leisure activities the wages earned in the previous acts make possible. Throughout, a "cross-section logic," which uses montage to concatenate many spaces articulated to social difference, predominates.[38] For example, in the lunch sequence, multiple classes and social groupings are observed, each in their proper place with their proper food: the rich in decadent dining halls lingering over multicourse meals, lower-middle-class workers enjoying a convivial discussion while eating sausages in beer gardens, and beggars bolting crusts of bread on church steps. The film implies that this spatialization and *naturalization* of class is the proper way to view the city and fend off modernity's disorienting effects through an afternoon scene in which a woman, fascinated and disconcerted by a pinwheel in a shop window, commits suicide.[39] The 1920s films' "perspectives, skewed angles, rapid and rhythmic montage, special effects, and iconography became a kind of shorthand for modern metropolitan life."[40] They strongly influenced the American city symphonies made in New York, Chicago, and elsewhere in the early 1930s, which tended to "realize urban views" that directly referred to their European predecessors.[41] The original cycle and its off-shoots were engaged with the kinds of urban structures that dominated the 1920s, and this engagement informed their aesthetics.

Therefore, it is not surprising that the next city symphony cycle's aesthetics are quite distinct from these first films; they changed along with the kind of urban development they engaged. The second city symphony cycle emerged in the 1940s and 1950s in concert with the rise of the New York avant-garde and what would become New American Cinema. These films engage, display commonalities with, and comment on the late modern period. Late modernity comprises the years 1939–1964, between the slowing and stabilization of modernity's technological and economic innovations in the late 1930s and the acceleration of global flows of capital and a service-based economy in the mid-1960s. Late modernity in the United States is characterized by the rescaling of capital to the regional and national level through the production of debt-financed infrastructure like the federal highway system. It is also shaped by the federal underwriting of suburbanization and ghettoization through the Federal Housing Act of 1949, the race, income, and ethnicity-based exclusionary policies imbricated with this and other housing policies, and the role urban planning played in them.[42]

This new embodiment of capital, racial discrimination, and state power was produced by and reproduced in spaces in which time pooled and evaporated unevenly, in which premodernity and the slow onset of a postindustrial mode of production built an uneasy, conjoined existence. Modernity proper, stretching from the 1890s through the early 1930s and attaining its most typical characteristics in the 1910s and 1920s, is a concentrated space bound together through evolving technologies and infrastructures, an ever-accelerating mechanistic force. Late modernity, by contrast, is organized by a time that is out of joint, by the proliferation of nonsynchronous spaces. Edward Dimendberg describes late modernity and its spaces "as a tension between a residual culture and urbanism of the 1920s and 1930s and its liquidation by the technological and sociological innovations accompanying World War II, as well as the simultaneous dissolution of this new social compact of the 1940s and 1950s by the society emerging in the 1960s, in which the simulacra and spectacles of contemporary post-modern culture are clearly visible."[43]

The New York city symphonies are produced by and against late modernity, and so it is not surprising that they disarticulate the rhythms that characterize the best known 1920s films. This second cycle affirms that, although city symphonies have been closely associated with European modernism, the form has always had an affiliation with American— especially New York–based—independent cinema. As Jacobs, Kinik, and Hielscher show, *Manhatta* has a strong claim not only as the first city symphony but also as the film that, through its successful and much imitated international distribution and marketing, truly provides the paradigm of the form.[44] In addition, several important New York–set city symphonies of the late 1920s to early 1930s indicate the importance of this form to the "lovers of cinema" who made up the prewar American film avant-garde.[45] The mid-century New York films, then, built upon a local symphonic tradition, but emerged out of a more organized and institutionalized avant-garde than their predecessors. They also tended to respond thematically and aesthetically to the 1920s European films rather than their more proximate ancestors.

The late modern New York cycle consists on the one hand of films like *Under Brooklyn Bridge*, and, on the other, films like Shirley Clarke's *Bridges-Go-Round* (1958). The former explore marginal areas through an observational documentary style and a focus on the human body while the latter engage the urban center through an abstract-expressionist experimental aesthetic and a focus on the built environment. *Go! Go! Go!* typifies this second group, and one of the major effects of its stuttering time-lapsed and single-frame images is to disarticulate and abstract human figures until they appear to be part of the city's architecture, as with the office workers discussed earlier. Whether concerned with the margins or the center, every film in the New York cycle tests the norms of the 1920s city symphonies. They distort their predecessors' grand panoramic views and pretenses to encompass the city through a curated selection of "typical" sites and sights. Instead, they emphasize, and empathize with, the exceptional and the grotesque. Fittingly, films of this cycle derive their impressions of the city's nature as much from sustained observation of and interaction with specific people or places as from adherence to a regimented temporal schema that allows for uniform spatial concatenation.

Following these two most coherent cycles, important city symphonies can be found in the work of California-based filmmakers like Bruce Baillie, Dominic Angerame, and Pat O'Neill through the 1990s. These filmmakers often focused on historical and geographic scale, as with Baillie's studies of the industrial spaces around San Francisco in *Castro Street* (1966) or O'Neill's evoking of the environmental pressures that reveal Los Angeles as an integral part of a regional ecology in *Water and Power* (1989). More recently, Singapore and China have been home to city symphonies like Tan Pin Pin's *Singapore GaGa* (2005) and Cao Fei's *Haze and Fog* (2013), respectively. These films engage with exceptionally rapid urbanization, its disruption of traditional social bonds, and the transformations of national space under globalization. The history of the city symphony maps the changing loci of political-economic and cultural power, forms of urbanization, and independent film across the span of the past 100 years.[46]

In addition to the cycles and clusters described above, city symphonies are central to commercial cinema's urban vocabulary across many different popular genres. Much of the lexicon of the cinematic city can be traced to the city symphony. Just as city symphonies crystallize a number of early cinema's attempts to represent the modernizing cities with which they were mutually constitutive, during and after the 1920s cycle popular genre film and art cinema alike drew on the form's established grammar to organize their urban depictions.[47] Thus, Scott Bukatman discerns a symphonic logic in MGM A-pictures such as Vincente Minnelli's *The Clock* (1945) and in the world-building of science fiction films like Ridley Scott's *Blade Runner* (1982), while Tom Gunning detects it in film noir like John Auer's *City That Never Sleeps* (1953). These scholars align such films with the symphony tradition because of their construction of the urban as a space of chance encounters among a diverse cross-section of people and places, as well as their foregrounding of quotidian rhythms.[48] Similarly, popular film critics use "city symphony" as a shorthand to describe commercial features that place narrative and thematic emphasis on urban environments and communities, as well as the impressionist editing style used to shape them. For example, reviews of independent films like Jim Jarmusch's *Paterson* (2016) and Kenneth Lonergan's *Margaret* (2011) describe them as displaying the logic of— or simply as being—city symphonies.[49] Outside their distinct cycles and attendant avant-gardes, city symphonies pervade the mediascape to the extent that they have become the default, even expected, language with which to denote an urban environment.

Given the city symphony's complex history and highly varied syntactic and semantic form, it is no surprise that studies of this genre conflict in terms of corpus and definition, perhaps even more so than studies of popular genre film. For example, Scott MacDonald understands the city symphony as part of a larger impulse within independent film to record, memorialize, and critique place. For MacDonald, the city symphony is "a film that provides a general sense of life in a specific metropolis by revealing characteristic dimensions of city life from the morning into the evening of a composite day."[50] This definition is widely shared across writing about city symphonies. It echoes John Grierson and Siegfried Kracauer's midcentury discussions of the form, which address the first city symphonies of the 1920s. It also informs Jon Gartenberg's survey of city symphonies in New York from 1905 to 2008.[51] Beyond this shared definition, however, major divergences in corpus and emphasis emerge. These range from Gartenberg's extremely inclusive definition to Stavros Alifragkis and François Penz's highly exclusive one. For Gartenberg, city symphonies are not part of historically determined cycles but instead a constant impulse within and aspect of the production of moving images in New York. They include early *actualités* and panoramas like *Coney Island at Night*, feature films like Ray Ashley, Morris Engel, and Ruth Orkin's *Little Fugitive* (1953), and contemporary documentaries like Mark Street's *Fulton Fish Market* (2003). For Alifragkis and Penz, by contrast, the term *city symphony* properly applies to films made during the original cycle. These authors understand the city symphony predominantly as an historical form that "makes it possible to construct a cinematic rhetorical argument about the city without resorting to traditional dramatic action, based on main protagonists."[52]

Like the above accounts, I understand the city symphony's core features to be the temporal boundaries of the day, spatial and narrative organization through montage, and emphasis of signifiers of modernity. However, my corpus and definition are based on a claim Penz made elsewhere with Andong Lu. Describing the frustration of trying to pin down the city symphony and its canon, Penz and Lu stated: "It is as though every film is having to reinvent the genre."[53] This exasperated insight guides how I understand city symphonies and which films I discuss. I ask how and why each city symphony reinvents its genre in terms of semantics, syntax, and industrial/institutional concerns. I highlight those films that most radically and comprehensively "reinvent" the genre, through new subject matter, formal strategy, industrial/economic context, or political orientation. Furthermore, I understand *the films themselves*, rather than programmers or scholars, as reinventing the genre, by which I mean that the critical work the films do is internal to them. I am chronicling the work that they do as historically specific representations of particular contradictions of capital as manifested in the rhythms that constitute the everyday. I ask less what a city symphony is and more what a city symphony does. As rhythmanalysis, a city symphony engages the rules and regulations that organize daily life. That life, and those rules, vary with urban development, and so too does the city symphony. Tracking changes in the city symphony's form discloses evolutions in forms of development; the films' aesthetics change to preserve their function. When a given city symphony has to reinvent its genre, the dimensions of that reinvention tell us something about how the city is being reinvented. At the same time, because city symphonies contribute to urban redevelopment as part of visual culture and challenge it as utopian critique, their reinventions also reshape the city.

These aesthetic and functional aspects are informed by questions of reception and generic evolution. That is, to what extent were the films produced within the city symphony tradition, marketed through it, and consumed with reference to it? To what extent is each film central to the form's dialectical elaboration of itself? For example, Lionel Rogosin's docudrama *On the Bowery* (1956) depicted a weekend in the life of indigent alcoholics in the eponymous neighborhood. It was made within an avant-garde film subculture that privileged the symphonic form and was consumed within a popular culture that acknowledged, positioned, and responded to it in the context of the city symphony, as contemporary reviews and interviews make clear.[54] The reception history of such films highlights the heterogeneous nature of city symphonies. As Jacobs, Kinik, and Hielscher argue, these films have been consumed in multiple contexts, from political clubs to Hollywood editing suites. Those contexts change which aspects of the films—their documentary footage, their montage editing, their use of social types—are emphasized by viewers, which in turn impacts future programming and production.[55]

The New York city symphonies were in some ways the most popular of the films made by local avant-garde institutions. They helped attract large audiences to Cinema 16 and other film societies. They also familiarized mainstream critics like the *New York Times* writers Howard Thompson and Bosley Crowther with the genre, which in turn gave the films commercial exposure and success unusual for independent cinema.[56] This popularity meant that the feature-length fiction city symphony *Little Fugitive*, about a boy who runs away to Coney Island, registered with viewers familiar with New York's street photography tradition as a documentary of the daily lives of poor children, and yet was reviewed by popular publications like *Life* and *Newsweek* as boasting "one of the best child actors to come along in years" and crafting a charming, "rich and funny" plot (figure I.2).[57] Readers of the specialist journal *Quarterly Review of Film, Radio, and Television* encountered the first description in a writeup of *Little Fugitive*'s debut at the Venice Film Festival, and commercial theatergoers saw the second on lobby cards that proclaimed the film "an all-American hit!" In this case, the film's use of symphonic montage and equation of its protagonist's circadian rhythms with the city's enabled its popularity with and consumption by varied audiences. On a textual level, these same symphonic aspects articulated a rhythmanalysis that excavated the regulations urban planning and capital imposed even on a space of leisure like Coney Island.

Little Fugitive reminds us that, while the fictional aspect of city symphonies is well known—ranging from scripted content in Alberto Cavalcanti's *Rien que les heures* (1926) to the soundstages of Cao Fei's *La Town* (2015)—predominantly narrative works generally have not been considered part of the canon.[58] In postwar New York, the confluence of increased location shooting by Hollywood productions and the importance of fiction feature films to the local avant-garde intersected with a robust cycle of city symphonies. As a result, many popular independent and genre features—including *On the Bowery*, *Little Fugitive*, Shirley Clarke's *The Cool World* (1963–64), and *Naked City*—drew on the grammar, themes, and politics of the city symphony. These films' relationship to the city symphony should be understood as a spectrum, one that takes

Figure I.2. Lobby cards for *Little Fugitive* exemplify the relative popular exposure and success independent cinema could achieve in late modern New York. (Original Lobby Card for *Little Fugitive*. Billy Rose Theatre Division, the New York Public Library for the Performing Arts. T-LC.)

into account their aesthetics, politics, and reception context. This spectrum ranges from, on the one end, films that are city symphonies in terms of their politics, aesthetics, and reception, to films, on the other end, that appropriate symphonic language, subsume it within the norms of a popular genre, do not articulate a rhythmanalysis of urban development, and were not produced or consumed within the institutional context of the New York city symphony cycle. In the middle of this spectrum we find films that combined the aesthetics of the city symphony with those of other genres in a way that primarily addressed the audiences and institutions associated with the city symphony and articulated a dialectic critique of extant conditions.

That is, on the near end of the spectrum are *On the Bowery* and *Little Fugitive*. As Gartenberg asserts, these films *are* city symphonies. As docudramas and neorealist adjacent fiction, they contribute to the "multiple genres" of experimental, documentary, and independent film that made up New York's long history with the city symphony. These films show "social and class contrast" through the city's changing spaces, linked through stylized montage.[59] They consistently associate their characters with social types and place them within a study of mass culture and crowds. Their temporality, including deadline structures, are worked into compressed time frames that emphasize the city's circadian rhythms. These aesthetic features articulate a rhythmanalysis that uncovers the workings of state power and capital in leisure areas—one an abject place of unemployment, the other a celebrated place of pleasure—usually understood as separate from the city's normative organization of space, time, and labor. These films' aesthetics and politics led programmers and critics to recognize and describe them as city symphonies, as noted above.

In the middle of the spectrum, *The Cool World* relates the story of a teenage Harlem gang member, combining crime genre plot beats with an extended use of symphonic aesthetics, particularly in opening, closing, and transitional sequences. The film's director, Shirley Clarke, was a key member of the New York avant-garde, showing her work at Cinema 16, collaborating with other directors of city symphonies, and making her own. This experience is reflected by the film's use of symphonic tactics. By wrapping the crime narrative in the symphonic form, *The Cool World* interprets its protagonists' actions as symptomatic of a city regulated by white supremacy rather than as a proximate cause of urban dysfunction, constantly juxtaposing the rhythms of the gangster film with those of the city symphony. As Nathan Holmes notes, the crime film "hyperbolizes social dynamics, throwing into relief the habits and assumptions of our behavior."[60] By combining the crime film with the city symphony, *The Cool World* cultivates this hyperbolic quality into a rhythmanalysis that negates the association of poor Black neighborhoods with criminality, instead defining white supremacy's denial of African American New Yorkers' right to the city as criminal.

At the far end of the spectrum are films like *Naked City*, a procedural noir that follows the progress of a murder investigation in New York over the course of a few weeks. Throughout the film, the case's progress is contrasted with the repeated patterns of work, commuting, and leisure undertaken by the city's population, who at times stymie the investigation with their sheer numbers. *Naked City* is not a city symphony. Its symphonic elements do not compose a rhythmanalysis and are subordinated to the norms of the noir. Here, a Hollywood genre film appropriates symphonic language, particularly the representation of the urban cross-section via montage, to lay claim to realism and authenticity without using that language to diagnosis or critique the rhythms that make up the city. Moreover, *Naked City*, unlike *The Cool World*, *Little Fugitive*, or *On the Bowery*, was consumed by general audiences in large commercial theaters primarily as entertainment, rather than as personal expression, documentary, or a critique of social ills in an art theater or film society.

Emphasizing the political function and reception context of city symphonies not only expands the kind of films I consider as city symphonies, it also leads me to reject the contention that city symphonies, particularly the New York cycle, squander their potential for political representations of, or interventions into, the city.[61] For many critics, such squandered potential is a sin of omission, a retreat into aestheticism, pure formalism, and indulgent self-expression, especially when compared with more recent, politically explicit, and often purely documentary work.[62] These authors—including MacDonald and Gartenberg, as well as Jacobs, Kinik, and Hielscher—argue that New York city symphonies either ignore the regulations of life in the city or celebrate them as charming, fascinating patterns without challenging the forces that organize them. They are ultimately reacting to early analysis by Grierson and Kracauer.[63]

Grierson in particular set the terms of the discourse with his 1931 review of Ruttmann's film, which was integrated into his 1941 critique of the genre. Grierson roundly excoriated *Berlin: Symphony of a Great City* for its fascination with industrial technologies and depiction of urban inhabitants as collectively resembling those technologies.

> By uses of tempo and rhythm, and by the large-scale integration of single effects, [city symphonies] capture the eye and impress the mind in the same way a military parade might do. But by their concentration on mass and movement, they tend to avoid the larger creative job. What more attractive (for a man of visual taste) than to swing wheels and pistons about in ding-dong description of a machine, when he has little to say about the man who tends it? And what more comfortable if, in one's heart, there is avoidance of the issue of underpaid labor and meaningless production? For this reason I hold the symphony tradition of cinema for a danger and *Berlin* for the most dangerous of all film models to follow.[64]

Grierson's analysis turns on the inverse relationship between the visual stimuli and sense of plenitude produced by the film's form and that form's ultimate, "dangerous," emptiness, which "avoids" grappling with social relations and dulls the viewer's awareness of them. For Grierson, Ruttmann's film naturalizes the crushing rhythms of industrialized urban modernity and extends their compulsion to the audience rather than diagnosing their effects. This analysis has proved definitive, particularly through the implicit connection Grierson makes between New Objectivity and fascist aesthetics, which Kracauer later made explicit.[65] Grierson's influence, however, extends beyond the reception of *Berlin: Symphony of a Great City*. It has aligned the symphony tradition as a whole with intimations of a shallow formalism that barely masks a malicious world view.

More recent discussions of the city symphony have combined Grierson's distrust of its fascination with surfaces with the sense that this fascination amounts to a claiming of those surfaces as the urban ideal.[66] As James Donald puts it, the city symphony is a cinematic entry in a larger tradition that imagines the urban as entirely transparent, logical, and rational, and as perfected or perfectible because of such characteristics. For Donald, this tradition falls under the ideological umbrella of "the utopianism of the Ideal City," an "extreme" to be avoided as it amounts to "a fantasy of pure space."[67] Similarly, Carsten Strathausen understands *Man with a Movie Camera* as a technotopia that is ultimately unable to grapple with or understand the uncanny aspects of the modern city that it seeks to deny and repress.[68] Even authors who write positively about city symphonies, like Alexander Graf, do so by focusing on the pleasure their visual play engenders, emphasizing montage's ability to provide the viewer with a complex, transportive experience that, like its musical namesake, lets the audience escape into a world in which opposed emotions and sensations are harmoniously resolved.[69] Despite the many nuanced analyses of widely varied films across a nearly hundred-year span, the city symphony retains the patina of Grierson's negative assessment, and does so because the form is understood to present a naive image of an idealized urban environment. That is, city symphonies are closely associated with the conventional wisdom of utopia as a shallowly conceived, impossible idealization.

If we instead understand the films as utopian instruments of Marxist analysis that articulate their social critique and their intimation of another world through rhythmanalysis, then both their potential and their limitations look very different. As Louis Marin argues of utopian fiction, they are "ideological critiques of the dominant ideology."[70] A city symphony suspends the usual working of ideology through representation by "bring[ing] into play through its textual structure the ideological organization by which it is itself caught."[71] City symphonies, like other utopian forms, mark the place of ideology by indicating, through negation and exclusion, what ideology makes impossible and removes from its representational field, and so from thought.[72] As utopian critiques, city symphonies face the same condition of limitation that Marin ascribed to utopian fiction. That is, city symphonies simultaneously critique the dominant socio-spatial order and indicate an alternative to it through a single representational field. However, that alternative is subject to and limited by the ideology it critiques and in which it is enmeshed; city symphonies, like all utopias, can only imagine a world that is otherwise through the language available to them in the world as it is. This limitation has its own critical function. As Ruth Levitas argues, utopia points beyond itself; its horizon of representation does not *only* mark its own condition of impossibility or ideological enmeshment.[73] Utopia allows "pure contradiction to be thought." It is a dialectic whose "empty place" of synthesis and resolution teaches us to want another world. Utopia "educates our desire," turning it away from reverie and imagined "elsewheres," and, by indicating the incoherence and intolerability of our present, trains that desire toward another way of being in the here and now.[74]

Like all utopias, the New York city symphonies' tether to the society they diagnose prevents the alternative social orders they point to from manifesting at their point of enunciation. In the case of the New York city symphonies, this tether is the films' treatment of race. The successive policies that remade late modern New York underlies and reinscribes America's identity as a space capital defines through whiteness and claims for white citizens. When the federal government began building new family housing outside the city in the 1930s, the towns were racially segregated. Privately funded middle-income developments like 1942's Stuyvesant Town that sought to keep such families in the city were also legally segregated, while the city's public housing often enforced de facto segregation, even in previously integrated neighborhoods. At the same time, suspicions of New York as un-American turned on a sense of its ethnic and racial difference from the rest of the country, particularly the idea that it was home to race mixing at the neighborhood level.[75] The New York city symphonies surface the ways in which not just the right to the city, but specifically the right of people of color to occupy and remake the city, was the absence that organized the five boroughs' redevelopment.

However, the films are not explicit in their condemnation of this absence or in the rejection of New York as a properly white space. Moreover, with a few exceptions, like Arthur Fellig and Amos Vogel's *Weegee's New York* (1948), the New York city symphonies fail to center people of color onscreen. As the final film in the cycle, *The Cool World*, attests, this diminution of race results in films that cannot imagine a world in which Black and brown New Yorkers remake the city according to their needs. The films illuminate race as the structuring absence of urbanism in late modernity. However, restrained by the nature of utopia as much as by the biases of their white directors and the film culture that sponsored them, they also reinscribe its absence and, in doing so, reach their horizon of limitation.

To Glimpse the Here and Now

To explore the New York city symphonies' utopian critical functions and limitations, this book is organized through two parallel maps of the late modern city. First, it charts the New York city symphonies in relation to the urban planning and visual culture they subject to rhythmanalysis. Second, it traces their aesthetic transformations from the 1939–1940 New York World's Fair to the 1964–1965 New York World's Fair. The first map examines several different forms of urban planning practiced in New York during this period, tracing the intertwining of the state and private capital throughout this period. During the New Deal and during World War Two, the federal government dominated planning theory and practice in concert with public intellectuals and professional architectural and planning organizations. After the war, capital increasingly took the lead in planning, until the federal government withdrew much of its funding and oversight from urban redevelopment to concentrate on the suburbs. This shifting partnership gave rise to multiple forms of urban planning, which included regional planning, urban renewal, slum clearance, and advocacy planning. Although these planning models are highly diverse in intellectual origin, method, and intent, they all intersect in the career of one man, who was involved in the remaking of New York's built environment and social space across the late modern period: Robert Moses.

Beginning in the 1920s, Moses used a series of appointments to city and state agencies to amass power and reshape the city. At the outset of his career, Moses was a reformer, taking on city and state machine

politics in support of progressive civic movements. One of his most celebrated early projects was the transformation of a huge ash heap in eastern
Queens into the bucolic site of the 1939–1940 New York World's Fair.
By 1939, Moses served as Parks Commissioner, chair of the Triborough
Bridge and Tunnel Authority, and President of the Jones Beach Park-
way Authority, among other posts. After the war, he went on to over-
see the construction of the United Nations and Stuyvesant Town, the
demolition of multiple city neighborhoods, and the erection of high-rise
public housing. Moses's selection of projects and use of funds helped
make New York an alternative national capital during late modernity.
His major infrastructure projects literally reshaped the city's skyline and
drastically redeveloped its public space. These projects displaced more
than a quarter-million New Yorkers and made it increasingly difficult for
New Yorkers of color to access public space or maintain private housing.[76] Eventually, resistance to these projects and the rise of new forms of
planning led to the diminishing of Moses's power. His last major project,
leading the 1964–1965 World's Fair Corporation, was something of a
private sinecure offered after he was forced to step down from several
state and city posts. His failure to make the Fair profitable contributed to
the end of his career. As Hilary Ballon and Kenneth Jackson put it, "The
good Moses of the 1930s is associated with the government's ability to
act on the public's behalf, and the bad Moses of the 1950s–60s mirrors
a loss of faith in government to act wisely, particularly in urban affairs
where governmental programs, however well intended, had destructive
consequences."[77]

Moses's trajectory, to which I return briefly in several chapters,
offers a kind of legend to the map of urban planning drawn across the
book, linking its different forms together and highlighting their differences, particularly the changing power dynamic between state power
and private capital during this period. Despite the distinct character of
each of the forms of urban planning active in late modern New York,
the mid-century was unified through the kind of vision Moses's redevelopment of the city generated. From 1939 to 1964, planners, city
workers, intellectuals, and activists, despite often very different political
orientations, all established a transparent, legible, and imageable city as
an urban ideal. This city-as-image produced and valorized a space that
is uninhabitable in practice and resists critical theorization as well as
transformative praxis.

The second map, drawn by the city symphonies themselves, shatters
this image and sets it into motion. This map is a utopian travel narrative

that allows us to recognize and desire what is excluded from thought by the late modern redevelopment of New York: the city as a collective work of art that the masses have a right to shape as they will. The New York city symphonies suspend late modernity's production of space and vision as they combine in the reduction of the city to an image, picking out the rhythms congealed within this image. Each chapter explores a different triad of planning, image, and rhythmanalysis. In every case, I begin with a dominant urban planning policy in its historical order of appearance. I explain how that policy generated a specific visual figure to reproduce and justify itself while reducing the city to an image. I then elucidate how a group of city symphonies estranged that figure, excavating the absented spatial practices that construct it and the policies that generate it while indicating socio-spatial alternatives to it. This interlocking, three-part model captures the central characteristics in the specific policy under discussion in each chapter and the figurative image it generated, as well as the vastly different forms individual city symphonies assume as they analyze these various types of planning and visualization.

Chapter 1, "Tomorrow Has No Smell: *The City*, Regional Planning, and the National Day," uses the 1939 New York World's Fair, specifically its popular attraction *The City*, to explore the relationship of New York and urban planning at the dawn of late modernity. Regional planning was the subject of multiple exhibits at the World's Fair. Its anti-urban logic was consonant with a white nationalism justified by the figure of the national day. *The City* purports to celebrate this kind of planning by presenting all of American history as a metaphoric "national day" that naturalizes the superiority of nonurban spaces it explicitly lauds for their segregation of functions and implicitly celebrates for their racial segregation. However, the film's regionally planned towns registered on screen as troublingly static, devoid of motion and, implicitly, of the possibility of lived experience within their confines. *The City* diagnoses the anti-urban, segregationist logic at the heart of garden cities, which defined a uniquely American future as a future limited to white citizens.

Chapter 2, "City/Text: *Weegee's New York*, Urban Renewal, and the Miniature-Gigantic," uses two films released during the same month in 1948, the city symphony *Weegee's New York* and the film noir *Naked City*, to explore how planners implemented urban renewal through projects like the United Nations headquarters and the figure of the miniature-gigantic.[78] *Naked City* typifies the ways in which urban renewal projects married abstracted, transparent, and highly legible views of the city (the miniature) to embodied and incoherent street-level spaces (the gigantic).

It obscures the alienating effects and rescaling of capital caused by the era's dominant social policy. By contrast, *Weegee's New York* imagines the city as a multiracial, queered, democratic assemblage. *Weegee's New York*'s disarticulation of the miniature-gigantic also results in splitting experimental and documentary aesthetics between its two sections, thereby reversing common concepts of space. The capitalist spaces of Midtown become a funhouse fantasy through optical effects while Coney Island becomes a fleshy republic through observational techniques. In using different techniques to produce the two spaces, *Weegee's New York* radically reformulates the aesthetics of the city symphony, tactics the city symphonies that followed it would imitate.

In chapter 3, "Secret Passages: Symphonies of the Margins, Slum Clearance, and Blight," *In the Street, Under Brooklyn Bridge, On the Bowery*, and *Little Fugitive* depict marginal spaces through observational documentary and fiction techniques. They focus on human bodies and communities to the exclusion of the built environment and deal with local festivals that break the rhythms of the everyday. Building on the techniques and politics of street photography, particularly those of the New York Photo League, directors like Helen Levitt, Rudy Burckhardt, Lionel Rogosin, and Morris Engel modified the city symphony's typical montage structure to document how everyday life in marginal areas was delimited by the figure of blight, which was central to slum clearance policies. They analyzed the bodily restrictions to which poor people and people of color were subjected by slum clearance, and the extent to which the image of a coherent city depended on the equation of these populations with blighted spaces.

Chapter 4, "Spectacle in Progress: Symphonies of the Center and Advocacy Planning," explores the films through which the New York cycle is most commonly defined: *N.Y., N.Y.*, Ian Hugo's *Jazz of Lights* (1954), Stan Brakhage's *Wonder Ring* (1955), *Bridges-Go-Round*, and *Skyscraper*. These films critiqued the figure of the spectacle and the advocacy planning then emerging to challenge the policies described in earlier chapters. For advocacy planners, to have the right to the city is the ability to sufficiently image the city and consume that image as spectacle. The symphonies of the center's concentration on surface allows them to atomize and estrange the spectacle. They do so by defamiliarizing human bodies, foregrounding monumental architecture, and using highly abstract experimental techniques. The films produce the center as an oeuvre that is a space of play and fantasy linked to a time outside accumulation.

Each of these chapters tracks changes in urban planning and particular images of the city, but they consistently reaffirm the ways in which
late modernity is characterized by attempts to produce an imageable city.
This changed with the end of late modernity and the onset of the urban
crisis in the mid-1960s. At this point, New York exchanged its role as an
economically expanding city of the American future, whose order generated and was guaranteed by its imageability, to a blind abyss with no
future that must be removed from the nation. Chapter 5, "Image/City/
Fracture: *The Cool World*, the Urban Crisis, and Nostalgia for Modernity,"
examines the onset of the urban crisis, the figure of the abyss, and the
continued longing for the perfect city as legible image it implies. This
new stage in urban history and its anti-image required a new rhythmanalysis. *The Cool World* teases out the rhythms that constitute the dawn of
deindustrialization and late capital as a production of space that cannot
be narrated at all. In doing so, the film depicts Harlem as a prototypical
New York space, rather than an alien threat to the city, and traces the
irrational restrictions placed on the movements of its Black residents.

In many ways, a utopian pause defined the quarter century between
the two Worlds Fairs. Between 1939 and 1964, very little significant utopian theory or fiction was published. Before, during, and after the war,
plans to comprehensively remake the world were instead the province
of totalitarian regimes.[79] In the United States, this led critics on both
the left and right to call "utopian" those federal programs they saw as
authoritarian. These programs included regional planning, urban renewal,
and slum clearance. The advocacy planners who decried these programs
explicitly defined themselves and their methods as anti-utopian. As a
result, they drastically decreased the federal government's direct interventions into urban development, but also enabled capital's claim to the
city unrestrained by state power.[80] The epoch ended as the urban crisis
rendered the possibility of utopia itself unthinkable for the American city.

The New York city symphonies provided the utopian content and
critique otherwise missing from the late modern period. Their most
important utopian operation was their diagnosis of this period as one of
stasis. As a whole, the New York city symphonies illuminate the extent to
which late modernity, a time of endless transition and attempts to generate social relations characterized by a harmonious rhythm, is defined by a
pathological stillness. In late modern New York, the plays of motion that
make up the everyday, the strong and weak patterns that determine our
experiences of different places and times, are ultimately futile and meaningless. These frantic movements compose social and political stagnation.

They accomplish nothing but to reinscribe capital's claim to the city and its inhabitants. The static rhythms of late modern New York ultimately deny bodies, both architectural and human, their time: their past, their future, and their occupation of the present as presences. The New York city symphonies not only make this deadened and deadly image visible, they help educate their viewers' desire toward a world in which these bodies take their time and their place.

1

Tomorrow Has No Smell

The City, Regional Planning, and the National Day

IN THE SPRING OF 1939, E. B. WHITE took a trip to see the future. He had a miserable time. "Carrying a box of Kleenex" as his "ethmoid sinuses broke down," White arrived in the far reaches of Queens, where the New York World's Fair of 1939–1940 had just opened. Unable to catch his breath or enter fully into the celebratory mood of his surroundings, temporarily experiencing his otherwise healthy, socially privileged body in terms of its "discomfort," White was not, perhaps, best suited to the charms of "The World of Tomorrow": "When you can't breathe through your nose, Tomorrow seems strangely like the day before yesterday." The 1939 World's Fair was held in what is now Flushing Meadows/Corona Park. Dubbed the "World of Tomorrow," it was dedicated to imagining ideal cities of the future. Perhaps because of its author's crabby and "clammy" state, White's account of the Fair was bathetic in the extreme. White continually juxtaposed the Fair's lofty claims to imagine the future and better the present with the petty annoyances and imperfections he experienced while navigating it with "embittered heart and slowed step." As White has it, there was "a wait of a few minutes to enter the future," and this bottleneck at the ticket booth only represented the end of a longer, unprepossessing journey: "The road to Tomorrow leads through the chimney pots of Queens."[1] Although he was enthusiastic about AT&T's long-distance demonstration, noting that

"I'd be there this minute if I were capable of standing up," his report-ing on the Fair's theme exhibits, such as *Democracity* and *Futurama*, was highly ambivalent.[2] These exhibits were dedicated to the Fair's central World of Tomorrow theme, which they imagined by depicting urban America's future. White dutifully described the impressive technology and cinematic wizardry in these exhibits without endorsing the kinds of societies they imagined. In fact, he critiqued them by noting that they lacked tactility or provision for social and personal intimacy. White summed up his experience by turning his hay fever into a summation of the Fair's overall sterility: "Tomorrow does not smell."[3] White's chronicle of his experiences at the Fair is unique in the emphasis he placed on his bodily discomfort. However, his criticism of the Fair for imagining a tomorrow with no quotidian imperfections, in which the human body played a subordinate role to a series of machines for living, was quite typical of other observers' reactions.

This chapter, inspired in part by White's experiences and insights, analyzes the regional planning concepts around which the Fair was organized. I show how exhibits like *Democracity* and *Futurama* embodied regional planning's tendency to reduce the urban to its conceptual dimen-sion, excluding experiential, especially embodied, aspects of space. Such a reduction allows the built environment to completely determine the way daily life is lived in the city. It impoverishes that life by enshrining and rationalizing structural inequality in urban design itself. Ironically, one of the Fair's theme exhibits, *The City*, which was commissioned by the American Institute of Planners—the preeminent advocacy organization for regional planners, later the Regional Planners Association—critiqued regional planning's core principles. The film did so by emphasizing a bodily rhetoric that echoes White's essay and by asserting the role of experiential space in daily life.

Regional planning was the unlikely offspring of a marriage between American exceptionalism and housing advocacy. It rose to prominence during the 1920s, was crucial to several New Deal programs, and influ-enced postwar urban renewal. Regional planners differentiated their theories from earlier forms of planning by arguing that effective urban design cannot occur when limited to a single structure, neighborhood, or even city. This is because regional planners understand a city as mutually constitutive with its surrounding area. They therefore espouse a model in which the city is a node within larger environs, both of which must be comprehensively planned if the region as a whole is to function. Regional planners aim to organize daily life—particularly the circulation of people and goods, as well as the use and scale of residential and natural space—within an area encompassing urban, suburban, and rural spaces instead of designing a city to function as an independent entity. Regional planning, as practiced and theorized in the 1930s, was closely associated with housing reform movements that sought to rehouse the urban poor away from the city within new, purpose-built communities. Such communities were intended to discourage social vices by decentralizing the population, discouraging multifamily residences, increasing green spaces, and encouraging home ownership.[4]

Regional planners idealized American identity, particularly its rural and agrarian aspects, which they imagined were threatened by rampant urbanization. Regional planning theory conflated this threat with immigration from Southern and Eastern Europe, as well as the migration of African Americans from the American South. This vision of America as a white ethno-state meant that regional planning favored the construction of entirely new "garden cities" where a socially and physically healthy population could live productively in small, decentralized communities close to nature. It also meant that, when these communities were actually built, as part of the New Deal's Resettlement Administration, they were racially segregated, sometimes ethnically or religiously restricted, and often favored middle-class nuclear families.[5] Henri Lefebvre argued that regional planning's internal contradictions—a progressive movement that depended on regressive social policies, an avowedly antisuburban theory whose implementation was the model for wide-scale suburbanization— can best be understood as the conflict between habitat and the drive to inhabit.[6] Regional planning ultimately elevates human habitats above their inhabitants, arguing that the proper location and construction of a town directly dictates the productivity and contentment of those who live there. Moreover, through prominent organizations like the American Institute of Planners (AIP), regional planning adherents took part in ongoing cultural and legal determinations of which kind of inhabitants were worthy of living in such model habitats in the first place. Regional planning, especially as represented at the Fair, advocated the dispersal of the working class from the urban core. It depended on and reinscribed a nostalgic ideal of American identity that enshrines racial segregation at its base.

Regional Planning and Cinematic Technologies at the World's Fair

At the Fair, regional planning advocated for its programs through the use of cinematic technologies and modes of vision in exhibits like *Futurama*

and *Democracity*. In these exhibits, techniques of aerial photography originally developed by regional planners in the 1920s mixed with cinema's
virtual and mobile gaze to align the audience's perspective with that of a
superhero-planner who can quite literally see the future.[7] The vision these
exhibits display, both in terms of the particular aesthetics they use and in
terms of the definition of the urban they articulate, is closely related to
one of eutopian urbanist Lewis Mumford's early theories. Mumford was
one of the foremost thinkers of the American city. His career stretched
from the 1920s to the 1960s. During those years, Mumford began as an
establishment figure and became increasingly iconoclastic. By the late
1930s, Mumford had authored eight books, was closely associated with
the powerful AIP, and was respected enough in federal circles to have
influence with New Deal programs like the Resettlement Administration.
Mumford's thought was notable for understanding the city within a wider
field of inquiry that included technics, sociology, architecture, and art.
Mumford's work continually expresses a tension between conservative
and progressive impulses, at once coming close to embracing both racially
tinged nationalism and liberal-left notions of radical governmental, labor,
and housing reform.[8]

The idea of Mumford's that was most central to the 1939 Fair,
the garden city or greenbelt town, typified these contradictions. Garden
cities are regionally planned, single-zoned (meaning that commercial,
residential, and industrial activities are physically separated), self-sufficient communities. They offer an alternative to the increasingly regimented existence demanded by industrialization and mass culture, one
that is collective as well as anticapitalist. Garden cities were the subject
of utopian literature like William Morris's *News from Nowhere* (1890)
and Ebenezer Howard's *Garden Cities of To-Morrow* (1902). These works
called for collective ownership of the means of production as well as
food independence. They modeled an anarcho-syndicalist urbanism that
never fully descends into nostalgic antimodernism.[9] Mumford's version
of the garden city downplayed or removed these aspects.

Mumford's garden city was not a utopian project in the sense I have
been using the term; it did not probe the contradictions of capital and
indicate an alternative set of socio-spatial relations. Rather, it was what he
called an eutopian form. For Mumford, eutopia exchanged the good place
that is impossible for a better space whose production is plausible, given
current social conditions. Mumfordian eutopias are projects or policies
that intervene into the current socio-spatial order to address fundamental
questions of civic life without necessitating a rupture from or within the

dominant social order.[10] Mumford understood regional planning projects that incorporated housing and de-urbanized the poor as eutopian. He used this eutopian logic to adapt the garden city to regional planning principles, imagining it as a way of regionalizing the entire nation and providing a more equitable distribution of space. However, the Mumfordian garden city also ensured that this space was privately held, dedicated to individual achievement and the amalgamation of capital.

These eutopian goals are especially evident in the Fair's World of Tomorrow theme, which Mumford provided. He hoped the Fair would produce conversations about key social issues that otherwise tend to escape identification and discussion, using it to "project a not-so-distant future where modern technologies would beget a harmonious, planned society."[11] In 1935, when planning for the Fair began, Mumford successfully asserted that the Fair would have purpose only if it could help articulate the full potential and danger of new technologies, as well as the need to subordinate them to planning goals.[12] This tenet, first developed in Mumford's 1922 book *The Story of Utopias* and continued through his 1938 work *The Culture of Cities*, permeated every aspect of the Fair, from its official theme exhibits, charged with embodying the central concerns of the planning committee, to its spatial organization. The layouts of past World's Fairs and Expositions mimicked orthogonal grids, Hausmann-style boulevards, or fanciful premodern winding streets enclosed in modern steel-and-glass Crystal Palaces. Unlike them, the 1939 site was fully single-zoned, with the sections radiating from the theme exhibits housed in the iconic Trylon (obelisk) and Perisphere (sphere) structures like the spokes of a planned community. Ironically, this also resulted in many related exhibits such as *Democracity*, *Futurama*, and *The City* being located far away from one another in different buildings and areas, which Mumford complained diminished their critical potential.[13]

One of these exhibits, Henry Dreyfus's *Democracity*, was an incredibly detailed miniature of an imagined future people's metropolis located in the Perisphere (figure 1.1). *Democracity* was a scale model of a Midwestern city, population 1.5 million. Its industry was located in the center, while "its workers are housed in nearby villages." Visitors stood on two moving platforms that revolved around the model every six minutes from heights of 52 and 64 feet. This perspective mimicked the view of "a citizen of Democracity coming proudly home to it in a plane 10,000 feet high."[14] For the first half of the show, H. V. Kaltenborn's narration described *Democracity* as "a symbol of life as lived by the Man of Tomorrow. No longer the planless jumble of slum and grime and smoke, but town and country joined for work and play in sunlight and good air."[15] When Kaltenborn's narration reached a climax, a color film by Kodak was projected above the platforms. It displayed "12 massed groups of figures [that] typify human factors in civilization," which consisted of farmers, medical professionals, school children, the civil service, unskilled laborers, and others. These figures were gender-segregated by profession and, with the exception of cotton pickers and Pullman porters included with unskilled laborers, depicted as overwhelmingly white.[16]

Democracity displayed the key aspects of regional planning: the separation of pedestrians from automobile traffic; high-speed motorways threaded around cities; the diffusion of the population from the city center; the separation of residential areas from commercial areas; a reliance on traditional gender roles as well as racial segregation. *Democracity* also incorporated characteristics of the nineteenth-century panorama and twentieth-century city symphony to produce what Anne Friedberg calls a mobile and virtual gaze. This gaze typifies and helps produce urban

Figure 1.1. An artist's rendering of *Democracity* at the 1939–1940 World's Fair emphasized viewers' elevated vantage point. (Theme Center-Democracity-Models of Town and Countryside. New York World's Fair 1939–1940 Records, Manuscripts and Archives Division, New York Public Library. MssColl 2233.)

modernity, transforming the city into a cityscape to be visually consumed.[17] This gaze expresses a male, bourgeois view in which space is a thing to be mastered and consumed. It is also one in which the viewer is everywhere and nowhere. Just as in much earlier panoramas and actualités, *Democracity* presents an apparently objective view that simulates the viewer's immediate proximity to the space an image depicts. The less the viewers physically move while being moved by a mechanical apparatus, the more they see, and the more they see, the more *what* they see appears to be naturally occurring and ideologically unmarked. In *Democracity*, this gaze was married to an elevated viewing position that mimicked the view from a low-flying airplane, making mastery of the space literal. *Democracity* connected Mumford-style garden cities to a proto-cinematic vision through an appeal to American identity.

It also utilized its audience's position to mimic the vantage point of the aerial photography that regional planners had long espoused. Regional planners found aerial photography particularly useful because it tended toward extreme abstraction and a sense of limitless space. These aesthetic aspects, combined with "the widespread assumption that *vertical* aerial photographs are particularly truthful and objective," as Sonja Dümpelmann explains, helped regional planners persuade city governments as well as the public of two things:[18] first, that their understanding of the city as a node within a much wider spatial context was obviously borne out by visual evidence of infrastructural patterns in the images; second, that the planners' ideas were the result of empirical, objective truths about space—truths that the distance of aerial photographs unambiguously disclosed. The model of *Democracity* was based in part on aerial photographs, particularly their panoramic, abstract, and vertical nature. By displaying itself like a photographic map to an audience that had been taught to accept such images as authoritative, and combining this map with the mobile and virtual gaze that encouraged audiences to perceive themselves as omniscient spectators, *Democracity* advocated for regionally planning the city of the future.

Democracity had many similarities to the Fair's most popular attraction, General Motors' *Futurama*, which was designed by Norman Bel Geddes. Both demonstrated why regional planning has been described as a subtype of "rationalist" or "totalized" planning.[19] It understands the city in the larger context of its immediate environment, a relationship that governs the forms development should take within and between specific urban ensembles. Such relationships, it claims, can best be achieved by leveling the built environments and social spaces that preceded them.[20]

Like *Democracity*, *Futurama* featured an intricate miniature of a Le Cour-
busian city of the future (in this case, of 1960), and imagined this city
as part of a newly designed region, one that linked the whole nation
together through an interstate system. Like *Democracity*, *Futurama*'s city
of 1960 was an avowedly anti-urban one. *Futurama* linked *Democracity*'s gleaming future of "town and country joined for work and play in
sunlight and good air"[21] to the advent of high-speed auto travel that
would "erase the signs of the city and replace them with the signs of
the country or village."[22] For Bel Geddes, such a city could not exist on
the East Coast. Bel Geddes conceived *Futurama* as the embodiment of
an urbanism that directly rejected New York as a possible model and
instead located a uniquely American future squarely in middle America.[23]

Like *Democracity*, *Futurama* drew on cinematic aesthetics, particularly the mobile and virtual gaze. Small four-seat cars, equipped with individual speakers, smoothly transported a daily audience of 28,000 through
the structure, logic, and benefits of the city of the future as the dynamic
narration contributed an additional authoritative dimension to the experience. From the level of a "low-flying plane," passengers encountered what
GM touted as "the largest and most lifelike model ever constructed."
This model used a scale similar to the one the Fairchild Aerial Camera
Corporation had developed for aerial photographs. Bel Geddes based his
model on these photographs in the hopes of having his exhibit described
in the same terms of authority and objectivity attributed to them. *Futurama* consisted of "more than five hundred thousand individually designed
buildings, a million trees of thirteen different species, and approximately
fifty thousand motorcars, ten thousand of which careened along a four-
teen-lane multispeed interstate highway."[24] Encountering them as though
simultaneously surveyors looking at photographs and pilots surveying a
city, visitors to *Futurama* became, as Adnan Morshed has it, "idealized
spectators of an idealized future."[25] Morshed argues that their vantage
point was reminiscent of images of futuristic cities from science fiction
pulp novels and superhero comics. Like Action Comics' new hero, Super-
man, and like regional planners, *Futurama* visitors could easily, instantly
visualize and comprehend a vast spatial expanse, identifying totalizing
problems and their solution with a single glance.[26] By aligning visitors
with superheroes and planners, Bel Geddes was enabling his audience to
momentarily identify with a viewing position—and a position of power—
he believed was the proper province of social elites.

E. B. White found occupying that viewing position distinctly uncom-
fortable. He described *Futurama* as employing a "modern technique of

site-seeing" that, like *Democracity*, requisitioned the tourist/viewer's voli-
tion and vision to move them seamlessly through a sterile space in which
both the literal touching of the exhibit and the metaphorical touching of
individuated, intense contemplation were prohibited. White's experiences
and impressions of these exhibits were quite similar to those of Lewis
Mumford, who reviewed them, as well as the Fair as a whole, in his
"Skyline" column for the *New Yorker* later that summer. Ironically, given
his role in planning the Fair, Mumford, like White, detected a kind of
sterility and shallowness in these marquee depictions of the urban future.
However, where White criticizes the impoverished imagination of these
exhibits, and their inability to represent or communicate a satisfying daily
life, Mumford regards them as the ruins of legitimate planning theories
poorly realized. For Mumford, these "wrecks" first disappoint because
they fail to realize the dream had by "a group of young architects" before
the Fair of "designing a whole community along modern lines," a fully
zoned and planned city that would exist as a series of interconnected,
physically linked spaces scaled less to the level of a miniaturized model
and more to the level of a prototype. This plan was not approved by
the World's Fair Corporation, and as a result the exhibits merely present
discourse about urban modernity or represent it in miniature; they do
not embody or perform it, and they are not integrated with one another.
Moreover, their content itself is lacking, featuring "stale conceptions of
capital cities" dating from the sixteenth century (*Democracity*) and a future
that is "just like the past" (*Futurama*).[27]

Mumford's complaints are grounded in the lack of attention the
exhibits paid to contemporary ideas about housing reform and their
indebtedness to European urban design. Mumford's critique speaks to
his insistence on the need for specifically *American* designs and solutions
to social issues as well as his distrust of European-derived solutions at
this point in his career. Mumford's complex treatment of and desire for
new urban designs, social reform, and the use of "authentic" forms to
achieve these goals was typical of the vexed relationship between urban
planning and housing reform in the United States since the turn of
the twentieth century. As Alexander Von Hoffman has shown, housing
reformers have always understood themselves to serve as the conscience
of urban planners.[28] However, when housing reform has been included
in urban planning, as it was in regional planning projects, its egalitarian
impulses toward racial and class equality have constantly been stymied.
This pattern can be seen in the future the Fair exhibits intimate, as
well as the drive toward suburbanization that would inform the fed-

eral programs that took up some of their projects, particularly those of
garden cities.

Garden cities were constructed in both England and America
beginning in 1909 but almost immediately employed racially restricted
housing covenants, denied loans to African American and Latino populations in an early form of redlining, and furthered the interests of
real estate syndicates and corporate landlords. By 1933, garden cities were closely associated with racially segregated rural or suburban
locations.[29] By the time Mumford critiqued *Futurama*'s impracticality
and downplaying of housing, urban planning and housing reform were
linked in several New Deal policies, such as the Urban Resettlement
Act, the Public Works Administration, and the National Housing Act/
Federal Housing Administration of 1934. All of these departments were
involved with or advocated for garden cities as a new form of housing
and community planning, bringing regional planning to national prominence. Yet the hegemonic relationship between urban planning and
housing continued, as Mumford's analysis implies, as did the recruitment
of garden cities to the reinscription of capitalist domination and racial
discrimination.[30]

Aside from the preeminence of the garden city, planners and housing reformers could not agree on what form future designs for American
living should assume. Yet exhibits like *Democracity* and *Futurama*, as well
as Mumford's own writings and his original impulses for the Fair[31] capture one of the few contentions shared by planners, reformers, and critics
alike: that any ideal future would occur outside, and in opposition to,
the modern city. In the rhetoric of the Fair, this malignant environment
was typified by New York, the very city whose outskirts it occupied.[32]
But just as the Fair in general proved significantly less popular than
predicted—attracting only 26 million visitors from April 30 to October
30 1939, instead of the projected 60 million—so too were its imagined
futures denied the reception their makers might have wished.[33]

The City typifies the Fair's putatively anti-urban agenda as well as
its ironic pro-urban reception. Fair organizers considered *The City* just
as important as Bel Geddes or Dreyfuss's exhibits in terms of its contribution to the World of Tomorrow theme.[34] *The City* was directed by
Willard Van Dyke and Ralph Steiner, experienced nonfiction filmmakers
loosely associated with the Left tradition of American documentary in
the 1930s. It was commissioned by the AIP on the advice of Catherine
Bauer, Mumford's protégé and a staunch advocate of housing reform, and
financed by a $50,000 grant from the Carnegie Corporation. Moreover,

The City boasted a scenario by Lewis Mumford himself. The film also makes use of some of *Democracity* and *Futruama*'s aesthetics, such as the mobile and virtual gaze and aerial views.[35] However, in *The City*, these aesthetics work to undercut, rather than support, regional planning theories. Even as Morris Carnovsky's voiceover narration, which predominates throughout the film, explicitly advocates for regional planning projects, the image- and soundtracks critique the nature of daily life that results when habitat is given unquestioned precedence over inhabitants. *The City* associates that situation with a static existence at odds with the fluid progress promised by regional planners. Simultaneously, it depicts an alternative to this model of American life through footage of New York—footage that audiences and critics have near-unanimously found more attractive and compelling than any of the spaces for which the film supposedly advocates.[36]

This city symphony uses the form's characteristic day-in-the-life structure and complex montage to tell the story of a national day through several sites. The national day was a theory used by early-twentieth-century cultural critics to allegorize a country or society's history and trajectory through the conceit of a circadian rhythm. This model was especially appealing to conservative European writers like Oswald Spengler, who imagined the decline of Western civilization as the setting of the sun and the fall of night. In the United States, regional planning advocates like Lewis Mumford took up the national day, but because of their belief in American exceptionalism, they modified its structure.[37] Mumford used the national day to narrate America's history as a movement from dawn through dusk and back to a new day, if his recommendations were followed—a potential cycle of origin, decline, and renewal. The national day's key allegorical and temporal components are pegged to specific places and forms of planning. The result is that particular areas and their inhabitants can be defined as properly or improperly American, credited or disparaged as responsible for the social conditions these habitats create. The national day's tendency toward spatial concatenation and its organization around a twenty-four-hour cycle aligns it closely with a city symphony's dominant tactics. *The City* draws on both the national day and the city symphony to illustrate regional planning principles. The film begins with an idealized colonial origin set in Shirley, Massachusetts, before continuing through a despairing industrial recent past attached to grimy Pittsburgh and Homestead, Pennsylvania, a potentially disastrous present embodied in New York City, and finally arrives at a redemptive future in the garden city of Greenbelt, Maryland.

Contemporary viewers and critics, as well as subsequent scholars, have consistently noted how uninspiring, and even unsettling, this future is.[38] As befits a popular exhibit with an intellectual bent, *The City* was reviewed by the national press, trade-associated publications like *Architectural Review*, magazines such as the *New Yorker* (by Mumford himself in his reflections on the Fair), and by documentary theorists and practitioners like John Grierson. Mumford understood the film as "a belated attempt at salvage," of the Fair's original ideals that "leaves off at the point where a new demonstration should properly begin," unable to actually depict the new way of life housed in Greenbelt.[39] Although the other reviews do not contextualize the film with regard to the Fair's larger project or the history of urban planning, they reveal a startling unanimity of opinion. All are generally positive about the film, laud its mission, and find it to be an important evolution in the techniques available to "films of fact."[40] Yet not a single review finds the pro-garden cities argument convincing. All prefer *The City*'s rendition of New York—whose function in the diegesis is to epitomize the soul-crushing automation and mass culture of modernity—to its depiction of Greenbelt, which served as a hagiography of the garden city and the regional planning ethos. As Howard Barnes wrote in his 1939 review for the *New York Herald Tribune*: "If the film has a flaw, it is that it lacks a certain unity in execution. The final sections, dealing with the potentialities of municipal remolding, are anti-climactic. In addition, they strike me as smacking strongly of wishful thinking."[41] Critical consensus has treated the uneasy representation of Greenbelt as the film's inability to effectively praise the AIP's plan.[42]

However, this does not make the film either a disjointed text or a failed endorsement. Rather, Greenbelt's unconvincing nature is the result of *The City*'s rhythmanalysis, and key to its articulation of a utopian critique of regional planning. *The City* indicates the contradictions inherent in the definitions of American identity and space on which regional planning depends. The film accomplishes this by producing the same kind of discomforted and resensitized perception White used to tease out the elisions and blind spots of the World's Fair. *The City* performs a rhythmanalysis that picks out the nativist thought and the preservation of capital's claim to the city that organize regional planning. The film analyzes the various disciplined rhythms that construct the urban everyday to make palpable an ethical knowledge of urban life. This knowledge reveals that life's structures and limitations, and the ways in which regional planning and the eutopian impulse behind it continues such structures rather than rupturing them.[43] *The City* educates our desire toward a world in which living in the city is a work of art within which the needs and wants of inhabitants determine what their habitat looks like.[44] *The City* diagnoses the extent to which the garden city, as implemented by regional planners and New Deal agencies, proposes rehousing workers and the poor to preserve their value as surplus labor while reserving housing rights and an authentically American identity for white citizens. Moreover, *The City* reveals these policies and theories as a symptom of the American urban environment's preextant condition. The film demonstrates that urban issues cannot be resolved by either disavowing urbanization or by approaching space primarily as a habitat. In these precepts *The City* uncovers a longing for preindustrial society that imagines all cities to be no more than codes—codes that justify American space as white.

The Dual Nature of Urban Space and the Reception of *The City*

The City mimics the structure of Mumford's *The Story of Utopias* and *The Culture of Cities*, which argue that America has built successive, flawed "social myths: the ideal content of the existing order of things, myths which, by being consciously formulated and worked out in thought, tend to perpetuate and perfect that order."[45] Following Mumford's model, *The City* depicts the transformation of America beginning with the preindustrial idyll of "the Country House," represented by small-town Massachusetts, before industrialization transforms it into the miserable grime of Pittsburgh/Homestead's "Coketown," which further automation and consumption transmutes into the crowded chaos of New York's "Megalopolis." The film reiterates Mumford's claims that only regional planning given a free hand to disperse the population to small, self-sufficient enclaves isolated by agricultural belts can reverse this disastrous progress and produce what the film's voiceover narration calls "the kind of city worth living in." In *The City*, Greenbelt, Maryland exemplifies such a city, the eutopia to the other locations' social myths.

By contrast, the film's lukewarm reception echoes Lefebvre's contention that Greenbelt, and the "new town" movement it exemplifies, is a result of the reduction of the city to a conceptual abstraction of habitat.

> In the new housing estate habitat is established in its purest form, as a burden of constraints. Large housing estates achieve the concept of habitat by excluding the notion of inhabit, that

is, the plasticity of space, its modeling and the appropriation by groups and individuals of the conditions of their existence. It is also a complete way of living (functions, prescriptions, daily routine) which is inscribed and signifies itself in this habitat.[46]

Once a city is understood only as a habitat, it is not capable of accounting for or incorporating its inhabitants as a constitutive aspect, and therefore loses its ability to transform social relations. Regional planning projects like garden cities, as practiced in the United States, are artificial microcosms. They insist that they are complete in and of themselves. *The City*, however, depicts its garden city and other habitats through the techniques of the city symphony, thereby opening a space for rhythmanalysis, for exploring the "burden of constraints" within regional planning and the national day. *The City* stages a collision of the national day and the city symphony, city as habitat and "to inhabit," and a Mumfordian, eutopian sense of continuous progress with a utopian diagnostic rupture. The film's structure gives the lie to its sponsor's principles.

Critical literature on *The City* traces these conflicts to the film's dueling images of Greenbelt and New York. For example, in his near-contemporaneous review of *The City*, first published in 1941, John Grierson judges Greenbelt on the distance between its screen reality and the promise of the film's premise.

They describe what they say is their road to heaven. It is, first of all, the rural paradise we have lost: and it is true enough that the rustic swinging with the seasons produced a harmonious art of life. But there is something wrong about the Steiner-Van Dyke paradise. There are fine shapes but no applejack. Van Dyke, as an old villager himself, might have at least remembered the smells that go with it.

The road to heaven twists. What is it now but a Washington suburb—neat and clean and tidy and utterly aseptic, with all the citizens practicing to be acrobats? No smells here either. Youth—how blessed a rhythm to the camera is youth—lit up in bronzed nakedness—gardens—sports—the old swimming hole—community centres. But what do they ever do in community centers? Is it only ring-o'roses?[47]

Grierson neatly limns Greenbelt's constituent parts, their relationship, the space that organizes and outlines them, and just as efficiently suggests their sterility. This last quality is emphasized by the oddly static nature of

Greenbelt in this description, despite Grierson's mention of rhythm. Grierson's dashed itinerary is a written recapitulation of the film's montage structure, which allows the viewer to assert a capacious visual mastery of the space through a series of "typical" sights and sites. *The City* thereby draws on the dominant visual logic of its heritage as a city symphony. It not only uses the typical montage structure, it also follows the tendency of many earlier city symphonies to separate scenes of work, leisure, and consumption. This segmentation mimics the single-zoning logic of regional planning. It also reduces the daunting complexity of the modern city to a unified and logical machinery.

Grierson was famously critical of earlier city symphonies for exactly this pretension to visual transparency, which he understood to derive from their fascinating arrangement of motion through montage. *The City* takes as its subject the exact people and issues—machine operators and meaningless production—that Grierson argued were absent from 1920s films like *Berlin: Symphony of a Great City*. One might expect him to embrace Steiner and Van Dyke's reformed and reforming city symphony. Yet Grierson's description of Greenbelt instead suggests a distinction from the norms of the city symphony without an appreciable difference. All of the "swing" of *Berlin* and other 1920s city symphonies has resolved into the staccato strobe of sites that, in Grierson's halting description, take on the characteristics of tableaux in a stage play, or postcard scenes from a souvenir book. The youth at once have "rhythm" yet are registered on screen only through the glint of light on skin that has been "bronzed," sculpted and frozen for our appreciation. Though the "ding-dong description" and "machine[s]" that troubled Grierson in *Berlin* have been dispensed with in favor of suburban still lives, the condition of the inhabitants and their labor remains obscured: what *do* they do in community centers? That is, what regulates the activities within them?

In contrast to his association of Greenbelt with still photography, or even sculpture and portraiture, Grierson's impression of *The City*'s New York is avowedly cinematic and, unusually for Grierson, highly uncritical of technology and the frenzy of motion it produces.

> I remember a lot of lyrical up-bubbling life in those children playing dangerously on New York sidewalks. . . . I remember the zingo of the switch from the—rather anemic—scenes of rustic bliss to the industrial world. . . .
>
> What I am getting at is I do not believe Steiner and Van Dyke believe a word of it any more than I do: and I have the proof of it the moment they shoot those children

on the sidewalk . . . or the open sesame of the automat. Like
myself, they are metropolitans. Their cameras get an edge on
and defeat their theories.[48]

Yet this "edge" of the cameras, this truth, does not resolve into a clear
image of the urban space so valorized. Instead, Grierson uses language
that is a far cry from his usual sober, deliberate style. Grierson's choice
of slangy, fantastic terms like "zingo" and "open sesame" suggest that
he needed to find a new vocabulary to describe the New York scenes.
These evocative phrases communicate some sense of the city's animating rhythm, but very little of its appearance, infrastructure, or organizing principles. Unlike Greenbelt, which, like *Democracity* and *Futurama*,
agreeably presents itself as a sightseeing series of masterful external views,
New York resists efforts to render it as an intelligible image.

As though he is cognizant of the incoherent nature of his praise
compared to the clear terms of his condemnation, Grierson attempts to
clarify himself. In the next paragraph he recalls a preproduction meeting for a never-completed city symphony called *The World Beyond War*,
which featured a scenario similar to *The City*. The meeting, in Grierson's
retelling, climaxed when he and his colleagues, Basil Wright and John
Taylor, rejected an architectural model of a garden city. The model seems
to have had a level of detail reminiscent of *Futurama*.

> It came to a head one day when a fine young bunch of men
> were showing us an ideal town they had planned. There were
> all sorts of good things in it. Your little mother did not have to
> risk her infants across main roads, the shops were just around
> the corner from the school, the factories were nicely detached,
> the town was sectioned into groups, and the decorative trees
> could have bred enough bugs to devastate a district. I was
> polite, as befitted the occasion. But young John Taylor had
> had about enough. "Christ," he said, "don't you have any fish
> and chip shops?"[49]

Grierson reports that this outburst was decisive, and that "we found
ourselves drifting back from the halcyon anemics of the architects to a
messier world that pleased us more."[50] Taylor's outburst, however, merely
reinscribes in Grierson's review the opposition between an all-too-clearly
describable, unlivable space, and one whose livability is bound up in its
resistance to clear description. It also deepens the mystery about what

Grierson's objections to regional planning are and why they—and the response to *The City* and the World's Fair that they typify—consistently take the form of a kind of poetic incoherence.

Taylor's fish and chip shop could be meant literally, pointing out that not even a fully planned community could possibly contain *everything* needed for a good life and that it especially lacks unplanned, implicitly democratic, working-class semipublic places. The comment could also be a sarcastic charge about the too-detailed nature of the model—it has planned the city down to the fake bugs on plastic trees, so why not the local chippie, too? The most compelling way of understanding Taylor's comment, however, is to match it with Grierson's complaint about *The City*'s Greenbelt. Just as with E. B. White's final judgment of the World of Tomorrow, Grierson finds that Greenbelt has no smell. The eutopian communities under consideration lack texture, grease, and bodies other than the "bronzed." They are abstracted, orderly, and idealized, habitats that reduce their inhabitants to décor by stilling their motion and with it their life force. Greenbelt, *Democracity*, and *Futurama* are perfect, jewel-like miniature images that make very "fine shapes" but simultaneously seem to forbid inhabitation with its attendant flesh, decay, and ability to shape its surroundings. These are cities reduced to thought and image that cannot be experienced or lived in because they banish rhythm along with its analysis. They are theories that exclude practice, as Lefebvre argued was typical of regional planning.[51] Grierson's flight from the architect's plans similarly indicates that physical or cinematic space built from such a center would, in a sense, remain a mere system of writing even if incarnated. But just as habitation's writing seems to leave inhabitation without a language, the fish and chip shop Grierson flees to resists translation into a clear concept of the urban. The gulf between the architect's plans and the fish and chip shop pinpoint an absence, something within eutopian urbanist projects like garden cities that structures them but cannot be named by them.

Grierson's linguistic failure is due to the atomization and stratification of space as a concept and space as an experience under mature capital. This fragmentation has given rise to a host of metaphors that allegorize the mutual incomprehension of conceptual space and experiential space through different kinds of vision or forms of communication. The best known example appears in de Certeau's *The Practice of Everyday Life*. De Certeau constructs a diptych of the view of New York from the World Trade Center Observation Deck and the negotiation of the same city at street level.

Beneath the haze stirred up by the winds, the urban island, a sea in the middle of the sea, lifts up the skyscrapers over Wall Street, sinks down at Greenwich, then rises again to the crests of Midtown, quietly passes over Central Park and finally undulates off into the distance beyond Harlem. A wave of verticals . . . it is transformed into a texturology. . . . on this stage of concrete, steel, and glass . . . the tallest letters in the world compose a giant rhetoric of excess in both expenditure and production.[52]

This description conjures the city as a huge art book, presented for the consumption of reader/viewers, rather than their inhabitation. The pedestrians de Certeau describes next, by contrast, "write" the urban text "without being able to read it. These practitioners make use of spaces that cannot be seen; their knowledge of them is as blind of that of lovers in each other's arms."[53] *The City*, Grierson's review, and de Certeau's analysis all enact an impasse Lefebvre argues is the hallmark of mature capital's production of space.

For Lefebvre, all space has internal division and difference, with space as concept, as opposed to space as experience, being simply one example. Conceptual space refers to how the built environment should be arranged and designed, how spatial relations should function, what the purpose of space is. Experiential space encompasses how users/designers negotiate space, how space structures the flow of daily life, and the movements that make it up. Lefebvre does not understand conceptual and experiential space as inherently inimical, nor as mapping onto specific places like center and periphery. A city that all citizens design according to their needs would necessarily include a concept of space as well as experiences of space with the two working in concert, mutually informing one another. One of the main ways capital asserts and reproduces its exclusive right to the city is by breaking apart conceptual and experiential space and then minimizing the latter. The New Deal policies to rehouse the urban poor, regional planning's desire to design the perfect habitat, the national day's identification of ideal American forms, and the garden city's implementation of these projects all typify the ways in which conceptual space has come to dominate and displace experiential space.

This domination and fragmentation leaves its traces on the ways in which we imagine space. Grierson and de Certeau's imperfect descriptions and evocation of binocular vision encode and testify to the ways in which estrangement has impoverished conceptual space and experiential space alike, robbing the former of tactility and the latter of language.[54] If, as Lefebvre argued, any successful and meaningful transformation of the relations of production requires that space first be transformed, then that transformation must reconcile conceptual and experiential space; it must include both theory and practice. When conceptual and experiential space are estranged, we cannot question the nature of space and perform spatial praxis at the same time. This means that any revolution of and in space is made impossible by the core characteristics of the socio-spatial order that necessitate such a revolution in the first place.[55]

Garden cities and other eutopian projects do not attempt to transform urban space, they make that transformation impossible by naturalizing, even valorizing, conceptual space's dominance of experiential space. Regional planning idealizes a pure, unimproved space that has no characteristics prior to the purpose-built communities constructed on it and therefore no history or populace that must be contended with. In erasing time, "this form of urbanism erases space."[56] This erasure is not merely one of physical space but also, and more important, one of social space. Regionally planned cities could only fulfill their potential to the extent that their engineers and designers enacted their plans free from political, governmental, and public oversight, razing extant social spaces and structures to the blank corners of a map. Only then could they produce, as *The City* has it, "a place fit for people to live in."[57]

In his revolutionary revaluation of urban planning, *The Right to the City*, Lefebvre argues that this goal is impossible for two reasons. First, despite this fetish for "the human scale, its measure,"[58] regional planning leaves behind the engagement any inhabitable space must have with the times and rhythms of everyday life. It actually operates without any reference to the "human scale" of the quotidian. Second, planners like Mumford, who Lefebvre names later in the same passage, mistake ideology for reality. As a result, "In the 'reality' which they critically observe—suburbs, urban fabric, and surviving cores—these rationalists do not recognize the conditions of their own existence."[59] That is, what regional planning perceives as an unworked and therefore perfect/unified space has in fact already been fragmented through the estrangement of conceptual and experiential space, producing a set of social relations from that fragmentation.

The City clearly references the estrangement of conceptual and experiential space by associating the former with Greenbelt and the latter with New York. However, the film is not merely an example of this production of space. Rather, it enacts a dialectic analysis, asking how and why these two spaces are opposed, and in what circumstances those oppositions could be resolved. It picks out the inherent contradictions of the social order that the opposition of Greenbelt and New York indicate, educating its audience toward the desire for another space and another way of being. As a utopia, the film puts conceptual and experiential space into "play," so that the gap they embody does not reproduce itself as an inherent limitation of and contradiction within language or vision. *The City* instead denaturalizes both kinds of spaces, indicating how their alienation came to be in the first place and outlining the social relations that result from this.

The film's rhythmanalysis arises from its welding of Mumford's national day onto the structure of a city symphony. In order to narrate the garden city as the apotheosis of American history, *The City* must produce three locations filmed in 1939 as a city of the colonial era, a city of the industrial revolution, and a city of the future, while New York stands both for mechanized capital in general and for the present moment in particular. To make this production more seamless, *The City* borrows the city symphony's twenty-four-hour structure to metaphorically associate Shirley with the dawn, Pittsburgh with a chilly twilight, and Greenbelt with a promising new day returned as a never-ending afternoon. As in several city symphonies, the twenty-four-hour structure is more figurative than literal. Just as Ruttmann's *Berlin* and other 1920s symphonies conflated late afternoon, the weekend, and the summer into the later passages of their four acts—the logic being that all represent or connote leisure—so too does Greenbelt. Similarly, the Pittsburgh section's slightly blue tinge, stark landscape, weak light, and bare trees simultaneously connote the early evening and winter, the end of the working day stretched to unbearable proportions. But the New York section fragments even this metaphoric logic, containing an entire working day. In doing so, *The City* takes one of the actions necessary to rhythmanalysis by juxtaposing the long epochal motions of the social order with the short, repetitive actions of daily life, surfacing the principles that regulate both.[60] Because New York always stands for the present within this structure, it is the axis on which *The City* turns, linking the film's rhythms together and exhibiting their differences and contradictions.[61] Coupled with the narration and cinematography unique to its section, New York emerges not as an event in the (time) travel narrative of the national day that leads to Greenbelt but as an alternate socio-spatial order. *The City* as a whole points out the structuring absence shared by the socio-spatial order of 1939 and the regional planning that purports to fix it. The New York section indicates the aspects of space both absent in order to function.

The City and the Utopian Uses of Rhythmanalysis

The City's critical use of a doubled historical structure is evident from its first shot. This shot does not draw on the same history and rhetoric of aerial photography as *Democracity*, *Futurama*, or regional planning in general. The opening shot depicts a low stone barrier in the foreground that shelters the town hovering just in focus in the background. This gesture of separation repeats compulsively throughout the film's opening moments. It's especially evident in *The City*'s editing, as with the opening shot's long lap dissolve into the exterior of a farmhouse. The dissolve is an apt tool for the figure of the national day, which dilates time. Its use here also continues the atomization of place, locating us immediately within the barrier yet disorienting us at the same time. The stone wall and the farmhouse signify the premodern period. The loose ungrouted stone of the wall, the faded shingles of the farmhouse, its colonial architecture, and the dry field around it associate the site with the New England revolutionary era.

At the same time, the image's temporal specificity, which signifies a particular moment in the past, clashes with the milieu-destroying tendencies of regional planning displayed in the third shot. This shot superimposes the only intertitle in *The City* over an anonymous image of a body of water: "Year by year our cities grow more complex and less fit for living. The age of rebuilding is here. We must remold our old cities and build new communities better suited to our needs." The text summarizes the credo of regional planning and adds a future-orientation to the first shot's invocation of America's socio-spatial origins. The image that accompanies the text forms an immediate rhythmic contrast between its own stillness—the camera is static and the only motion in the frame is the ripple of the millpond—and the dynamic development the text promises. It articulates the central tenet of regional planning: that space does not preexist its working or planning, that sites themselves are brought into being by planning out of the void, and, if any physical or social space once occupied what planned space will appropriate, it must first be reduced to a state of nothingness. Regional planning, unlike utopia, claims to *start* from a void rather than narrate toward it.[62] Yet for all these claims of creation ex nihilo, *The City*'s advocacy for garden cities is justified by the national day. Greenbelt's status as eutopia depends simultaneously on the erasure of historical space and the erection of a very specific history of space. The pairing of the contrasting rhythms of everyday and epoch required to create this impossible place creates contradictions the film cannot resolve. They ensure that, even without the presence of the crucial New York section, *The City* analyzes and critiques the garden city and the national day.

The remainder of the opening sequence obscures the annihilating aspects of regional planning. Rather than starting from a completely blank slate and a fantasy of empty land, the opening sequence instead aligns the national day with American history. Following the opening text, the next shot depicts a waterwheel suspended over the pond, figuring the relationship between the mechanical and natural world that serves as Mumford's thesis in miniature. This tableau dissolves into a tracking shot that begins the visual analysis of a farmhouse located in Shirley, Massachusetts, and culminates with a close-up that captures a plaque reading "Sias Farm 1791" on its roof. Despite the critical assessment of this section as lyrical and languid,[63] in a sequence that lasts no more than thirty seconds the viewer has been fully transported into the revolutionary era, with the plaque functioning as a diegetic title card. After a visual tour of the farm's environs, Carnovsky's voiceover begins, claiming that "a century or two ago we started building cities to suit our needs." The film then presents a series of activities associated with colonial New England, including barrel making, town meetings, and so on. The sequence culminates with a tracking shot of light through maple leaves taken from the bed of a moving horse-drawn wagon. The reverse shot reveals this to have been the point of view of the young white boy laying on his back in the wagon, who then rises from it and walks across the crest of a hill, surveying the town beyond in an extended mobile point of view shot (figure 1.2). This shot begins the film's tendency to associate positive social relations, forms of production, and idealized spaces with white children. While this rhetoric reaches its height in the final Greenbelt section, it is fully formed here, as the camera consistently emphasizes the boy's childishness through the slight overlargeness of his clothes and his whiteness through lighting that halos his head and reflects off his blondish hair. The shot of the boy and his town—and the metonymic relationship implied between them—capture and compose the sensory data and visual observations compiled by *The City*'s prelude,

Figure 1.2. A point of view shot provides a survey of the town of Shirley, Massachusetts in the opening section of *The City*. (Ralph Steiner and Willard Van Dyke, Dir. *The City*. 1939; New York: Naxos, 2009. DVD.)

providing an organizational external vantage point that mimics *Democracity* and *Futurama*.

    The Shirley section superimposes the image of the colonial past on a present-day community. By stilling the progression of historical time, this section mummifies the rhythms of both colonial New England and contemporary Massachusetts until their experiential aspects can be frozen and captured as a concept and a code. As Shirley indicates, the figure of the national day depends on banishing rhythm, on absenting the patterns and regulations of daily life—as well as the organizing principles and forces behind them—that give each epoch its character. Paradoxically, as a cinematic exemplar of the national day *The City* can only delineate what separates the past from the present, and what makes it useful, by producing rhythms: those that mark the difference between the past and the present, and those that characterized daily life in the past. *The City* constructs a metonymic relationship between these rhythms by having the differing quotidian rhythms in each section stand for the rhythm of the epoch that section represents. This not only heightens the rhythmic contrast between sections, it also causes a doubling within each section. This ambiguity is first felt through the figure of the boy, whose point of view composes a shot of Shirley as a colonial still life even as his body drags it partially back into the present. This occurs in several ways. The first is the clothing worn by the boy, who is dressed in denim overalls and a plaid shirt, looking more like Tom Joad than Johnny Tremain. The second is the remainder of the voiceover narration, which is delivered in the present tense, so that "a century or two ago" is also today. While this aural present describes the progression of the seasons over the course of a year, the mise-en-scène and cinematography indicate that the entire section occurs during a highly compressed period of time. The gradual acceleration of activity from quiet natural scenes, the brief arrival sequence featuring the boy, the selection of activities like churchgoing/town meetings, and the elision of meals or sequences visibly set at night all evoke the first movements of 1920s city symphonies. They also associate Shirley with a national dawn.

While Grierson and later critics describe the Shirley sequence as constructing an overly simplified space, its rhythmic structure becomes ever more complex. For example, the rhythm of a single lifespan is intimated through the initial image of the boy, who is joined by increasingly older adults and walks through a graveyard toward the end of the segment. But this visual intimation of the passage of time is offset by the narrator's invocation of a repetitive, season-based work cycle; the graveyard appears as Carnovsky completes his description of harvest time. Thus, the seasonal nature of agrarian labor is extended to the lives spent in it, which are implied to be as renewable as the products generated by their labor. This link between laborer and production is crucial to *The City*'s equation of preindustrial labor to nonalienated labor and its naturalization of that labor's regulation.

The transition from the colonial to the industrial era amplifies this equation. The narrator completes his collapse of an individual lifespan and centuries-long political history: "First we built the church, and then we built the town hall, so we could discuss what needed to be done. We disagree sometimes, but there are no serious differences. We work for ourselves, if you can call performing such healthy and vital tasks 'work.'" This description begins over images of a town meeting in which all inhabitants are white, overwhelmingly male, and are dressed in "Sunday best" clothes that associate them with an ethnically unmarked, unclassed, rural identity. The sequence intimates who "we" are, who originated the national day (and America itself), and for whom its benefits are intended.

The voiceover ends with an establishing shot of a blacksmith's forge. The next images dispense with the Shirley segment's long, smooth tracking shots in favor of a series of four abrupt shots that cut increasingly closer to the forge, eventually framing out the smith and leaving only the image of fire in the frame. The voiceover drops out and the image cuts to black, with Aaron Copeland's triumphant main theme fading out, only to reemerge in a minor key. Both image and score reappear over a series of shots that cut back out from the fire to reveal the ravaged outskirts of an industrial city[64] with its steel plants and coal mines. This cityscape is composed through the device of a steelworker's fraught commute home at the end of his shift, just as the boy's wanderings introduced an external view of Shirley. The industrial city, rather than emerging out of a bucolic natural scene, is literally birthed by darkness. This sense of darkness continues throughout the sequence. The temporal cue of the miner leaving work resonates with the omnipresent coal dust and low winter sun, giving every image in the sequence a patina reminiscent of the late afternoon and evening—no golden hour, but a perpetually dingy half-lit twilight that betrays the promise of Shirley's morning. The section's overture reinscribes the logic of the national day and imposes a continuity between Shirley and Pittsburgh. However, the conjunction of multiple rhythms points out the illogic of a dual insistence on American cities' historical evolution and simultaneous coexistence.

As important, the Pittsburgh section indicates which lives are excluded from the nation's (every)day, and on whose labor the nation depends. Unlike the inhabitants of Shirley, whose whiteness is foregrounded by cinematography and mise-en-scène, the miner's racial identity is obscured by the copious coal dust that darkens his skin and clothes. This darkening associates the worker and his milieu with a stain on urban America as a white and ethnically unmarked space. Compounding the disjuncture evident in the image, a concomitant major shift occurs in the narrator's vocabulary. His diction drops, evoking the working and immigrant classes, and the dominance of first-person narration is replaced by a series of commands: "Machines, steam, power! Block out the past! Forget the town and peaceful country!" William Alexander argues that the disembodied nature of these commands effectively offers an alibi to their real-life issuers, who include *The City*–sponsoring Carnegie Corporation, a company partly responsible for the oppressive conditions endured by workers in Pittsburgh and Homestead.[65] Indeed, on the image track, the directionless and inhuman nature of the commands is juxtaposed with looming close-ups of heavy machinery in which no people are visible. It is as though these directives issue from the newly dominant machines themselves, which are no longer subordinated to human need or closely tied to use value.

By implying that the machines themselves are responsible for the dysfunctional rhythms of modern life, the shots obscure the flows of capital and state power that determine when, how, and where the machines are operated. The alienation workers experience in this situation is echoed in the voiceover's description of the populace. For the first and only time in the film, the script not only refers to them as "we" but also as "you."[66] While the second person can denote an ambiguous first- or third-person referent, the image track makes it clear that "you" is better understood as "them." In this section, the visual track contains only bodies that deviate from Shirley's idealized figures—an amputee, dirt-streaked children, obese women—who are never represented as collectively constructing a body politic, as with the church meeting shots in Shirley.

Like the steelworker, every person who appears in the sequence is covered in coal dust, and this contagion comes to stand not so much for illnesses like black lung as for a more metaphoric pollution of the American dream and an implicit call for the restriction of that dream to middle-class whites. This section features medium shots and close-ups of individuals and small groups that recall the depiction of immigrants and the poor that formed a major strand of New York photographic practice at the turn of the century. Photographs in that tradition, like those of Jacob Riis in *How the Other Half Lives* (1890) or the photo essays of Ellis Island entrants, document untenable living conditions and potentially engage the viewer's outrage on behalf of their subjects. However, those images were also caught up in the discourse of typology, control, and criminology—often associated with phrenology and similar pseudoscientific discourses—that justified and amplified urban America's fantasy of itself as a pure, white, middle-class society negotiating the impurities of ethnic white immigrants and African American emigrants.[67]

The Pittsburgh section participates in this tradition by attempting to expel these pollutants from the national day that the rest of the film constructs. For example, in order to further distinguish and distance this section's "you" from the rest of the film's "we," the narrator adopts an accented, nonstandard English: "It don't make us any happier to know there's millions like us living like this." Here, the apparent inclusive use of the first-person plural is blunted by the disjuncture between the narrator's assumption of a nonstandard diction and the continuation of his stentorian, omniscient tones. The narrator speaks for the populace even while continuing to abject that population; the use of "we" in this section connotes condescension and mimicry. The montage of individual Pittsburgh citizens accompanying this voiceover emphasizes racial and class difference. In addition to the prominence given to coal dust, the camera also focuses on several nonwhite figures, most notably a middle-aged Black man seen drawing water from a well and taking it inside a shack (figure 1.3). This man's lower-right leg has been amputated, and he walks using a wooden prosthetic. The voiceover here describes the substandard housing of the workers and is part of a generally sympathetic recounting of their inadequate living conditions. However, combined with the dulling of skin and hair of white bodies throughout the section and the camera's focus on the man's injury, the film constructs his presence as a

Figure 1.3. A Black miner, wearing a prosthetic leg, enters a shack in *The City*'s Pittsburgh section. (Ralph Steiner and Willard Van Dyke, Dir. *The City*. 1939; New York: Naxos, 2009. DVD.)

Black man, along with that of other people of color in the section, as an unnatural injury the industrial revolution has dealt to the nation—one that must be corrected.

Over the image of another Black worker entering his shack, the voiceover asks, "surely there must be a better place than this?" *The City* positions Greenbelt as such a better place. However, while Carnovsky continues, "We're asking," he does not state the question as "surely there must be a better place than this *for us?*" This omission reminds us that Greenbelt, like other New Deal Resettlement Administration locations, was restricted to occupation by whites only, implying that this better place was made better, in part, by its exclusion of people of color. Greenbelt and its cohort represent the beginnings of the federal government's "other subsidized housing" program: the suburbs. Some participants in the Resettlement Administration, particularly commissioner Rexford Tugwell, wanted to produce suburbs as new cities that served groups who had previously struggled to find suitable housing, particularly the working class and African Americans. As actually implemented, however, Greenbelt and other resettlement projects were avowedly anti-urban in design and intent, had financial requirements that only the middle and upper classes could meet, and were legally segregated.[68] The segregation embedded in Greenbelt anticipated the segregationist policies of northern postwar suburban developments like Levittown.[69] *The City*'s Pittsburgh section implicitly demonstrates these policies with its ejection of the residents from the American body politic and the American future of the garden city.

By overdetermining the spatial and bodily differences between sections, *The City*'s symphonic structure reveals the logic governing such coding. The health of the bodies in Shirley match the health of the town, the health of the particular social ordering for which the town stands, the "health" of the Revolutionary Era, and thus of America itself. Similarly, the sickness of the bodies inhabiting the Pennsylvanian cities proves the sickness of Coketown and the sickly, atypical qualities of social relations during the industrial revolution—to which America's future will not be subject and which has no bearing on the country's "true" nature. Grierson's description of the architectural model *The City* reminded him of abruptly takes on more weight. As he notes, that garden city was characterized by its single-zoning, every location "nicely sectioned off" from the others. *The City* decodes this sectioning as segregation. It thereby reveals the structures that shield the ethnically and economically homogenous originators and inheritors of the American dream from the unhealthy interlude of poorer, diverse, alienated labor. By juxtaposing the rhythms of the nation's history with the rhythms of daily life—especially in relation to labor—in each section, *The City* asks which forces and principles make the rules that determine America's epochal and quotidian existence.

New York and the Incongruous Present

The first two sections of *The City* unbundle the contradictory rhythms the respective formal logics of the national day and city symphony assemble and double. In doing so, these sections point out the exploitation of labor and the racial oppression on which regional planning and the national day depend. They also indicate how this policy and its attendant figure make it impossible to imagine the city as a site of racially inclusive, nonalienated labor. In the New York section that follows the Shirley and Pittsburgh sections, their doubled rhythms converge, and shatter the film's temporal conceit. New York does not bear the burden of doubled representation; it is not required to simultaneously depict another time and its own, both the metonymic space of the entire nation in an earlier epoch and its own distinct local character. Its epochal and daily rhythms do not relate to each other as they do in other sections. Here, the rhythms of the modern age are almost indistinguishable from its daily patterns because the nature of an epoch is difficult to discern from within it. This merging rebukes the eurhythmia of the national day, which supposes not only that a prior period's space can be reproduced in the present, but also that it may be so reproduced because the present has no innate qualities of its own aside from its difference from the past. By contrast, the New York section shows how daily rhythms are what makes the present the present; to destroy one is to destroy the other. In doing so, this section affirms that experiences of space conducive to encounters in and ownership of the center as a collective work are the constitutive absence shared by the present and the eutopian regional planning that seeks to replace it. However, by virtue of its position in *The City*'s larger time travel narrative, the New York section does not stop at this diagnostic step. Its contrasts from the remainder of the film educate our desire toward a way of being otherwise, for a society built on what this one absents, and the kinds of rhythms it would produce.

This education begins with the transformation of the earlier sections' images of segmentation and external, masterful views into images that encompass multiple scales and intermingled sites of action as well as internal, partial views. Rather than the extended transition of cut-ins that joined Shirley and Pittsburgh, the Pittsburgh to New York transition is managed with a single, abrupt hard cut. This cut joins a horizontally composed pan across the trains and railyards the coal miners' misery makes possible and the narrator's exhortation to abolish the slums they generate to the film's first vertically composed images. The first two shots of the New York section are static low-angle shots of different skyscrapers, their top floors lopped off. The first is seen through the girders of another building being assembled nearby, and the second is compressed between the shadows cast by the buildings across the street (figure 1.4).

These opening shots throw into relief exactly how far *The City* has deviated from an image consonant with regional planning. They emphasize an embedded, grounded view, very much that of a pedestrian/citizen rather than of the superhero/planner. At the same time, they remind the

Figure 1.4. The second shot of *The City*'s New York section, which composes an internal, embedded viewpoint. (Ralph Steiner and Willard Van Dyke, Dir. *The City*. 1939; New York: Naxos, 2009. DVD.)

viewer that the shots that began the previous sections, while originating from a somewhat more elevated position, certainly did not use aerial or traditionally panoramic vantage points. More important, the shots that began Shirley and Pittsburgh were implicitly embodied. They followed specific inhabitants of those areas as they undertook itineraries tied to their lived experiences (going into town for a meeting and going home from work, respectively) rather than an overarching, "objective" survey determined by a planner's concept of the future. The opening shots of the New York sequence ensure that we do not visualize or regard New York from afar, but rather begin already within it, subject to its unique spatial logic and practices. This space cannot be narrated as or reduced to a coherent concept and image for regional planning to interpolate.

Unlike the first two sections of the film, this one cannot have its symphonic structure recruited to the national day. New York is not, as *The City*'s logic would seem to demand, the "night" section that follows Pittsburgh's twilight, the crescendo of alienated mass production arising from the industrial revolution. Instead, the New York section produces its own day and its own rhythms, a present that remains liminal and cannot be recruited into the national day's future-past. Because the section's opening shot fails to provide contextual cues or a sense of orientation, it is clearly intended to communicate the overwhelming and alienating qualities of modernity, establishing the contemporary city as foil to the garden city. However, by eschewing an outside vantage point and an establishing shot, locating the viewer at street level and composing the city as an engulfing environment rather than a thought experiment, the opening shots of the New York section instead convey the qualities of spatial practices and the encounters that arise from them, insisting on their presence here and absence from the eutopian Greenbelt.

The New York section depicts appropriated, monumental spaces. The other sections excise any built structure that could function as a recognizable landmark or symbol of the particular real-life city under examination, because including one would disrupt their status as a metonymy for an American historical epoch. By contrast, New York nominates itself in all its specificity through signage and monument, with the Woolworth Building, the Stock Exchange, and Broadway prominent throughout, but glimpsed in their context, from the point of view of the crowd passing by them on the street. These structures do not stand for the city, but rather appear as one progresses through it. They thereby resist hegemonic conceptual space's tendency to reduce physical and social space to a code dependent on metaphor and metonymy, wherein place always stands for something rather than being or doing something in and of itself.[70]

In *The City*, the "nice sectioning" of regional planning, in addition to its sinister resonance with segregationist housing policies, reproduces this coding, so that, as we will see, each zone of Greenbelt *stands for* the home, labor, or leisure, rather than actually deriving its nature from the spatial practices and rhythms that make up inhabitation. Similarly, the bodies and homes in Pittsburgh represent dysfunction, the church meeting in Shirley democracy, and so on. The New York section makes the workings of this code and the insufficiency of the image it produces legible. The monuments in the New York section do not stand for the city, or industry, or production. Rather, they are part of a collaborative work produced by the spatial practices of the people who negotiate and thereby activate it. These itineraries in turn combine and contrast the linear rhythms of commuting, labor, and leisure with the cyclic rhythms of the buildings, which add their own longer and slower measure of time. The space of the city is also multiplied by the symphonic structural markers of commute, work, lunch break, and so forth. Unlike Shirley or Pittsburgh, New York lays claim to an entire day.

The section individuates inhabitants as having their own spatial practices, rather than constructing them as abstracted representations of an historical concept of space or a generalized population demographic. The New York section is the only one in which citizens actually speak for themselves rather than through the questionable ventriloquency of the narrator. The soundtrack is dominated by the voices of telephone operators, doctors, waitresses, and others, whose accents and jargon mark them as New Yorkers. For example, the short-order cooks and waitresses whose voices are heard over images of the lunch rush at a diner—which Grierson refers to as the "open sesame of the Automat"—call out orders associated with New York, in the brusque shorthand associated with the perpetually busy city: "two swiss on rye, Russian." Their words are paired with images of toast being mass produced and coffee hurriedly drunk by a variety of customers, shown in rapidly edited close-ups and medium shots. These customers, however, are a mixed-gender, multiracial crowd. They navigate the diner space with perfect ease, smoking, chatting, and enjoying their meals. These images and voiceovers are intended to indict the mechanistic nature and frantic pace of the city. However, like the doctors and nurses whose calm diagnoses are heard over footage of a street accident earlier in the section, the words of the diner staff establish them as confident, socially specific, locally embedded New Yorkers expert at navigating their city. They represent themselves as locals, rather than being represented by the narrator as an undifferentiated "we the people," or an abjected "you."

Just as the voices of the citizens overtake the space of Carnovsky's expository voiceover, their movement within shots often contrasts with Aaron Copeland's score, whose dissonant and threatening chords are challenged by the competence and happiness displayed by the bodies it attempts to encode. This is particularly evident in the section's "street problem" scenes, where the score's insistent horns—whose rapid increase and decrease in volume mimics a passing car's Doppler effect—evoke the never-ending onslaught of traffic as a quotidian rhythm problem. The subjects of the shots, however, are pedestrians whose purposeful strides across the street and rapid left-right-left scans for vehicles and navigational opportunities create a rhythm tethered to the body and its negotiation of urban life. These images depict a mastery of the environment at odds with the aural cues. Moreover, these voyagers are always acting in a frame filled with complex action and background sights; the sheer unruliness of space the voiceover decries finally seems to overcome even its rhetoric.

The New York section displays the exact kind of dense, mixed-use space against which *The City* inveighs, and it includes racially integrated crowds as well as women at work outside the home. However, racial and gender difference in the New York section is relatively unmarked. Because of the concentration on the crowd, which the voiceover assures us removes individuality, the pseudo-scientific taxonomy of racial difference as expressed by portraiture in the other sections also disappears. The multiple classes and races in this section may not be properly American in the calculus of the national day, because their city represents the opposite of an American space, but they are citizens of New York rather than symptoms of its degradation, and they are not represented as being the reason for its expulsion from the national imaginary. Similarly, the section does not produce mixed-use space as a concept, but rather foregrounds the daily strategies used to negotiate and live within this space and the rhythms that develop from it. It is this experiential aspect of the space that appears so at odds with the concepts that attempt to denigrate it.

The contrast between the narrator's discussion of a rhythm out of control and the visual depiction of New Yorkers' rhythmic competence produces a critique that originates *within* the film. It establishes the New York of 1939 as a series of citizen-presences that each take their own time and trace their own experiences of space in the face of both the mechanized capital that largely dictates the city's daily and epochal rhythms as well as the regional planning that would obliterate urban modernity and all its rhythms. The New York section produces space along the axis of experience rather than concept. It suggests that space can be known through the kind of encounter and habitus expressed by the diner patrons rather than mastered through an abstracted study. Lefebvre describes this as the difference between a knowing through space (*connaître*) and a knowledge of space (*savoir*).[71] These two ways of knowing space result in yet another break in *The City*'s carefully managed temporal rhythm. Greenbelt, unlike New York, stands for another time (an ideal future), as well as the present. Because it, like the other non–New York sections, narrates a knowledge *of* space, it comes to look like an alternative to New York, rather than its successor, rupturing the conceit of the national day.

This is evident even in the transition from New York to Greenbelt. The transition between Pittsburgh and New York is instantaneous, accomplished through a cut that articulates the movement between each section as a step forward in time. But although New York and Greenbelt appear to occupy the same epoch, they are emphatically separated in screen time and space in an attempt to preserve the proportionate logic of the national day and the single-use dicta of the garden city. Carnovsky's voiceover insists that garden cities are not suburbs, but the images that accompany it show Greenbelt being reached by exiting New York in cars and driving on the highway. Like the fictional settlements of *Futurama* and *Democracity*, the real suburbs that Greenbelt heralded were dependent on highways that allowed transportation of a labor force between home and work. Even though the narration will later insist on Greenbelt's self-sufficiency and claim that its residents work in all kinds of industries housed within the town proper, the film preserves a trace of the truth: that this new city is not a city at all, but merely a bedroom community.[72] To further the fiction that this is not the case, Greenbelt must be entirely dissociated from both current infrastructures and the extent city, so the New York segment concludes with a series of accidents shot on stock footage or presented as still photographs. Motion restarts with an aerial shot that depicts the Hoover Dam and a series of parkways, which are delinked from any previously represented space by intervening shots of forested mountains. With these shots, *The City* at last deploys images aligned with the dominant aesthetic of regional planning. Yet this montage very quickly disorients the viewer. Rather than produce the sense of abstraction, limitlessness, and spatial linkage that *Democracity* and *Futurama* draw on, these images isolate the various infrastructure and environments they depict. A hard cut between each shot and a lack of continuity editing make it very difficult to ignore the borders, distance, and difference between them, or to interpolate them into a single panoramic view.

What is important here is not any logical spatial orientation—the Dam is much farther west than any other site in the film, and the highways take the familiar knotted form of "the cloverleaf" that exists from New Jersey to Los Angeles. Rather, they typify extant successful federal projects, ones that Greenbelt will emulate, and even surpass. It is as though while a low stone wall was sufficient to make an anachronism of Shirley a much larger barrier is required to separate the eutopia of Greenbelt from its urban contemporary. In this case, the barrier of the Hoover Dam has the added virtue of representing a successful contemporary spatialization of government power and investment in infrastructure and planning. This concentration on large-scale infrastructure also helps rearticulate the film's American exceptionalist viewpoint. The specificity of New York must be replaced by monuments at once iconic yet not specific, which signify America's national might rather than any local rhythm. The overdetermined islanding of the sequence helps produce the conjoining of nostalgia and technology, an amalgam that gives the suburbs a strange temporality suggestive of both the past and the future.[73] Only through this aerial vantage point of an impossible time and place can America itself be transformed into a eutopian figure, just as the returned voiceover helps to obscure the lack of real difference between the extant world and the eutopia Greenbelt must realize.

The City's structure positions Greenbelt as the American city's future, and the closing voiceover makes this explicit, as a possible future that must be chosen by the viewer. However, *The City*'s attempt to trace the proportionate qualities of the garden city, and fit it into the miniaturization of American history as composed by Mumford's national day, results in an extreme heightening of temporal ambiguity and the collapse of spatial differentiation. If the national day attempts to artificially induce eurhythmia and to use this harmony to justify and characterize regional planning, then the Greenbelt section reveals this false unity as the total erasure and cessation of both daily life and the lifecycle. Throughout the Greenbelt section, Carnovsky again speaks of "we" in the present tense: "There are no cars here. We can walk to work and come home for lunch, just like the kids." The end of this sentence accompanies the depiction of a baseball game played by physically fit white men, all of whom are in their twenties and thirties; the images confirm that this is play undertaken *like* children, not with them. The doubling of the national day and the city symphony results in the final halting and compression of time, to the extent that even the difference between adults and children is suppressed.

Like the rest of the Greenbelt section, it affirms that this eternal leisure is reserved for true Americans, which is to say white Americans. This scene, and the section as a whole, removes people of color from the frame and ensures that their presence as laborers in the Pittsburgh and New York sections is their only representation on screen: leisure and fun, an existence outside productivity, is not possible for them. The dilation of rhythm not only reaffirms Greenbelt's status as a spatial concept, it also illuminates another dimension of the false harmony of the dollhouse that is the garden city. Guy Debord argues that suburbs disperse history. Cities, as much as they are the site of more intensive exploitation of labor, are also threats to the accumulation of capital because, in the density of workers and these workers' appropriation of the urban center, they are also the loci of history. Cities contain memory and with it the seeds of substantive historical change.[74] Greenbelt goes a step further than the typical suburb, depicting a place where not only the collective development of history, but also individual biological development, ceases.

Where the Pittsburgh and New York sections depict the problems arising from the mixed use of spaces and the difficulty of moving from spaces of production to spaces of leisure, the Greenbelt section features the segregation of uses and the ease of navigation in which this will result. However, the Greenbelt section also collapses the rhythms that will constitute and animate such uses and spaces. The slow yet disjointed pans used to convey the differentiation of spaces and facilitation of movement depict what the voiceover describes as laboratories, houses, and public buildings. It is impossible, however, to determine the spatial relations of one to the other, and shots of each structure include nearly identical backgrounds. This stasis is emphasized by the lack of temporal progression in the section, and the interruption of the national day built by the first two sections. If Shirley is morning, Pittsburgh evening, and New York an entire day, then Greenbelt is an unsettling afternoon that refuses to end. This time of day, in the section's melding of youth and young adulthood, labor and leisure, is also simultaneously the weekend and the summer, a perpetual break from the rhythms of labor and a collapse of the rhythms of the seasons and of a lifetime. This lack of rhythmic differentiation results in the regionally planned, self-sufficient garden city coming to resemble a disorienting, nightmarishly claustrophobic Möbius strip in which schools look exactly like factories (figure 1.5). The Greenbelt section reveals that the schools *are* factories that produce an uncomplaining surplus labor force, far from the restive city and its potential for utopian rupture.[75]

By the end of the film, as if to overdetermine the "naturalness" of the production of this atomized labor force and to justify the whiteness of American identity in the past and future alike, nature metaphors dominate the voiceover and the visual track. As the narrator claims that "human beings need good food, light, and space to grow," shots of white workers leaving factories dissolve into shots of trees. The Greenbelt section articulates whiteness, Americanness, and preferred social formations even more insistently than does the Shirley section. Almost every person is dressed in spotless white or light colors, and, unlike the varieties of ages and body types on display in Shirley, the only figures seen are of children or younger adults. These figures are idealized: backlit, shot from

Figure 1.5. A school from the Greenbelt section of *The City*. It closely resembles the other municipal and office buildings in the section. (Ralph Steiner and Willard Van Dyke, Dir. *The City*. 1939; New York: Naxos, 2009. DVD.)

lower angles, and often depicted in motion under bright natural light to emphasize physical prowess and light skin tone. Similarly, traditional gender roles are emphasized in the insistent depiction of women within the home and in the act of mothering, while the workplace and outdoors are largely reserved for men. The Greenbelt section makes it unquestionably clear that the American future is restricted to those who best match a narrow, fetishized idealization of its past in race, gender, and class terms. In the film's pretend paradise of unalienated, gender-differentiated, and racially homogenous labor, the identity between producer and production has been so strengthened that there is finally no difference. The workers are as much of a crop as the ones they plant and are cultivated and grown in much the same way. Regional planning has succeeded in constructing the ultimate eurhythmia through the obliteration of rhythmic difference, just as the national day abjected the racially mixed, heterogeneous spaces of Pittsburgh and New York as un-American historical aberrations.

But Greenbelt must function not as a true utopia but rather as a *eutopia*. Greenbelt is not a counterfactual historical alternative, well-islanded from current society so that its borders and vanishing point speak the conditions of its own impossibility. It is a place that is possible within the extant socio-spatial order. Therefore, the section is also narrated as a potential future emerging from the Shirley-Pittsburgh–New York lineage, and so is intercut with images from that lineage to strengthen its contrast from earlier sections. This intercutting rises to a climax at the film's conclusion by alternating images of Greenbelt and New York. These images are intercut so as to communicate Greenbelt's superiority in all areas of life: clean blond children playing in grassy fields are juxtaposed with shabby, ethnically ambiguous waifs jumping into a dark river; factories disgorging white-jacketed workers versus black smoke. Yet this crosscutting also directly stages the contrast that Grierson and others described in their critiques. The presence of multiple rhythms in the New York footage being placed directly against the stillness of Greenbelt undermines the latter's claims to be a true alternative socio-spatial order. Rather, the contrast provides *The City*'s culminating critique of regional planning. The film not only reveals a space in which workers are themselves a product, but also that this space is no different from the real world it purports to correct. Simultaneously, *The City*'s production of New York as social, experiential space with its own synchronic day subverts the conceptual space of modernity as a stop on the film's mythic itinerary from the prerevolutionary pastoral to the garden city.[76] The result is that the present cannot be successfully integrated into the film's map of American history, but rather exists as an equal, alternative figuration of space outside of this map, an experiential space that points out conceptual space's limits. *The City* may have been commissioned to serve eutopian urbanism, but it enacts a utopian critique of that very concept.

The City as Progenitor of the New York City Symphonies

The City visualizes the extent to which regional planning and the national day are incapable of truly transforming social relations, or even effectively critiquing them, because they reduce space to a concept and idealize it as a transparent, cross-sectioned image.[77] The tactics that *The City* uses to critique these eutopian concepts were adopted, modified, and promulgated by the city symphonies that began to emerge in New York in the early 1940s and became a recognized cycle associated with an organized avant-garde in the postwar years.[78] *The City* became an important part of the formulation of this cycle, occupying a prominent place in the New York avant-garde's primary exhibition venues and its programming discussions. *The City* lent its descendants the complication of structure it introduced to the twenty-four-hour organization of the original 1920s cycle, its production of New York as a space that related to America as a utopia, and its inscription of race as a key spatial dynamic. *The City* also bequeathed the limits of its racial representation to its descendants. That is, like *The City*, the postwar New York city symphonies continually exposed racism as a major component of extant cities as well as the policies that sought to remake them. However, *The City* only critiques the segregated spaces of the national day and the garden city by exaggerating them in the Shirley, Pittsburgh, and Greenbelt sections and then unmarking and deracializing space in the New York sections; it cannot fully articulate a city or nation to which a multiracial multitude has a right. The postwar New York city symphonies inherited this limitation, and, as we shall see, failed to fully register the extent to which the policies that followed from regional planning disproportionately impacted people of color.

If these postwar films inherited *The City*'s organizational aspects and political limits, they also differed from their ancestor in two key ways. First, the postwar city symphonies reacted to and critiqued urban planning and social policies as they existed in the built environment and popular culture. They did not make them their topic and perform an autocritique of them like *The City*. Second, *The City* produces New York as a series of spatial practices that reveal the film's other spaces as unified codes and images that lack inhabitation, life, and what E. B. White might recognize as smell. In the years after *The City*, in part because of the dominance of regional planning–descended policies like urban renewal, New York began to be conceptualized in both commercial cinema and urban planning very similarly to the garden cities that it once opposed: as a unified, encoded image. Thus, the postwar city symphonies could not merely juxtapose New York with other American spaces as an experiential space at odds with conceptual spaces. Rather, they had to contend with a New York that, like the World of Tomorrow before it, had been reduced to an antiseptic, complexly coded, unified image that forbade inhabitation.

$$2$$

City/Text

Weegee's New York, Urban Renewal, and the Miniature-Gigantic

In March of 1948, two films that would redefine their respective genres opened ten days and a mile or so apart. On March 4, Jules Dassin's film noir *Naked City* opened at the Capitol, a large commercial theater at the north end of Times Square. On March 14, the first American subscription-based film society, Cinema 16, screened Arthur Fellig and Amos Vogel's city symphony *Weegee's New York* as part of its inaugural program at a Chelsea art gallery.[1] Both films are remarkable for their formal innovation. Each draws on striking cinematography and editing that depicts the city as an ensemble, a whole greater than the sum of its parts. In these films, New York cannot be adequately visualized, understood, or developed based on a single perspective, even if that perspective duplicates the aerial, allegedly objective view of a prewar regional planner. Rather, both these films posit a city resonant with the one postwar urban planners were beginning to define, celebrate, and change. For those planners, as for these films, New York could only be apprehended through the use of multiple, flexible scales because its character consists in part of interior spaces, complex lives, and "labyrinthine streets" that only a "lively document" could capture.[2] As Sonja Dümpelmann describes, these planners understood the city as a living thing whose physical and social structures are intertwined. Therefore, any adequate cinematic depiction of it must not only survey it from above, but also "look down *and in*."[3]

Naked City and *Weegee's New York* both exemplify postwar visual culture and urban planning in rejecting the idea that to visually encounter the city from above is to translate and master it; that the conceptual aspect of space is sufficient for understanding, designing, and living in the city. However, *Naked City*, like postwar forms of urban planning and popular visual culture, proposes a new image of the city that reasserts the rights of capital and state power to urban space. By contrast, *Weegee's New York* substantively revises the norms of the city symphony to challenge the postwar visual regime and urban renewal projects with which *Naked City* is aligned. *Naked City* demonstrates how popular genre film echoed the logic behind postwar urban planning, in part by appropriating some of the city symphony's traditional aesthetics. In response, *Weegee's New York* and the city symphonies that followed it devised new aesthetics that asserted residents' right to a city in the process of being radically reimagined and reinvented.

Naked City typifies postwar noir's reliance on police procedural narrative and location shooting. The film also features a sly, hectoring, running commentary by its producer, Mark Hellinger. This voiceover at once "humanizes the voice of god" and brings the hyperstylization of noir into its closest contact with the earnest authority of expository documentary.[4] This enables the film to run on parallel tracks, at once following the linear progression of a murder investigation from beginning to end as well as the cyclic repetition of the city's everyday as residents' lives continue largely undistributed by this investigation. These conjoined rhythms determine the film's form, which articulates the space of the investigation and the space of the everyday through two distinct aesthetics: the elevated view and the street scene. For its part, *Weegee's New York* popularized the use of time-lapse and optical effects to depict iconic New York infrastructure and sites. It also used observational portraiture to empathetically document poor neighborhoods.[5] In doing so, *Weegee's New York* disarticulated the comingling of modes and subjects that had previously defined the city symphony.

Throughout the 1920s and 1930s, city symphonies integrated experimental, documentary, and fictional techniques. Combined with their cross-section logic, these films used the wide array of cinematic modes they incorporated to equally encompass human and architectural figures, monument and outskirts alike. Early city symphonies' concatenating structures helped viewers interpret and master the socio-spatial relations they depicted, making them legible and often suggesting them as ideologically neutral. Some first cycle films nuanced or elided individual aspects of the aesthetic described above. Yet even films like Liu Na'ou's *Man Who Has a Camera* (1933) that were more explicit about their status as entries in a well-defined genre, or ones that concentrated on a particular subculture or neighborhood like Jan Koelinga's *De Steeg* (*The Alley*, 1932) still strongly tended to the dominant combinatory, decoding aesthetic.[6] *Weegee's New York* dispenses with almost every norm of the city symphony genre. It separates experimental and documentary techniques, the built environment and human inhabitants, the center and the periphery, into two different sections of the film, each of which composed their own day-in-the-life structure independent of one another. Rather than offering viewers a sense of the city as transparent and legible, *Weegee's New York* problematizes the city, putting connections between people and places into question, and suspending normative visual and spatial hierarchies.

The import of these generic evolutions—and their political divergence from one another—is most palpable in a further, improbable commonality *Weegee's New York* and *Naked City* share. Both films have sequences in which a "bright, hot light begins to shine" on the massive crowds that constitute one of their central subjects (figure 2.1). In *Naked City*, this light is figurative. Hellinger uses the phrase to describe the police department's efforts to isolate, identify, and locate a suspect based on a somewhat vague physical and occupational description. The line is spoken over long shots of pedestrians slowly edging their way along the sidewalk in the summer heat. The short sequence alternates between such shots and close-ups that isolate small groups or individuals in the frame so that Hellinger can mimic the often futile questioning that accompanies investigations: "Lady—you ever see a guy looked like this?" Here, the film proposes that to master or read the city is to attend to its specific details at ground level, later abstracting them into patterns. This is a very different way of conceptualizing the city as an object of control than the one at play in regional planning and its attendant visual culture—but it still articulates the individual inhabitants of New York as requiring outside control and interpretation, here in the form of the narrator's disembodied voice. In *Naked City*, the bright, hot light belongs to agents of state power, a metaphor of intensified scrutiny that allows them to parse the synchronicity of life lived en masse in the postwar metropolis. The film exposes the entire population to a look that renders every member legible with regard to the threat each does or does not pose to the continued accumulation of capital in the urban center. It also obscures capital's need of those very crowds in order to function.

In *Weegee's New York*, by contrast, the bright, hot, light is quite literal. It takes the form of a rainbow effect stretching across two-thirds of a slow-motion shot's center in an otherwise desaturated image. This light is cast by the skillful application of in-camera optical effects, especially the use of a diffracting prism. The fragments so illuminated include the faces, hands, and head coverings of several members of a pedestrian crowd as they seem to rise and fall in the frame rather than walking forward. In *Weegee's New York*, the increase of attention to members of the crowd displays the irreducible differences that remain within the bodies of urbanites as they are subjected to the demanding rhythms of a corporate economy and mass culture. Their movements draw attention

Figure 2.1. A "bright hot light" shines on a midtown crowd in the "New York Fantasy" section of *Weegee's New York*. (Arthur Fellig [Weegee] and Amos Vogel, Dir. *Weegee's New York*. 1948; New York: International Center for Photography. 16 mm.)

to the variety of gaits, desires, goals, and rhythms at play in what is no longer a unified crowd. This shot articulates the urban center as a series of fleeting encounters through momentary alignments of bearing and touch on a busy street. Where the bright, hot light in *Naked City* compels New Yorkers to present themselves before the classifying eye of the police and the forms of capital they defend, the same light in *Weegee's New York* renders urban dwellers as presences in Lefebvre's sense, as having unique rhythms that generate and link their own past, presents, and futures. In *Weegee's New York* urbanites possess and generate their own rhythms. They have the right to *take their time* as they see fit, without reference to the demands of capital, the regimentation of daily life it imposes, or the decoding images that secure it.

Naked City's depiction of New York and *Weegee's New York*'s subversion of it can be traced to immediate postwar planning policy and the image it generated. Postwar planning in New York generally took the form of urban renewal, which had many components. Its related programs included slum clearance, infrastructure expansion, suburbanization, ghettoization, public works, public housing, and public-private funding structures. This chapter deals with public works, infrastructure expansion, and public-private ventures. Such projects reshaped the built environment and iconography of New York, as well as the ways in which New Yorkers imagined themselves. These projects, and urban renewal in general, precede from, and reproduce, a particular kind of vision.

This vision is putatively pro-urban, focused on a present and future lived within the city, and is multiscalar in terms of time and space.[7] Urban renewal is concerned with the everyday rather than with a national day, and it visualizes the city through an engagement with images limited and interrupted by borders and edges. For example, as Samuel Zipp shows, public-private urban renewal projects like the United Nations campus were intentionally designed to avoid referencing American identity/ history. Their designers considered this avoidance necessary to eradicate the extant kinships ties and patterns of behavior that allegedly led to international armed conflict and intergenerational poverty.[8] These sites were prepared, imagined, and documented through photographic and cinematic images that consistently presented a limited view. These images concentrated on detailed streetscapes and on elevated or aerial depictions of specific infrastructure or monuments that stressed their context within the larger space of the city rather than using the limitless aesthetic of prewar aerial surveys.

Urban renewal proponents had come to believe that the city was not a problem that could be solved simply through dispersal, but rather that "urban centers needed improvement and renewal."[9] For example, the city planner Percival Goodman and his sociologist brother Paul greatly admired Lewis Mumford. But, in their 1947 book *Communitas: Means of Livelihood and Ways of Life*, they laid out three transformative plans for American life that proudly centered on the city. These plans were informed by the brothers' disdain for garden cities in particular and the dispersal of the urban population in general as workable forms of planning.[10] As well, postwar urban planners like the Goodmans had come to distrust the skyline view and dizzying height of regional planning in both its policy aspects and visual language. Urban renewal advocates concentrated on the city itself, and they dispensed with the once-standard 1–400 scale of aerial photographic maps in favor of a more three-dimensional and penetrating visual culture that peeked behind the skyline into individual streets, neighborhoods, and monumental sites alike.[11] The city in regional planning doesn't have to be read. Its meaning is self-evident, obvious to the planner-viewer through the instant, sweeping gaze of an aerial image. By contrast, the postwar city of urban renewal has to be laboriously decoded through multiple scales, different kinds of images, and somehow incorporate and explain even that which resists encoding.

The visual and temporal logic of urban renewal does not dispense with experiential space, as does regional planning and the figure of the national day. Rather, it falsely claims to *incorporate* and reconcile experiential space with conceptual space, asking us to take concept for experience. Urban renewal literalizes conceptual and experiential space into two linked figures: the miniature and the gigantic. In doing so, urban renewal reduces two fundamentally distinct socio-spatial modes into mere matters of scale, scales that can be combined into a single, textual image. In this chapter I demonstrate how *Naked City* alternates between elevated and street views to effect an apparent reconciliation of conceptual and experiential space, one that resonates with the rhetoric, description, and visualization deployed by key urban renewal projects as well as contemporary popular photography and film. I argue that *Weegee's New York* forcefully disarticulates the miniature-gigantic figure to show how experiential space is still excluded from postwar New York, explore the forces responsible for the shaping of the city's daily rhythms, and indicate an alternative structure for daily life.

The Secretariat and the Willow:
Urban Renewal and Visual Culture

The miniature and the gigantic, unlike habitat and inhabitant or other binary terms that I have used to discuss the atomized nature of conceptual and experiential space under capital, are primarily narrative terms. As originally described by Susan Stewart, they describe how we tell stories about and with space, what kinds of stories we tell, and what kinds of social space those stories create and permit.[12] They capture the process of how capital reasserts its claim to the city by consistently transforming space into narrative, so that physical and social spaces, and the relations they produce, are reduced to codes. When the miniature and the gigantic are conjoined, as they were in the policy and imagery that remade postwar New York, they gain the ability to dissimulate the lived experience of space as being preserved within, rather than overwritten by, these stories. The miniature-gigantic operated within postwar urban renewal policy as well as popular culture, particularly photography, literary essays, and genre film. It had significantly more penetration of mass culture than did the prewar figure of the national day, and forged a close tie between urban renewal policy and popular culture. This connection makes it possible to understand both policy and popular culture as drawing on and propagating the same visual vocabulary. This visual vocabulary established the city as something that could and should be remade within its current borders because its very built environment and vantage points could make it legible—and therefore controllable by the conjoined forces of capital and state power. That is, *Naked City* and *Weegee's New York* respectively contribute to and contest postwar urban planning largely through the miniature-gigantic figure rather than by engaging specific urban renewal policies or projects. To understand how this occurs, we need to first explore the policies behind postwar urban renewal projects, and how these projects promulgated the miniature-gigantic within visual culture.

After World War Two and the end of New Deal programs like the Resettlement Administration, the federal government's involvement in urban planning increasingly became a matter of funding and legislation, not direct involvement in the building of specific communities or the movement of populations. Yet with the passage of the Federal Housing Act of 1949, the American government deeply committed itself to the remaking of its cities, with private enterprise reaping many of the financial benefits: "the business welfare state eroded the insulation between government and business and allowed urban redevelopment—and other public/private schemes—to become a way for private enterprise to avoid maintaining equality under the law."[13] As recounted by Zipp, this new relationship underwrote the construction of two massive post-war projects on Manhattan's east side. The first was Metropolitan Life Insurance's Stuyvesant Town and the second was the headquarters of the United Nations. Both projects exemplified the kind of image on which urban renewal depended.

Stuyvesant Town was a segregated middle-income housing development of eighteen square blocks that contained more than 30,000 rooms. Described by its opponents as "a walled city," the massive, inward-looking residential community was also avowedly *not* a garden city. Rather, its planners and proponents described it as "a suburb in the city" meant to avoid the need for the white middle class to abandon the urban core. One of Met Life's goals for Stuyvesant Town was to maintain this class as potential customers, employees, and shareholders. Their presence would supplant that of the restive and racially mixed working class in the urban core, and with it the rent riots and grassroots organizing that had inspired regional planning's taste for urban dispersal in the first place. Met Life understood itself to be undertaking an investment in "the New Manhattan," one secured for its white, middle-class clientele by the presence of "anchor families."[14] Stuyvesant Town was possible because New York state officials passed legislation that made urban redevelopment lucrative for corporations. These officials, led by Robert Moses, believed that the influx of private capital was more salutary for urban health than the timely construction of low-income public housing.

In the case of Stuyvesant Town, Moses collaborated with Met Life executives to ensure that Stuyvesant Town could legally restrict black New Yorkers from residence. Met Life justified its segregationist policies by appeals to property value, the detriment racially integrated housing posed to civic order, and the need to prioritize housing for white veterans and their families. This was of a piece with the company and the state's deep investment in the daily lives of Stuyvesant Town residents and interest in their abilities to generate profit as surplus labor.[15] For state and corporate power, improvements might be made to urban lives, but only insofar as those lives could be articulated to actuarial formulas and matched to the dominant class and racial group—if they signified, as worthwhile expenditures of capital in perpetuity, beyond the ability of the human eye to view.

This visual logic is embedded in Stuyvesant Town's origin story. Before and during the project's construction, Met Life executives brought visitors to their building's roof to look down on the gaps in the urban text Stuyvesant Town would fill: the crowded low-rise tenements of the Lower East Side and low-density buildings of the Gashouse District.[16] This encompasses the same viewing position as Bel Geddes's *Futurama*, with the "planner-superman" surveying the site of future intervention, its very topography making its problems and their solutions evident. However, as the description of Stuyvesant Town as a "walled city," and the strong opposition to its construction by the 3,400 families it displaced suggests, such a transcendent viewpoint was no longer sufficient to justify or celebrate an urban planning project. Instead, advocates like Lewis Mumford wrote appreciatively of the shared tranquility and natural rhythms to be found in the interior courtyards, whose vast walls dwarfed the inhabitants yet delineated a communal experience and identity.[17] Stuyvesant Town's designers and users avowed the superior life it afforded residents by combining two modes of vision, one external and elevated, the other internal and embedded.

The visual figure of Stuyvesant Town typifies aspects of both the miniature and the gigantic. Susan Stewart defines the miniature and the gigantic as exaggerations that mark the disjunction between language and lived experience and that reinscribe certain bodies and ways of being as normative. The miniature is a textual image that foregrounds a sense of closure and proportion by offering the comforting sense that signification continues beyond the point of human perception. Contrary to utopia's education of our desire, the miniature marks "our desire for desire" and falsely presents language's referent as the world, helping to obscure ideology's construction of that world.[18] Stewart argues that the miniature absorbs the gaze of the viewer into an endlessly dilating moment of contemplation and a fantasy of multiplicity that obscures its univocality and closure. The view from the Met Life roof and the agenda of Stuyvesant Town's planners typifies these aspects of the miniature. The miniature promises that the sign holds a world within it by erasing the rhythmic difference the sign inscribes.[19]

The gigantic, in turn, miniaturizes the body itself and severs referent from synecdoche to make the sublime—including the public, the infinite, the natural, and, at times, the grotesque—intelligible in conventional (visual) language. It exaggerates the experiential space the body writes but cannot read or make legible. In doing so, the gigantic transforms this aspect of space normally rendered mute under capital so as to return it, in comprehensible narrative form, to the social construction of reality.[20] In Stuyvesant Town, Grierson's fish and chip shop becomes intelligible as Mumford's courtyard. The miniature-gigantic encapsulates postwar urban renewal's differences from prewar regional planning. Regional planning purported to *rationalize* experiential space and thus render it extraneous to the daily lives of inhabitants. Urban renewal claims to *incorporate* experiential space into its concept of the city. Such a production of space, whose defining characteristic is its synthesis of apparent opposites, offers a mirage in which experiential space has always already been reconciled with conceptual space, abrogating any need to rupture the socio-spatial order.

This role of the miniature-gigantic is especially prominent in the United Nations headquarters. The UN construction secured New York's postwar claim to world-capital status. Its construction was a key test ground for urban renewal's project of modernizing, centralizing, and capitalizing on the city. It proceeded through private land purchase by John D. Rockefeller with easements secured by Robert Moses. The UN was deliberately designed as a "vertical city" that mimicked an office building, one whose steel-and-glass curtain wall and eschewal of ornamentation or any reference to an "American style" was meant to proclaim its freedom from both national identity and the confines/legacy of the past.[21] In order to construct this placeless future, the hyperlocal, very much embodied, past would have to be torn down.

Building the UN headquarters meant razing the far eastern part of the Turtle Bay neighborhood, known as the Slaughterhouse District. This area was home to a mostly white-ethnic mix of working-class and lower-middle-class families and small business owners. Though the slaughterhouses themselves were largely shuttered by the 1940s, the neighborhood retained the name. It had unusually robust social ties, low population density, and fairly high rates of home ownership as well as capital accumulation on the spot through small businesses. The Slaughterhouse District did not meet any of the legal or cultural definitions of a neighborhood that required razing and rebuilding under federal, state, or local law. Instead, a new kind of photographic tactic was used to depict it as a slum. Photo essays in the popular press described it as a deserted, ruin-like space that was, as several captions proclaimed it, "a dead end." The images used were largely taken from street level, featured oblique angles, and tended toward medium or long shot, foregrounding looming buildings, framing out the sky, selecting empty stretches of the street, and capturing details like broken or missing windows.[22] These images invoked bombed out European and Asian cities and positioned the neighborhood as a kind of alternate history New York, one in which the city had been ruined by war, social disintegration, or both. In this case, images typical of the gigantic seal the Slaughterhouse District's fate, while the temporal dilatation and abstraction of the miniature bolster the UN's claims to global order.

To celebrate both the UN and Turtle Bay in his classic essay "Here Is New York," E. B. White further links the miniature to the gigantic. White's writing in this essay, like the photographs of the Slaughterhouse District, is haunted by the specter of aerial bombardment, specifically the possibility of a direct nuclear attack on New York. Against these bombers, White marshals two defenses. The first is the bulk of the UN headquarters, which he describes as solving war, "the greatest housing problem of them all."[23] The second is a decrepit willow tree in a courtyard in Turtle Bay Gardens, the racially restricted development where White lived.[24] White's diptych recalls Met Life's vision of the superblocks of Stuyvesant Town, as well as Mumford's celebration of its trickling fountain and seedling trees. Here, the Secretariat represents the kind of ballast, solidity, and wholeness evoked by aerial photography, while the willow recalls the kind of detail that such images use to allow the viewer to imagine themselves as secure and emplaced. The two also figure divergent but mutually supportive temporalities, with the UN securing a constantly receding, as yet invisible future (reminiscent of the miniature), while the willow attests to the worthiness of the daily life hidden/sheltered by that future (the gigantic). By producing the two figures as symbiotic opposites and symbolic duplicates, White not only makes the endlessly complex "diurnal rhythms" of this urban "concentrate"[25] legible, he also elides the ways in which the construction of the UN was made possible by razing the Slaughterhouse section of Turtle Bay (including, of course, local plantings) in the name of urban renewal. White's essay conjoins the glass-and-steel construction designed to come from nowhere and speak for the world with the homely, long-rooted willow tree while suppressing the enmity between them as well as the class and racial prejudice that ensured the latter's survival and its neighbors' destruction. "Here Is New York" typifies urban renewal's ability to falsely induce a unity or mutually supportive relation between conceptual and experiential space by imagining them in terms of the miniature-gigantic's diverse scales.

These uses of the miniature-gigantic were especially evident in late 1940s aerial photography and street photography. Aerial photography has played a key role in the transformation of the city into the cityscape since the 1910s. As described in the last chapter, for regional planners, the vertical landscape and the abstracted, limitless, "view from nowhere" of aerial photography was key to legitimating and advancing their theories.[26] Aerial photographic surveys remained crucial for urban renewal planners after the war but their aesthetic changed, abandoning the idea of abstraction and the god's-eye view. Teresa Castro argues that after World War Two aerial photography participates in a wider visual culture that valorizes aerial views as a literal and figurative "oversight." Castro associates this oversight with New York and describes it as "suggesting a city that needed to be seized in its complexity and sensorially explored. A city that ultimately demanded to be planned, managed, and surveyed from above."[27]

Castro's "above" is precisely located both geographically and socially. After the war, aerial photography moved closer to its objects, concentrating on a single structure or limited area, a view reminiscent of the human scale of Met Life officials looking down from the roof. That geographic limitation also pinpointed social loci. It embodied New Yorkers' anxiety in the historical wake of bombed cities. As Edward Dimendberg notes, these images modified earlier traditions of urban pictorialism as well as aerial photography by emphasizing "photojournalistic detail." Postwar elevated views of New York compulsively conjure and then dispel the anxiety of death from above by returning to sites popularized in prewar imagery, duplicating one another to such an extent that "their repetition of standard views proposes them as a kind of photodocumentary cliché, an image of the city instantly recognizable by everyone."[28]

Such clichéd images favored monumental shapes and structures like the UN and Stuyvesant Town. These photographs preserved the detailed and multiscaler orthography of the built environment such that each structure, street, and tree in the photograph was legible to viewers in all its specificity, as unique as a signature. At the same time, the photographs emphasized the density, depth, and complexity of the city as a coherent space, one whose distinct borders and contained differentiation granted it unity and stability. This combination of telling detail and synergistic wholeness—the miniature and the gigantic—granted the viewer mastery over an endlessly legible and logical city while ameliorating the sense of anxiety or even dread otherwise associated with aerial and elevated images of the postwar city.[29]

As the dissemination of this imagery across institutional and commercial use suggests, the figure of the city central to urban renewal was part of an overall popular visual culture with which urban renewal policies were mutually constitutive. Therefore, a film like *Naked City* need not directly engage urban renewal to articulate a miniature-gigantic image that reproduces its rhetoric, nor must *Weegee's New York* explicitly discuss such policies to offer a critique of them. Urban renewal and the miniature-gigantic lay claim to the present as well as the past and the future, experiential as well as conceptual space. *Naked City* and *Weegee's New York* reinscribe or challenge this claim through their analysis of the quotidian rhythms it produces, particularly the idea that these rhythms can be wrested into normative language and made to tell the story of the unified city.

New York as Tall Letters:
Naked City and the Narration of Space

Naked City chronicles a methodical police investigation undertaken by a veteran-rookie detective pair, Lt. Muldoon and Det. Halloran (Barry Fitzgerald and Don Taylor), into the murder of Jean Dexter, a model. It was the first full-scale Hollywood production shot in New York after the war. James Sanders argues that, unlike previous films that had shot a few location sequences in the city, including noir procedurals like Henry Hathaway's *House on 92nd Street* (1945) or social problem films like Billy Wilder's *Lost Weekend* (1945), *Naked City* "conveyed the true sense of a city of millions."[30] *Naked City* turned these millions into a plot point by detailing the obstacle New York's anonymous crowds pose to police work, associating such crowds with Times Square in particular and Midtown Manhattan more generally. Moreover, while the film produces the repetitive movements of the masses as erasing individual identity and desire, it also reframes those anonymous faces in the crowd as stories placed in and given meaning by a preextant urban text. As Hellinger's closing voiceover, paired with an image of a mostly deserted, early-morning Times Square, states, "There are eight million stories in the naked city. This has been one of them." *Naked City* was not created as a city symphony. However, this film noir's emphasis on location shooting, exploration of the behavior of crowds, and explanation of quotidian New York as a series of simultaneous, geographically distinct phenomena all align it with the symphony tradition, if not the New York cycle's politics.

The film's aesthetics double and concretize these narrative gestures toward the miniature and the gigantic. *Naked City* spatializes its central murder investigation as a continuous movement between two vantage

points. One is the literally and figuratively raised position of deduc-
tion, authority, modernity, and morality (figure 2.2). For example, the
detectives consistently discuss the case, plan their next steps, or chew
over confusing material evidence while exploring the victim's high-rise
unit, staring out a window of person of interest's office, or smoking on
the roof of their apartment building. The other is the sunken, illegible
space of bodily experience, criminal disorder, and the linguistically and
culturally distinct milieu of immigrants and racial minorities, which the
film articulates to the cramped streets of the Lower East Side. *Naked
City* produces these two poles as a series of clues and interpretations, as
mysteries to be solved within the current socio-spatial order by integrat-
ing these spaces and their associated modes of vision in the joint figure
of the miniature-gigantic. This detective story ends happily when the
power of rationality, order, and the city rendered as a totalized, legible

Figure 2.2. Det. Halloran ponders the case from an elevated vantage point that
mimics an urban planner's position and miniaturizes New York in *Naked City.*
(Jules Dassin, Dir. *Naked City.* 1948; New York: The Criterion Collection, 2007.
DVD.)

image combine to make sense of *all* New York's spaces and inhabitants. *Naked City*'s successful murder investigation holds out the hope that every urban space can be fully encoded, decoded, narrated, and known—that a sufficiently capacious concept of the city can account for experiences of it.

Naked City's generic affiliation with the detective story means that the hegemonic relationship of conceptual and experiential space embedded in the miniature-gigantic takes on a metanarrative dimension. Detective fiction has a close connection with existentialism and the potential to articulate an anticapitalist nihilism.[31] However, it also enacts and thematizes the transformation of space into narrative. Whether examined as a type of the Oedipus myth[32] or as a strategy for negotiating urban modernity,[33] narratologists understand detective stories as metafiction whose subject is the construction of a narrative. Detective fiction begins when the detective starts his inquiry into a crime that has already been committed.[34] The story then told is doubled: it relates the progress of the investigation and simultaneously (re)constructs the story of the crime. The end of the text is the point at which plot and story coincide, as the end of the investigation is also the solution of the crime. The detective text ends when the traversal of space has successfully been written as story, has been "solved" by its transformation into signifying-bearing differences. To get to this solution, the detective and the audience traverse the city, attending carefully to its material reality, but always for the purpose of transmuting experience into evidence—into language and concept.[35] As is perhaps not surprising for a genre so closely associated with urban modernity, detective fiction, like conceptual space under capital, finally reduces everything to the sign of a sign. Moreover, like the miniature-gigantic, detective fiction authors another fiction on the reader or viewer's behalf: that to decode and conceptualize space is also to experience space. Detective fiction produces a fantasy where to read the city, to consume the city, is not only to write and (re)produce the city, but also to improve or restore the city to an imagined perfection.[36]

Naked City transforms the space of postwar New York into a story of the miniature-gigantic. Lt. Muldoon and Det. Halloran's investigation eventually leads them to Frank Niles (Howard Duff), an amateur jewel thief, his regretful accomplice Dr. Stoneman (House Jameson), and Jean Dexter's murderer, Willie Garzah (Ted de Corsia). This police procedural is elucidated, critiqued, and contextualized in terms of the city's daily life by Hellinger's voiceover. In fact, the latter frames the former. Borrowing from the photodocumentary clichés of its cohort, *Naked City* begins with a celebrated triptych of shots that produce New York as a miniature.

Naked City's first three shots produce an impression of the built urban environment as a structure in which the whole subsumes the parts, yet those parts remain individually intelligible. The first shot approaches the island from due south over Battery Park. This shot displays Manhattan's southern cluster of skyscrapers in the financial and civic districts, as well as the flatlands beyond, in what are now SoHo and Chinatown. The second shot begins at the north-central fringes of this lower area, moving north from the Empire State Building and concluding at Central Park. The final shot moves back down to the southern tip of the island along its west side. The skyline serves as an establishing shot in countless postwar location-shot New York films, from Mervyn LeRoy's *East Side, West Side* (1949) to Robert Wise's *West Side Story* (1961). In these films, the skyline provides a sense of "constancy," a "reassuring familiarity" because it depicts "an entire place—the very thing being symbolized."[37] The skyline shot is a type of miniature, dilating time and confirming infinite signification, encoding the city.

Naked City preserves this aspect of the skyline shots found in other New York films, but undercuts their evocation of constancy. For example, to present the city as fully intact, the film's first three shots truncate their circuit of the island. They avoid the far east side, where the newly razed Slaughterhouse District and incomplete UN Headquarters would have complicated the impression of unity, closure, and timelessness. Even with its avoidance of this site, the opening sequence still recalls White's spectral bombing run while evidencing the survey logic of (equally destructive?) urban renewal planning photographs.[38] The three shots are also typical of urban renewal's emphasis on multiple scales and a "down and in" view. The camera angle is never perpendicular to the ground, and the plane is making a noticeably slow circuit from an elevation that seems not terribly higher than the skyscrapers. Because of this, the shots have a remarkable sense of three-dimensionality and mass; the impression is of the individual buildings in relation to one another, not a generic landscape. Moreover, the three shots are joined by slow dissolves that emphasize the ways in which each view is partial. They insist that to render the city naked requires a skyline view that can somehow also access the places behind it in all their depth.

This sequence also includes the equivalent of White's willow tree, the emplacing text of the gigantic. Immediately following the three-shot aerial sequence, the camera loses its elevated vantage. The next shot is of the east side at night, taken from the level of the water, the city looming above the camera instead of exposed beneath it. If we are to truly understand the city as it is, then the camera must also have access to the ground-level, human-scale view. That vantage point is further embodied and tied to a particular class and historical position in the following shots. These shots depict a deserted Wall Street, empty newsroom, silent factory, and vacant theater. As Hellinger says, "A question—do the machines in a factory ever need rest?" This question and the shots it accompanies locate the viewer squarely in the postwar urban working and middle classes, working nine-to-five jobs and pursuing leisure activities in the evenings. These images bespeak a comfortable anonymity on an individual level. But they also intimate the viewer as belonging to a particular community, nestled comfortably within and beneath the built environment and social structures, aligned with their anthropomorphized tools. *Naked City* takes the gigantic sensorium that White describes as exceeding sight and reassures the viewer that, although parts of the city may lie beyond our senses, they never lie beyond our common sense or past our power. *Naked City* produces New York as an infinite text, as a city generating endless explanations of itself—and requiring that its citizens explain *themselves* within the confines of this text.

Naked City's conjunction of the miniature and the gigantic depends on this constant oscillation between two kinds of vision, which is also a movement between two distinct film genres. Tom Gunning has argued that postwar procedural noirs "often present themselves as panoramic presentations of the urban environment, city symphonies within the noir series."[39] This quote offers an effective description of *Naked City*'s structure, but I would add that *Naked City* is not a city symphony within the noir cycle. Instead it demonstrates how commercial cinema and popular visual culture could borrow tropes and tactics associated with the city symphony, strip them of their utopian function by suppressing their rhythmanalysis, and, by reducing them to a "panorama," inscribe them within the visual culture of urban renewal. By appropriating aspects of the city symphony, such as the day-in-the-life structure, popular genre films like *Naked City* could present and parse typical and extraordinary aspects of urban life alike, including sensational, initially inexplicable phenomena like murder.[40] Here, the false reconciliation of conceptual and experiential space yields a city whose idealization is not predicated on the planned eradication of social ills and locations said to exceed logic but rather their containment within a universally legible narrative. *Naked City*'s viewer learns to read the serial rhythms of the city, to recognize disruptions of those rhythms, and to appreciate the city's ability to account for and counteract those disruptions. At the same time, Hellinger's knowing commentary on the homicide squad's activities produces their management of exceptional or shocking crime as routine, as possessing its own rhythms, rules, and space. The city becomes a problem that solves itself through the decoding of rhythm into text.

As the film continues, aerial views increasingly motivate street scenes, the miniature generating the gigantic as the crime is solved. *Naked City*'s main crime scene is set in a high-rise apartment building. After examining Dexter's body, Halloran and Muldoon return to the precinct. They step to a window, and examine the busy intersection at their feet in an image that recalls the Met Life executives planning Stuyvesant Town and its demographics. Hellinger's voiceover notes the view as a challenge: "There's your city. Take a good look at it. Jean Dexter is dead. The answer must be somewhere down there." This scene elucidates the miniature's assurance that signs—people and places—continue to signify no matter their physical size, that streets are stories. At the same time, "The answer must be somewhere down there"; effective policing of the city cannot be completed with the miniature alone. The detectives must descend to the street, activating, traversing, and experiencing urban space if they are to master and restore the city's normative function, entering the realm of the gigantic. Throughout the proceedings, street views come to be associated with the gigantic's excessive, disproportionate, and often grotesque detail, which threatens to overwhelm the investigation and engulf the viewer.

This is particularly evident in one of the film's final sequences, set in the Lower East Side. Halloran, hot on Garzah's trail, must descend fully to find himself "at the feet of the giant,"[41] going downtown, leaving the clarity of the grid for the jumbled, crowded warren of sidewalk vendors and street life. The sheer abundance of sensory input obscures Halloran's goal; old crumbling buildings refuse to display their numbers, peddler carts make it difficult for patrol cars to penetrate the area, and not all residents speak English. At the same time, however, the area's status as a residential neighborhood with strong kinship and communal ties—the same ones that urban renewal projects like Stuyvesant Town and the UN Headquarters disrupted—aid the detective. As Hellinger's voiceover notes, a simple picture and description of a man shown on a major, anonymous Midtown avenue is unlikely to yield a positive result. In the Lower East Side, however, the corner store is still a repository of connections and information, and the proprietor is able to narrow Halloran's search to a single block. Later, children on a playground direct him to the proper building.

Although the Lower East Side yields up the murderer, he must be physically extracted from the mesh of the city's routine before he can be apprehended. Thus, his capture and death occur halfway up the west tower of the Williamsburg Bridge in a sequence that provides a close approximation of the aerial shots that open the film. In the sequence's final shot, the "street detail" of Garzah and the murder/disruption he represents appears in the foreground, isolated against the backdrop of the miniature-gigantic view of the cityscape. The gigantic bridge miniaturizes Garzah's body and returns it to its appropriate place and time: Garzah falls to his death, leaving city's text behind him undisturbed.[42] Throughout *Naked City*, the street is treated as a kind of lexicon, the repository of all facts and information. These facts cannot be transformed into artifacts, cannot be parsed or used to solve the crime, until they are removed from the gigantic sensorium of the street and examined in the light of abstraction generated by miniaturizing views.[43] Experiential space is always already the raw material of conceptual space and worthwhile only to the extent that it can be narrated.

Hellinger's closing voiceover—which Stewart cites in her description of the miniature—makes this apparent by reducing the diverse and divergent experiential space produced by murderer, victim, and investigator to a unified narrative, one story out of an impossibly huge store of them. This voiceover accompanies an extreme long shot of Times Square in deep focus, pairing the verbal description of the city's huge, anonymous population with footage of an area that evokes this. The bottom of the frame features a tabloid headline about the case, literally performing the reduction of spatial practice to story. While the investigation sure-footedly followed a narrative thread through experiential space, Hellinger's voiceover recontextualizes the thread as one among many. Hellinger intimates that even those inhabitants of the city appearing in the film as experiential detail extraneous to the case—the radio DJ wondering if he has an audience, the fashionable young women musing about Halloran—themselves have a secret narrative life of their own. Their stories could just as easily have been told as Jean Dexter's, incorporating the inchoate rhythms of randomness, contingency, and coincidence into the urban text. *Naked City* demonstrates the ease with which the postwar visual culture of popular genre texts, aerial surveys, literary essays, and urban renewal projects includes and tames experiential space.

These very extraneous lives are *Naked City*'s most direct borrowings from the city symphony. The city symphony and the film noir have been discussed as mutually opposed traditions of representation, noir associated with what James Donald calls the "Uncanny City" tradition and the city symphony with the "Concept City" tradition.[44] *Naked City* not only inverts these usual affiliations by associating the detective portions of the film with conceptual space and the symphonic portions with experiential space, it also demonstrates how such two seemingly opposed mappings may mutually support one another and structure the same production of space. A symphonic critique of urban renewal and its attendant visual culture must therefore develop a new kind of rhythmanalysis that decouples the miniature and the gigantic. It must reinvent the city symphony, evolving beyond those structural aspects that have been appropriated by the dominant production of space, exchanging them for a sight that exists beyond binary models of the urban.[45]

Weegee's New York and the Reinvention of the City Symphony

Weegee's New York disrupts space's subordination to narrative by producing a new utopian relation in which space narrates. Marin argues that utopian narrative is always doubled because it does not conceal its origins. In this, utopian narrative differs from narrative encodings of space like the miniature-gigantic.[46] Utopia generates a narrative *of* spaces so that "a place is a tale's trace" and language retains its architectural nature rather than utterly displacing the lived reality of space.[47] In *Weegee's New York*, rhythmanalysis points out the structuring absences on which the extant city is founded and points toward an alternative way of living, instead of urban space being narrated by the demands of capital and state power.

    Weegee's New York undoes the urban narrative *Naked City* conjures in part by evoking several key themes of detective fiction. Weegee's photographs, which often appeared in left-leaning tabloids and magazines—including *PM*, edited by *The City*'s codirector Ralph Steiner—had a "curt familiarity" that spoke with the cynicism of a knowing character in a police procedural.[48] However, his photographs also played with the idea of voyeurism, exposing the pleasure the viewer took in the taboo subjects they looked at while emphasizing the public gaze and public space that defined urban encounter. For Arthur Fellig, known as "Weegee the Famous," living in the city was a matter of contractual, consensual looking, constantly submitting to another's gaze. At the same time, he construed his images as *seeing* what a casual, blasé, or averted look merely passed over without registering.[49] Such acts of detection are very much present in *Weegee's New York*, where quotidian rhythms and the manner of their regulation are the subject and object of the camera's inquiry. The film's first segment, "New York Fantasy," shares *Naked City*'s focus on Midtown Manhattan, especially the Times Square area. The second segment, "Coney Island," is set in Times Square's mirror opposite. *Weegee's New York*'s first section deals with the city's sensory assault on its population, dramatizing the tight cluster of Midtown skyscrapers and the crowds these buildings disgorge. Its second section depicts those crowds outside of the built environment, further emphasizing their numbers. *Weegee's New York* refuses to hierarchize its two sections and their divergent spaces and vision. Instead, it wrests the city from the binaries that urban renewal and the miniature-gigantic impose upon it.

Producing a utopian critique of urban renewal and the miniature-gigantic's subordination of experiential space to conceptual space requires a new film language. *Weegee's New York* was one of the earliest, and certainly most influential, of the postwar city symphonies. While its fame can in part be attributed to Weegee's celebrity, its impact lies in its structure and production context. *Weegee's New York* unpacked not only the rhythms that made up daily life under urban renewal but also the structure of the city symphony itself. Moreover, its success helped ensure the stability and longevity of its distributor and exhibition venue, Cinema 16. At Cinema 16, the diagnostic dialectic that shapes utopian critiques extended beyond the films being screened to the very logic of the programming and the audience it attracted.

Cinema 16 was instrumental to the development of New American Cinema. It was where members like Francis Thompson, Ian Hugo, and Shirley Clarke met, viewed the independent film of the day, honed their own craft, and eventually screened their own films. It provided Lionel Rogosin with a model for contemporary political filmmaking as well as the idea of the art house and reparatory theater as a communal, pedagogic space. He would use these concepts to guide his own exhibition practices at the Bleecker Street Cinema, founded in 1960. Similarly, Cinema 16 helped inspire Jonas Mekas and Shirley Clarke to create the Film-Maker's Cooperative and the Filmmakers' Distribution Co-op. All these organizations were dedicated to realizing the feature film as a key aspect of avant-garde cinema, one that could develop the New York avant-garde into a true alternative to Hollywood's product.[50] In this way, Cinema 16 helped to reproduce its Greenwich Village neighborhood as a space with its own rhythms, and one that resisted inclusion in the taxonomizing models of urban renewal. Through organizations like Cinema 16, the

Village provided a space in which inhabitants encountered each other as mutual contributors to the construction of an oeuvre. Here, the originating point of view did not come from above, and did not write the viewing subject into a predetermined legible urban text. Instead, it set out to record lived experience as well as new concepts without reducing either to the ready-made narrative of the miniature-gigantic.

The confluence of these personalities and artistic practices not only made Cinema 16 an important subcultural space in New York, it also suggests it as a utopian figure, an other space for American cinema and the other of the space of Hollywood. This utopian character is affirmed by Scott MacDonald's description of Cinema 16's programming strategy, which is reminiscent of rhythmanalysis.

> [I]ndividual programs and seasonal series were usually structured as if each were a meta-film meant to confront the audience in a manner reminiscent of Sergei Eisenstein's dialectic editing . . . at Cinema 16 presentations, one form of film collided with another in such a way as to create maximum thought—and perhaps action—on the part of the audience.[51]

Amos Vogel, Cinema 16's founder and the editor of *Weegee's New York*, pursued this strategy through the individual films he selected. As he arranged each program, Vogel habitually juxtaposed films that contradicted, challenged, or complicated each other. Cinema 16's films could not help but estrange postwar New York because their exhibition was designed to disarticulate and analyze the rhythms that constituted daily life as well as cinematic renderings of it. From the beginning, the making, screening, and discussing of city symphonies was key to this project, as it was to Cinema 16's success and very identity.[52]

The crucial role city symphonies played in the life of this institution is evident in the June 3, 1948 program, which included *The City* and *Weegee's New York*. *Weegee's New York* was screened several times by Cinema 16, and garnered enough of a reputation among the society's members that it was advertised in the fall 1955 program as "the fabulous press photographer's legendary impressions of the metropolis, including his famed candid study of life and love in Coney Island."[53] However, at the moment of its original premiere in 1948, Cinema 16 introduced the film with the dual lures of Weegee's celebrity status and its distinctive contrast to its program mate *The City*: "This classic provides a striking counter-point to Weegee's film."[54] The June screening began Cinema

16's tradition, which continued through the early 1960s, of juxtaposing critiques of urban planning and the popular visual culture with which it was mutually constitutive.

Cinema 16's juxtaposition of *The City* to *Weegee's New York* throws the latter's transformation of symphonic aesthetics into high relief. Like its screening venue, *Weegee's New York* depends on a series of conjunctions that fragment the possible meanings of individual images. The juxtapositions and estrangement within *Weegee's New York* proceed from its reinvention of the city symphony's large formal structures. This makes it possible for the film to perform rhythmanalysis on a production of space whose defining characteristic is its artificial wholeness and completeness. Unlike earlier films in the city symphony tradition, *Weegee's New York* does not integrate experimental, documentary, and fiction techniques. It does not display classical unities of space, time, and theme, and it refuses to produce a sense of omnipresence for the viewer via spatial concatenation. The film also eschews the contrastive schema older symphonies develop and resolve. In pre–*Weegee's New York* city symphonies this resolution might occur in several ways, including accelerated editing, a focus on public spaces or unified crowds/audiences, or a return of earlier subjects now advancing through their day. Of all these concluding rhythms, *Berlin: Symphony of a Great City's* is perhaps the best known, as it expresses the city's transcendence of its component parts in a fireworks display. Even films without such obvious punctuation reach a resolution by their end, restoring the city to a unified whole, often by foregrounding the illuminated cityscape and the public space associated with electrification in the 1920s.[55] In order to combat the miniature-gigantic and urban renewal's claim to incorporate experiential space, *Weegee's New York* eschews these earlier tactics and instead disarticulates every space and movement into arrhythmias that resist the easy explanation and textualization of narrated space.

Across its two sections, the film isolates Midtown Manhattan and Coney Island, winter and summer, architecture and bodies. *Weegee's New York* also displays a formal disjuncture across the sections, reserving special effects and dizzying montage for the first section and observational documentary and tabloid portraiture for the second. The film teases apart postwar New York's spiral of flesh and concrete, disrupting the epochal rhythms of architecture and bodies as well as the quotidian rhythms that otherwise determine spatial practices. It contests the apparently logical division of labor and leisure time, spaces of consumption and spaces that are themselves consumed. This, in turn, surfaces experiential space that cannot be incorporated or, more properly, *narrated* by the seemingly endless signifying capacity claimed by urban renewal and the miniature-gigantic. *Weegee's New York*'s expression of the city as a place of illogic, erotic play, and joyful oddities depends on the irreducible difference of the two spaces it produces, but they are differences that explode the distinctions that postwar urban renewal had already encoded in them.

This refusal of closure and perfection enables the film's transformation of the city symphony's structure, and it is evident from its first frames. Appropriately for a film shot by a popular postwar American photographer, *Weegee's New York* is organized like a photography book. Both of the film's sections, "New York Fantasy" and "Coney Island," are introduced by brief explanatory text against a black background, just as images in a photography book are proceeded by captions or descriptions. For example, "New York Fantasy" begins with the caption "At Five in the morning . . ." followed by several shots of disembodied headlights and streetlights as cars zip around the corner and speed toward the camera before disappearing out of sight. The ellipsis in the title card, as well as its text and subject, duplicates the opening chapter of Weegee's first photography book, *Naked City* (1945). This book, like the detective film that bears its name, produces a miniature-gigantic figure. Its structure, based around chapter titles like "Fire," "Murder," and "Persona," which allude to dangerous, scandalous, and/or spectacular aspects of the city, enunciates the typical classifying, oblique gaze of postwar photography. Its method, the photographing of unsuspecting, unwilling, or unusually confrontational subjects with a Speed Graphic camera, reinscribes this logic.

In *Naked City*, Weegee promises to lay the city bare, to induce it to narrate its truth, and to implicate the reader in it through the frank, returned gaze of figures in the image: "In [Weegee's] photographs we watch spectators watching themselves being photographed."[56] As multiple critics have noted, the book's title is meant to evoke both sexuality and truthfulness, and to link the two.[57] The notion of the naked city, the one that has to be exposed to reveal its meaning (or code), also implies that a legible truth is there to be read off the city's skin. Weegee's photographic work not only displays how miniature-gigantic rhetoric claims to decode the city, it also suggests how sexuality and reproduction can be yoked to the discipline instilled by urban renewal. *Weegee's New York* differs from Weegee's contemporary photography in this regard. The film foregrounds spatial practices that frustrate concepts of competition, exposure, and accumulation. These practices dispel the assumptions of the "naked city" and emphasize the subversion of voyeurism already at play in Weegee's photographs of public space.

Weegee's New York's rejection of perfection, closure, and encoding also reinforces its rupture from earlier city symphonies. When *Weegee's New York* premiered in Chelsea in March 1948, it may have run as long as an hour and seems to have lacked a fully developed Coney Island section as well as a soundtrack.[58] By June, *Weegee's New York* still lacked a soundtrack—which it would not gain until the early 1950s—and ran a total of twenty minutes, divided into one section of eight minutes ("New York Fantasy") and one section of twelve minutes ("Coney Island").[59] Even the length of each section indicates the lack of proportion characteristic of earlier city symphonies or appropriations like *Naked City*. The single location of Coney Island receives half again as much screen time as the varied landscape of midtown Manhattan and its bordering waterfronts. *Weegee's New York* divides New York into built structures and citizens, overview and detail, and accentuates these differences of content through contrasting film forms without ever associating one with the miniature and the other with the gigantic. The film jettisons the tactics of *Naked City*. Neither section has the status of lexicon, as with the Lower East Side in *Naked City*, a space that merely serves as a repository of stimuli to be abstracted and analyzed in spaces of power and capital.[60] There is no drawing back to a miniaturizing vantage point from which the city may be read as a text. Instead, remaining embedded in experiential space, *Weegee's New York* surfaces the contradictions and structuring absences of life under postwar urban renewal.

"New York Fantasy" begins by analyzing commuting. In the immediate postwar period, commuting produced space that is neither leisure nor labor, yet connects the two, dissolving the border between them. Commuting helped extend the time of labor into all areas of life, reinscribing the endless present with which urban renewal concerns itself.[61] "New York Fantasy" induces an arrhythmia in commuting by focusing on a built environment that resists it and by displaying rhythms seemingly generated outside of accumulation. Following the opening title card, the first shots feature low-contrast, natural lighting. They depict a barely visible exit ramp populated by equally invisible cars, whose presence is indicated by their headlights. These cars at five in the morning seemingly lack drivers, and their points of origin and arrival are only undifferentiated darkness. As they zip past on the left side of the screen, their smooth motion and skittering headlights sharply contrast with the steady, equally disembodied illumination of the street lamps on the right side of the screen. These first frames set the city into a motion that cannot be decoded or fit neatly into a miniature-gigantic figure. As well, the opening segment noticeably dispenses with the aerial shots and photo-journalistic views that *Naked City* and its cohort articulate to the ideal of a legible, textual city. "New York Fantasy" continually insists on a city that resists narration either as an infinitely signifying miniature or an emplacing gigantic. Instead, this section depicts the collective time that both those exaggerations absent.

Throughout the section, Weegee defamiliarizes central and mon-umental structures including the Flatiron Building, the main branch of the New York Public Library, the Empire State Building, and the Rockefeller Center ice skating rink. "New York Fantasy" reorients the viewer to them as a series of ludic sites opposed to the time of capital. For example, the opening segment of the section features the Patience

Figure 2.3. Optical effects diffract light around the lion sculptures that guard the New York Public Library in "New York Fantasy." (Arthur Fellig [Weegee] and Amos Vogel, Dir. *Weegee's New York*. 1948; New York: International Center for Photography. 16 mm.)

and Fortitude lion sculptures outside the New York Public Library (figure 2.3). These sculptures are the kind of scaling detail integral to the miniature-gigantic. Moreover, the library they guard organizes its hours of operations around the demands of the industrialized working day. They also enact the displacement of space by narrative encoding. The lions are a metonym of the library (they are currently its trademark) and serve as a metaphor for New Yorkers, as expressed by Mayor Fiorello LaGuardia when he bestowed their names at the height of the Great Depression. Weegee films each lion in near isolation. Bereft of crowds and the monumental, centering force of the building behind them, the statues loom disproportionately in the shot. The lions appear to waver in the frame. They are photographed using prism effects Weegee pioneered, which create diffracted color around objects in otherwise desaturated or black-and-white images. The lions are surrounded by a nimbus of color that radiates their edges outward and blurs their details. These effects are especially striking given the stillness of the shot, which stands in sharp contrast to the frenzied movement and time-lapse photography that otherwise characterizes the section.

These elements suggest the shots as depicting the ghostly remnants of the lions' past, present, and future, the bones of the city that do not change with the anonymous and repetitive movements that otherwise characterize it. They produce a time of contemplation and an understanding detached from the time of accumulation, undisciplined by the demands of exchange value, and not narratable within the current socio-spatial order. "New York Fantasy" draws attention to detail without allowing that detail to either enter into a metonymic relationship with the city as a whole or to be transformed into an artifact/sign that explains experiential space, as with the "bright, hot light" shot.

Throughout "New York Fantasy," the pace of editing between shots and of movement within shots is characterized by jarring and unmotivated changes of speed and direction. This rhythm turns the act of negotiating a central space of production into a spatial practice more reminiscent of an amusement park ride. This section transmutes the drudgery of commuting into the exuberance of movement for its own sake. Similar tactics even succeed in revaluing the Empire State Building, the kind of landmark included in any miniature, whose bulk provides the comforting sense of context and textual inscription on which the gigantic turns. The modern skyscraper disciplines the perception and lived experience of space around it to the eurhythmia of white-collar labor and touristic gawking. "New York Fantasy" depicts the building in every way but the traditional one: as an insubstantial apparition glimpsed fleetingly between buildings, as an attenuated shadow cast on passing cars, as an attenuated needle shot through a heavily distorted lens. *Weegee's New York* takes this icon of the miniature-gigantic and uses it to force the figure open, revealing a space that is fluid and incomplete. Seamless editing turns a vertical pan up the side of the Empire State Building into a horizontal tracking shot of the underside of the Park Avenue viaduct several blocks to the northeast. The sequence continues with another attempt to complete the survey of the building; this time a pan down its side results in a dissolve of fifteen blocks north to the Rockefeller Center ice skating rink. Utilizing visual distortion and the rearticulation of disparate locations, the camera defies the regimentation of space, time, and rhythm that Midtown engenders. Instead, it engages in an aimless drift that is defiant precisely because it *is* aimless. The film eschews the scurry of the commuter, the consumption of the shopper, and even the regimented itinerary of the tourist. This scene's camera movements and their rhythms lack the potential for exchange value. The textual, legible city that urban renewal and visual culture produce shatters.

"New York Fantasy's" closing treatment of Times Square is similar. Though commonly discussed as a monumental landmark, Times Square is, as the sobriquet "the crossroads of the world" reminds us, one defined by emptiness.[62] Formed by the intersection of Seventh Avenue and Broadway, Times Square is framed by buildings and, more important, billboards. Times Square is technically an absence, an opening in the built environment, yet full of endless symbols and the traces of capital's claim on the city. Its increasing centrality and use in the postwar era was a direct result of suburbanization, which, backed by the same federal policies that made urban renewal possible, began emptying the city's residential base. At the same time, as the cases of Times Square's cross-town counterweights—Stuyvesant Town and the UN Headquarters—suggest, urban renewal prioritized the city for commercial and industrial use as the suburbs were increasingly construed as the proper place for residential use. Times Square's increased prominence was also due to Robert Moses's efforts to attract additional corporate capital to the city and assert the local government's authority over Wall Street tenants by producing Midtown as an equally viable center of white-collar industry.[63]

Weegee's New York subverts Times Square's status as the place of empty production and anonymous crowds using the same optical effects that dominate the rest of "New York Fantasy." It also relies on intensified and varied time-lapse. This technique, when applied to the area's neon signage, displaces these advertisements' traditional function as signs of consumption. It turns the luminescence of the billboards themselves into an amusement or an attraction without abstracting them. Subsequent shots shift their framing to include the very bottom edge of the elevated ads or leave visible only their reflection on the pavement while accelerating the time lapse. The result is a confusion between the surface of the street and the surface of the billboards. Suspended on a black background, the crowd appears to pulse and dance rather than trudge home. The segment calls to mind not only the illuminated evening conclusions of early city symphonies like *Berlin: Symphony of a Great City*, but also the alluring, dangerous whirl the electrified metropolis posed to rural populations in 1920s fiction films like F. W. Murnau's *Sunrise* (1927).[64] Twenty years after *Berlin*, the chaotic neon, klieg, and other lights of Times Square are routine, not novel, and part of daily annoyances rather than potentially lethal revelations. This closing segment of "New York Fantasy" not only unbundles the rhythms of tourism, leisure, and commuting, it also subverts the usual triumphal, unified nighttime climax of a city symphony.

Reinforcing this remaking of symphonic grammar, "New York Fantasy's" final scene focuses on the marginal and the arrhythmic. Rather than dwell on the monumental backdrop of skyscrapers that frame Times Square, or the outline of the then-headquarters of the *New York Times*, the camera grants the window of a small, shabby tourist shop command of the screen. The totalizing, oblique, panoramic view crucial to the miniature-gigantic is nowhere to be found; instead a sense of smallness and strangeness emerges. What are we to make of this grubby neon sign behind which "live turtles and cut rate souvenirs" can be acquired? The shot organizes nothing, addresses no totalizing cliché, constructs no metonymy. Walter Benjamin once associated the turtle with the gaze and unique rhythm of the flâneur. In that context, the turtle represented a touch of the surreal within urban mundanity, as well as the flâneur's privileged, unworried, and unhurried gait.[65] In *Weegee's New York* there are no turtles, merely an advertisement for them that suggests a tired parent or tourist purchasing a last-minute gift on their way home; Times Square as carnival midway. The sign reveals the oddity and pleasure at the heart of this space and its activities, returning encounter to the center. The sequence highlights the difference between the humble local turtle ad and the overwhelming lights and ads for internationally sold products that define the space in which the shop exists. Times Square's main functions are recessed but not elided as its surreal, disorienting qualities come to the fore. In doing so, "New York Fantasy" uncovers the polyphony of experiential space that exists even in a space otherwise produced for and by the forces of urban renewal and through the miniature-gigantic.

"Coney Island" exchanges abstract-expressionist optical effects for tabloid-like portraiture aligned with observational documentary. That it does so while also exchanging the built environment and spaces of accumulation for fleshy assembly in a space of leisure is not incidental. Rather, these inversions produce spaces and modes of representation that are incommensurate without privileging one over the other. Like "New York Fantasy," "Coney Island" borrows the logic of a photography book and, following the title card, begins with an intertitle: "A million people on the beach of a Sunday afternoon, is normal." This intertitle goes out of its way to establish objectivity via typicality—what we are about to see is a common occurrence, a normative one. It is, in fact, the only content explicitly presented this way in the entire film. The next shot is an almost exact duplication of Weegee's famous photograph *Coney Island, 22nd of July 1940, 4 o'clock in the afternoon* (1941). Max Kozloff describes this image as a gathering of the citizenry posing for a "collective portrait"—"an off-work swarm of bodies, mingling every physique, age, and background, though not color. If they can be designated a mass, still this is not a united assembly."[66] With the parachute jump in the background to provide scale and to balance the elevated angle from which Weegee takes the photograph, a seemingly endless crowd covers the beach from the immediate foreground into the far distance.

The first shot of *Weegee's New York* differs from the photograph it references in several minor but important ways (figure 2.4). Shot from roughly the height of a lifeguard's raised beach post, the take begins with an image of Deno's Wonderwheel, stark against a cloudless sky, with the crowded boardwalk pushed into the lower fourth of the frame and the beach itself reduced to the top of beachgoers' heads glimpsed just above the frame line. The camera then tilts down until the multitude on the beach occupies the entire frame, waving and smiling at the camera in a subtle slow motion that fuzzes the otherwise crisp depth of field in the shot. A jump cut is followed by a static shot of another section of the crowd, even more vast than the last. Here, both the crowd and the boardwalk are included, as well as a larger expanse of the beach.

These images recall Dimendberg's typical postwar photographs in all their photojournalistic cliché. However, they substitute people for the built environment, robbing the image of the contrastive scale on which the miniature-gigantic depends. The whole cannot be extricated from,

Figure 2.4. The opening shot of "Coney Island" asserts the normality of the huge crowd it features. (Arthur Fellig [Weegee] and Amos Vogel, Dir. *Weegee's New York*. 1948; New York: International Center for Photography. 16 mm.)

or rendered more important than, its parts, and those parts stubbornly retain their individuality, assembling a collective or an ensemble, but not a unified whole. Moreover, opening the section with two near-duplicate shots suggests that even a relatively homogenous, limited-use space like Coney Island cannot be represented from a single vantage point, elevated or otherwise. Even with the cooperation of his subjects and the mobility of a 16 mm camera, Weegee must still draw on multiple shots to introduce this space and communicate exactly how large the "normal" crowd that frequents it is.

This crowd, importantly, also differs from the one depicted in the 1941 photograph in that it is multiracial. White bodies predominate, but there are also people of color present throughout the shots, including a group of Black children in the right foreground near the beginning of the first take—as well as throughout "Coney Island" as a whole. Moreover, the combination of glare, summer tans, and a range of skin tones blur obvious racial distinctions, drawing our attention to race as a lived experience rather than as a set of visual signifiers. The multiethnicity and ambiguity of this crowd stands in sharp contrast to the taxonomized, racialized logic of the miniature-gigantic, as well as the sharp lines of segregation drawn by urban renewal projects like Stuyvesant Town.[67] "Coney Island" presents the citizenry as a mixed multitude, explicitly names this multitude and its makeup as "normal," and challenges visual signifiers of whiteness as normative, elevated, or self-evident.

"Coney Island" reimagines a space consumed as amusement as a space that produces a plethora of new social forms, a democratic assemblage in the flesh. Amusement parks in general and Coney Island in particular were constitutive loci of urban modernity.[68] In popular cinema ranging from King Vidor's *The Crowd* (1928) to Stanley Donen's *On the Town* (1949), Coney Island has been both valorized as a place of total escape from the pressures of modern life and denigrated as a paradigm of the alienation and anonymity of mass culture.[69] In early cinema, it was both a break from and intensification of the city's sensory onslaught. One of the forms this took was Coney Island's use of electricity, which predated domestic and civic uses of electricity in the urban core. As a result, even in films as ambivalent about mass culture as *The Crowd*, Coney Island "represents, in part, a social site where alienation is suspended, where electricity is used for play instead of work, providing an atmosphere where people can bond with one another."[70] Typical of its tendency to reverse the signification of sites, *Weegee's New York* reserves the spectacle of illumination for centers of production, and depicts Coney Island only during the day, with none of the nighttime illumination that it was known for even in the postwar era. However, it reaffirms Coney Island's status as a space of collective affection and bonding, one outside of capital's alienating effects.

Weegee's New York's production of Coney Island as normative experiential space requiring no decoding or explanation is especially important because of the role the area played in the popular culture of the time as a signifier of integrated public spaces as degraded.[71] Moreover, the crowd in *Weegee's New York* cannot be encoded as a sign of modernity, or even the sign of a quotidian urban experience that must be analyzed for it to have social value, as in *Naked City*. It is not produced as an overcrowding problem to be resolved, as in urban renewal policy. Rather, "Coney Island" produces its eponymous space as paradigmatic—but crucially not metonymic—of New York as a whole. It insists that the city can be represented through the bodies of its inhabitants alone, dispensing with the miniature-gigantic. Describing the million people on this particular beach as normal challenges the fear of interracial and interclass bathing spaces—an anxiety that informed several of Robert Moses's postwar recreation projects in the city and his prewar development of Long Island's beaches, which could not be reached using public transportation.[72]

As important, making this very long summer afternoon the entire subject of a full day at Coney Island intervenes into the classic city symphony structure. *Weegee's New York*'s focus on the beach's inhabitation inverts public and private behavior, exchanges the phallic power of the camera for ludic performativity, and heteronormative, patriarchal reproductive rhythms for a queered communal eroticism. In doing so, it stages a series of spatial practices that are unassimilable by even the miniature-gigantic. "Coney Island" educates our desire toward a concept of space in which "the center" of the city moves with its population, where the center no longer refers to the concentration of capital and power, or even of residential real estate, but rather where inhabitants gather at any given time. Moreover, this gathering occurs according to those inhabitants' desires for encounter with physical space and with one another, outside the logic of exchange value as well as the demands of accumulation and social reproduction.

"Coney Island" begins this process by defamiliarizing the crowd rather than encoding it as a symbol of alienation. While the crowd has perennially signified urban isolation and atomization in modernity, including in *Naked City*,[73] in "Coney Island" enforced proximity engenders a kind of intimacy. A series of shots of beachgoers adjusting their bathing suits, arranging their towels, and undressing follows the opening shots. After seven of these portraits, a second explanatory intertitle appears: "Everybody's doing it." The text is clearly meant to evoke sex, yet the images are not sexualized, but rather matter of fact, and even awkward, attending to the ungainly bends, lunges, and pinches that accompany the shedding of shoes and adjusting of bathing suits. Every *body* is, in fact, doing it; the camera dwells predominantly on women, but subsequent shots feature several men. The subjects are of all ages and races. All demonstrate a striking lack of concern with their appearance and freedom in their bodily display.[74] The subjects display what is usually private behavior in public, inverting dominant quotidian rhythms by undressing in public in the middle of the day. In addition to these portraits of individual beachgoers, the camera continually catches others on the edges of the frame. The 1 million from the opening shot have disbursed themselves from the cluster of the crowd, but they still form a multitude that fills almost the entirety of the available space, reminding the viewer that behavior that seems to be observed by only the camera, or recorded illicitly, always already exists in view of fellow citizens. This undercuts the camera's voyeuristic power and its claims to photographing the objective, "naked" truth. How could it, when each subject is already aware of and consenting to their own exposure, quite literally letting it all hang out, removing the restraints of suspenders and shapewear as they go?

Weegee's autobiography and photography foreground voyeurism and the penetrative power of his camera's "truth."[75] Critical assessments of Weegee's work also acknowledge the extent to which many of his shots were staged, and the lengths to which he went to disavow this.[76] Yet in "Coney Island," the film's subjects continually interact with, hail, perform for, or challenge the camera without necessarily posing for it, engaging in an act of mutual, and mutually acknowledged, creativity. For example, in a striking shot, one of the longest in the section, a kissing couple is observed from mere inches away; their faces fill the frame. This couple is perhaps the most "conventional" in the section. Both members are young, white, of opposite genders, physically fit, and more modestly dressed than the other couples Weegee singles out. Moreover, unlike other couples, in which the woman is depicted as more sexually aggressive, initiating or intensifying kissing or groping, here she assumes a more passive role. As Weegee's shadow falls over the couple, the woman looks up at the camera, laughs, covers her face with her hands, looks away, spreads her fingers, looks back, looks away, drops her hands to her mouth, and looks up, holding the camera's gaze, as her partner and their friends wave. In this instance, the camera serves a tutelary purpose, helping its subject leave behind restrictive notions of the performance of white femininity and instead acclimate to the more permissive environs of Coney Island. Even when the subjects of shots appear unaware of the camera, as with the older people of all races who slowly traverse the tide line, the Black parents teaching their toddler to walk, or the white male couple who smile and murmur to one another as they slow-dance together, they are still in a crowded outdoor space in which mutual observation is a given. There is also a rhythmic contrast between the usually quick, jerky cuts of people interacting with the camera, and the lyrical, medium and long shots of these intent, unaware beachgoers. These contrasting rhythms are intercut with one another, but do not create any kind of clear encoding of space or people: the tideline cannot be mapped and captioned as the space of the elderly, just as dancing is not the exclusive province of queer men or parenting that of African Americans.

These unmotivated changes in rhythm are familiar from the first section of *Weegee's New York*. However, while their use in "New York Fantasy" produced immobile, monumental skyscrapers as a ride or amusement, here they serve to individuate members of the crowd and destabilize the already hazy temporal structure of this day "off," lending it a sense of syncopation. *Naked City*'s fetishized reduction of the city to an image to be read through the form of a white woman under threat cannot be easily reproduced here. "Coney Island" does not produce "the City," but rather a plethora of "cities" composed by each of the million New Yorkers assembled on the beach. Each "city" has its own rhythm and each pursues different activities. The section's final sequence depicts the setting sun, which renders swimmers indistinct from water, silhouettes onlookers against the pier, and mingles the natural colors of the sunset with the artificial red of the parachute jump. The day ends several times: people empty the area, a seagull chases the tide, the moon rises, and a single couple remains cocooned under a suggestively moving blanket on the darkened beach. Just as with the conclusion of "New York Fantasy," there are no fireworks—except the figurative kind of the couple's furtive coitus—no triumphal conclusion, no transformation of the day's end into a symbol for the city's fundamental unity and textuality.

Scott MacDonald argues that the "generous, unashamed" display of bodies in the Coney Island scenes mark their historical distance from today's body consciousness.[77] As important is these bodies' resistance to the repetitive, mass rhythms on which the reproduction of late modern capital and its labor force depend. "Coney Island" features many images of parents and children, but usually sequesters them in separate shots. The parents exchange lazily erotic caresses without the urgency or possibility of immediate reproductive sex, while the children wander in aimless groups, freed from the nuclear family unit for the afternoon to the observation and protection of the million other beachgoers. Similarly, neighbors' extremities regularly intrude in the close-ups of couples, and occasionally other subjects will intervene into or change the space of the couple, putting up bunny ears or miming their activities. This group participation becomes more overt in a sequence of seven shots that feature groups engaged in erotic activity. The sequence includes a young man and woman who kiss, curling together on their sides as another man rests his head on the male partner's lower back and buttocks (figure 2.5). Another image features a threesome consisting of two women and a man. The women lay next to each other as the man kisses the one nearer to him and draws his arm across the other, circling her waist. Interestingly,

Figure 2.5. One of the casual threesomes that populate the middle section of "Coney Island." (Arthur Fellig [Weegee] and Amos Vogel, Dir. *Weegee's New York*. 1948; New York: International Center for Photography. 16 mm.)

like the couple described above, all these figures tend to be younger, more conventionally attractive, and whiter than the bulk of the subjects of this section's portraits.

This suggests a further troubling of the "normal" aspects of this "typical" Sunday by attributing deviations from heterosexual norms to more privileged subjects rather than racial and sexual minorities. This sequence can also be read through what Christopher Bonanos argues were Weegee's relatively progressive ideas about sexuality and gender expression. For example, Weegee's images of men in drag, including under arrest, highlight the subjects' defiance rather than condemning them. Similarly, Bonanos recounts an anecdote in which Weegee rejected a men's magazine's request for photographs of "abnormal fellows who liked to dress in women's clothes." Weegee refused and responded that "what was abnormal to [the magazine's editor] was normal to me."[78] The threesome/moresome sequence from "A Day at Coney Island" implies

Weegee's embrace and extension of this idea. The images deliberately blur the lines between platonic, tactile affection with romantic and intimate acts, presenting each as equally acceptable in public, and the participants in each as equally *part* of the public.

The penultimate sequence continues to produce Coney Island as a space in which the private is made public, and celebrated in and by the public, through the depiction of large groups dancing. There are two distinct groups—one performing an Italian folk dance, and the other a Salsa, which associates the dancers with white-ethnic and Latino identities, respectively. These groups are intercut with shots of individual dancers of multiple racial backgrounds, often children, who dance while seated or engaged in other activities, as with three young Black children who watch and cheer while piled into a beach chair. The reverse-shot of the Italian dancers that follows brings the children into the group activity as an appreciative audience. The dancers generally dance in groups rather than in pairs, and when they do they change partners frequently; the only couple extensively featured in the sequence is the male one previously mentioned. This sequence refuses to unify all the beachgoers as it attends to their differences, even as they engage in the same activity, but neither does it encode them in their differences. It collects amorphous performances of gender, sexuality, and family in extensive formations while refraining from comparing them. This sequence, like the rest of the section, estranges the encoding on which the miniature-gigantic depends because it produces rhythms governed solely by the pleasure of encounter, not the requirements of exchange. Unlike leisure, which is always defined by its difference from labor, pleasure demands its own time, creating spatial practices that educate our desire toward another way of being.

Together in the Crowd

As the use of the Lower East Side in *Naked City* indicates, the program of urban renewal and the miniature-gigantic figure it generated had already incorporated spaces of difference so as to mimic an alternative socio-spatial order and obviate the need or desire for it. When urban renewal began to wane in popularity in the late 1950s and early 1960s, its critics would turn to the Lower East Side and spaces like it to valorize the residential neighborhood as an alternative to the space produced by top-down social policy. *Weegee's New York* eschews spaces like the Lower East Side, instead staging its utopian critique of urban renewal and the miniature-gigantic through Midtown Manhattan and Coney Island. These spaces embody urban modernity and encapsulate its increasing division in the late-modern period into spaces dedicated to the accumulation of wealth and consumption of goods, on the one hand, and spaces that are consumed as recreation, natural beauty, or leisure, on the other.[79] Although nearly inverse images of one another—a mutual opposition that would only increase as their fortunes diverged throughout late modernity—they share several important features. Each experiences an especially intensive version of mass rhythm, as the workforce flows into Midtown during the working week and out to Coney Island during the weekend. Each, at certain times of the day, week, and year, has a legitimate claim to serve as New York's center because of its vast number of inhabitants. Each is almost an entirely commercial space oriented less toward the industrial economy of the past and more toward the service economy of the future.

Neither space, that is, lends itself to the idealized notion of the small-scale urban village that critics would later invoke against urban renewal. Instead, both spaces evoke Iris Marion Young's concept of "being together with strangers." Young defines "being together with strangers" as an experience of urban space that allows for tactical alliances, mutual support, and safety, while preserving a certain degree of anonymity, plurality, and freedom of movement beyond the confines of communities.[80] Such relationships are not exclusionary or antimodern, as those imagined for and produced as "communities"—including Stuyvesant Town—often are. Rather, they are incomplete. Like the irruptive instants of utopia, they may be momentary, or extend only to certain parts of our lives, or be only half-acknowledged. More important, they resist encoding. *Weegee's New York* estranges Midtown and Coney Island to produce them as experiential spaces in which being together with strangers is possible. These spaces indicate a city in which the masses have the right to the city because they produce and reproduce it as an oeuvre. The right in question is the right to determine how the city is conceptualized, perceived, and experienced with reference to the needs of residents and users rather than the demands of capital, racist state power, or the reproductions of extant social relations. This is the very right that urban renewal takes for itself, and which the figure of the miniature-gigantic simulates. In opposition to it, *Weegee's New York* depicts the city as a collective work of art that remains forever unfinished and receptive to the myriad, undisciplined, pleasurable rhythms of its inhabitants.

As the template for the postwar city symphonies, *Weegee's New York* pioneered a new aesthetic and mode of rhythmanalysis that educated viewers' desire for an alternative way of being through both its exhibition site and its structure. Cinema 16 produced the concept of the center as a collective work of encounter through its very location, its institutional identity, and its aid to other societies across the country in establishing their own venues. Cinema 16 and other avant-garde institutions like it would go on to play a central role in the production, distribution, and exhibition of the city symphonies that followed *Weegee's New York*. These films were part of an ongoing process of estranging late modern New York's production of space and revealing its structuring absences. They did so by constructing spaces that, rather than being transformed into an encoded narrative, narrated an alternative space. That is, *Weegee's New York* and its descendants depicted the quotidian realities of spaces like Times Square and Coney Island through aesthetic forms that disarticulated and analyzed the rules and regulations that constituted them. In doing so, they enabled the material of everyday urban life to point toward another way of living, another set of rhythms and therefore relations of production. The city symphonies that performed this utopian narration between 1948 and 1964 did so in large part by extending the insistent lack of completion that marked *Weegee's New York*. They built on the landmark break their progenitor made with the structure of the traditional city symphony to separate documentary and experimental technique, margin and center. These films continued *Weegee's New York*'s dismantling of urban renewal's reduction of the city to a code, instead producing spaces that told other stories.

3

Secret Passages

Symphonies of the Margins, Slum Clearance, and Blight

Those who go there do not send back dispatches.

—Elmer Bendiner, *The Bowery Men*

I N THE 1940S AND 1950S, THE street photographer and filmmaker Helen Levitt based her practice in poor New York neighborhoods, most notably East Harlem. There, she shot the city symphony *In the Street* (1948–1952) with James Agee and Janice Loeb. In that film, as in much of her output, she foregrounded images of everyday life as it is lived in public and improvised spaces by members of multigenerational, racially integrated communities, especially children. Her work focused on what the photographer Henri Cartier-Bresson called "the decisive moment": the ephemeral instant, action, or gesture that captures the nature of an event. In Levitt's photographs and films, these decisive moments illuminate ideas of belonging and how social and spatial marginalization delimits that belonging.[1] For Agee—a writer, film critic, and social gadfly—Levitt's subject matter and her approach to it were a major ethical and aesthetic intervention into image making. Agee argued that

Levitt's "way of seeing" amounted to "a unified view of the world," in which depictions of poor people are never "psychological or sociological documents," but rather render their subjects as "wild vines upon the intricacies of a great city."[2]

Two aspects of Levitt's depiction of poor neighborhoods are especially important as critiques of capital's claim to such space, particularly via urban planning. The first is her dedication to capturing such areas in motion. Her decisive moments explore how marginalization and belonging manifest on the level of rhythm, documenting how the social regulation of quotidian spaces plays out in the uses of those spaces. The second is her representation, as intimated by Agee, of the lives of the poor as a series of improvised, interstitial acts that occur in the small openings left in the urban fabric. These acts add surprise, beauty, and grace to an otherwise uniform landscape.

These two qualities define not only Levitt's *In the Street*, but also other postwar city symphonies filmed in poor areas like *Under Brooklyn Bridge*, *On the Bowery*, and *Little Fugitive*. The directors of these films (Lionel Rogosin, Rudy Burckhardt, Ray Ashley, Morris Engel, and Ruth Orkin) like Levitt, had experience with street photography and were aligned with Left causes and organizations such as the New York Photo League.[3] Their city symphonies depicted the economically, socially, demographically, and/or geographically marginal neighborhoods of Fulton's Landing, the Bowery, and Coney Island. These films have had a fitful relationship to the category of the city symphony. For example, Scott MacDonald rejected *In the Street* as a city symphony because "its focus is not New York City in general."[4] However, *In the Street* is part of a single-neighborhood tradition that stretches back to the first city symphony cycle. These films, which include American entries like *A Bronx Morning* and European films like Joris Ivens's *De Brug* (*The Bridge*, 1928), focused on a single location. That location could consist of a single site and its environs, as in Ivens's film, which deals with a railroad bridge, or a larger area linked by demographic or architectural similarities, as in Leyda's film about neighborhoods around Grand Concourse Avenue. The films in this chapter are city symphonies in this sense, even if their production of an urban cross-section differs from more famous films of the first cycle.[5] In addition to their generic instability, these films, particularly *In the Street*—but even the feature film *Little Fugitive*, described in *Film Comment* as a "thin sketch"—have loose, opaque structures that downplay the dawn-to-dusk or twenty-four-hour norm.[6] By recognizing the films' commonalities as "symphonies of the margins," we can understand these traits as important modifications of symphonic norms, discern the logic of their organization, and surface their power as utopian critiques.

The symphonies of the margins depict poor neighborhoods as the sites of festivals that benefit the urban ensemble as a whole. Such a way of seeing is a direct inversion of how postwar urban planners envisioned such areas. Under local and federal policy, East Harlem, Fulton's Landing, the Bowery, and Coney Island were defined as slums. They were dealt with as social ills that had to be removed through a process known as slum clearance. This meant razing the extant built environment, including housing stock, businesses, and sometimes industrial areas, to the ground, and removing former residents. The rhetoric slum clearance proponents used to justify these policies was complex, if not contradictory. For urban planners, slums were obstinate, unchanging areas frozen in an unhealthy past, devoid of any kind of motion, including both the generational/figurative movement of social advancement and the daily/literal movement of people and goods. At the same time, they also held that the condition of the slum was infectious, capable of seeping into other areas of the city at any moment and dooming them as well.

This doubled figure of stagnancy and invasion is evident in the statements and policies of the agencies responsible for overseeing slum clearance and determining which neighborhoods qualified as slums. New York City's Committee on Slum Clearance, headed by Robert Moses, used stable and abstracted metrics, especially concerning population density and the age of housing stock, to determine which areas qualified as slums. Such statistics encapsulated the idea that slums and their residents could not speak for themselves, nor change themselves; they remained as frozen as the numbers used to represent them.[7] The nongovernmental organization American Council to Improve our Neighborhoods understood slums in equally scientific terms. However, they drew on medicalized discourse rather than statistics to portray slums as threateningly dynamic, associating them with an "insidious decay" that can "set in" anywhere people do not take sufficient care to keep up the value of their property.[8] For its part, the federal government, in the form of the Housing Authority and the federally backed mortgages its associated institutions facilitated, understood certain neighborhoods as slums based solely on their demographics. These were poor, Black, or Latino areas that could never qualify for bank or federal loans and mortgages because their inhabitants' very identities posed an inherent, inborn risk.[9] Adding to this complexity, the institutions whose job it was to identify slums, even those that understood slums as fundamentally resistant to transformation, sometimes *created* them. For example, Moses added the

Gas House District, the area eventually replaced by Stuyvesant Town, to the rolls of New York slums slated for clearance even though it fit none of his own Committee's criteria for a slum.[10] Redlining policies led to the creation of slums—by which I mean areas with extremely high population density, major public health issues, and substandard housing stock—in a far more material way. Because residents could not secure home improvement loans or mortgages, they were subject to a rental market whose prices were consistently artificially inflated and landlords who had no incentive to improve or maintain their property, leading to overcrowding and crumbling apartments.[11]

The paradoxical nature of the definitions used by slum clearance officials indicates a structuring absence at the heart of these criteria. How can a slum be both virulent and stagnant? How can it arise from the inaction of any homeowner and yet also be a reason to deny specific groups of people the opportunity to become homeowners? By 1965, the sociologist Scott Greer proposed a more functionalist definition that implied the underlying logic binding these contradictions together. To describe something as fulfilling the conditions to be designated as a slum, he claimed, is simply to say "This land is too good for those people."[12] Greer's comment implies that a slum is any place the state or capital wish to possess at the expense of the people who already live there. That is, a slum is a place whose exchange value cannot be maximized given its current habitat and inhabitants. Slum clearance is inextricably bound up in capital's assertion of its right to determine what a city is for and how a city is structured. The more conservative sociologist Herbert Gans, also writing in 1965, found that slum clearance is a mechanism by which institutional racism reinscribes structural inequality in urban spaces.[13]

Greer's and Gans's critiques are especially notable because, in New York, slum clearance was conceived as a way of *diminishing* the role of capital and white supremacy in city life by establishing housing as a human right.[14] Slum clearance was supposed to be a means to an end, removing substandard rental stock owned by exploitative real estate companies so that the city could build federally subsidized, modern rental housing for the poor—housing that would help people of different classes and races live together equitably, and with a high standard of material comfort. This subsidized rental housing would offset the harm done by redlining and the rising costs of city living in general.[15] It would also "surgically remove" the disease and threat posed by the slum to the rest of the city, excising the source of the contagion and thereby inoculating both the former slum and the areas around it.[16] Those hopes went unrealized because the housing reformers and progressive politicians who espoused them were stymied at the federal and local level by real estate interests, the prevalence of racism in popular and juridical discourse, and the competing agendas of urban renewal planners invested in building infrastructure, cultural centers, and luxury apartments.

In this chapter, I explore how the symphonies of the margins assert the rights of poor people to their neighborhoods as the sites of festivals and as places of mutual care. In doing so, the films critique the impact of slum clearance on the neighborhoods they document. The films articulate this critique through observational documentary and fiction techniques. They focus on human bodies and communities to the minimization of the built environment, modifying traditional symphonic tactics and topics. The symphonies of the margins vary significantly in form and length, ranging from the short documentary subjects of *In the Street* and *Under Brooklyn Bridge* to the feature-length docudrama of *On the Bowery* and the neorealist narrative of *Little Fugitive*. Similarly, the latter two films focus on a few central characters, whereas the former encompass whole communities. Yet each is structured by the abstract time of the festival, which, rendered through montage, accompanies, and sometimes substitutes for, the familiar classical unities of the city symphony. All of these single-site city symphonies foreground an event set apart from the normal quotidian flow of time and its everyday concerns, instead detailing an extraordinary celebration. Each festival is distinct, matched to its film's form and content: *In the Street* takes place during Halloween, *Under Brooklyn Bridge* over summer break, *On the Bowery* on a lost weekend, and *Little Fugitive* on a birthday. When depicting these festivals, the symphonies of the margins also subvert normative iconographies associated with the neighborhoods in which they occur. Part of this subversion involves restricting their depiction of New York to these neighborhoods. By refusing to represent the geographic relationship of marginal areas to the rest of the city or to offer a visual comparison to the rest of the city in terms of the economic, racial, or social status of their inhabitants, these films contest the slum status of the neighborhoods they depict.

The Motionless City

The symphonies of the margins depathologize and recenter poor areas while positing their inhabitants' right to these neighborhoods as places of encounter rather than of exchange. They indicate the ways in which the production of space slum clearance inscribes is dependent on such places remaining marginal. In particular, they uncover how slum clearance policy generated a way of seeing the city just as coherent as Levitt's, and diametrically opposed to it, through the figure of blight. The figure of blight combines both characteristics attributed to slum areas: stillness and infectiousness. It makes sense of the potentially paradoxical nature of these elements through its ecological metaphor. Blight originally referred to any number of plant diseases. A blighted plant has been infested by a parasite, often borne by external environmental conditions, due to which it can no longer photosynthesize or grow, leading to its death.

When Catherine Bauer and other housing reformers first applied blight to a discussion of urban neighborhoods in the early 1940s, they hoped this scientific, objective terminology would convince governmental institutions to treat the spatial manifestation of poverty as a medical, rather than moral, condition, one for which the habitat, rather than inhabitants, bore responsibility. In the rhetoric of housing reformers like Bauer, a slum had been blighted by external social ills and, now infected, had ceased to generate growth. Clearing the diseased housing to make way for modern, subsidized units would cure the neighborhood and restore its growth.[17] Bauer's model, however, was inverted when it was taken up by agencies like Moses's Committee on Slum Clearance, disseminated by trade groups like the Home Owners' Improvement Association, and relied on for legislative and legal purposes by the Housing Authority and Supreme Court. This discourse, which dominated planning policy and visual culture until the mid-1960s, reversed Bauer's model. In this new figure of blight, a slum was an inherently static space, unable to modernize or generate productive activity. This motionless area took on the poisonous qualities of a brackish pool, breeding social diseases that would rapidly infect any adjoining areas.

For Bauer, blight was a way of advocating for investment and improvements in slums. For those advocating or adjudicating slum clearance, blight was a way of justifying the destruction of neighborhoods. As the Supreme Court held in 1954's *Berman v. Parker*, blight was such a threat that a local government wishing to exercise eminent domain seizures of property in a blighted area was not responsible for proving that whatever replaced the property would constitute a distinct benefit to the community. Rather, a city could seize and level any area it proved to be a slum, because blight was so dangerous that simply *removing* an afflicted area benefited the general public. As Wendell Pritchett has argued, *Ber-*

man and the function of blight in legal and popular discourse especially abrogated the property rights of immigrants and racial minorities, who were excluded from "the general public."[18]

To understand how blight justified such an exclusion, we need to understand how it manifested in popular culture around slums: as a conjoined threat to motion and to vision. For example, *New York Times* articles on Coney Island and East Harlem characterize them as "airless"[19] and "congested."[20] These same pieces attribute the difficulty in remediating these conditions to the impossibility of visually accessing or mastering the areas in which they occur. Similarly, for over a decade the paper's coverage of the Bowery described it "dark and gloomy" or "grim and dark." This gave the area the nature of an "immovable obstacle," impervious to social improvements.[21] These descriptions indicate how blight as a figure and the spaces it defined related to the dominant visual culture of the postwar era. Urban renewal and the miniature-gigantic produce the city as a space that functions as a text, where the built environment and its users can be fully imaged and accounted for. Under this policy and figure, even potential threats to the rhythms of capital as they are instantiated in daily life can be rationalized, apprehended, and neutralized using the same visual schema.

Blight positions slums as spaces that are threatening precisely because they interrupt this schema. Neither the "down and in" miniaturizing gaze of elevated images nor the emplacing gigantic gaze of crowd-based images can adequately depict or narrate a blighted place. Where postwar visual culture in New York and urban renewal is defined through conceptualization that accounts for and includes experiential dimensions of space, slum clearance and blight posits poor areas as simultaneously resistant to conceptualization and devoid of meaningful experience. The conflation also manifests in zeugmas that collapses the built environment and its inhabitants. Rather than the wild vines Agee describes, the urban poor become overgrown by their environment, tangled within it until habitat cannot be distinguished from inhabitant. This elision helps justify slum clearance as a cure-all policy and obscures the extent to which residents were subject to displacement. It also alibis the racist logic at the heart of the "scientific understanding" of slums that blight afforded courts, governments, and planners.[22]

Fully embracing the figure of blight, New York emerged as a leader in slum clearance, displacing as many as 250,000 people between the late 1940s and mid-1960s.[23] By 1965, backed by federal funding and private sponsorships, the New York City Housing Authority (NYCHA) had completed 152 public housing developments, with 146,653 units, which were largely dedicated to housing those displaced by slum clearance.[24] The terminal arrhythmia that blight attributes to the slum obscures and disavows the rhythms that structure *slum clearance*, which are based on the circulation of capital rather than the movement of people. Even as housing reformers attempted to redefine housing as a human right, they persisted in thinking of the bodies so sheltered, even in public housing, as use value and surplus labor.[25] Calling slum areas motionless describes their prevention of the maximization of their properties' exchange value more than it does the lives of those who live there.[26] The removal of the populace simultaneously frees this capital and disrupts the usual smooth rhythm that structures property—the right of transfer through sale or inheritance. This disruption and recirculation intensifies the movement of capital back to the urban center and directs it toward accumulation as wealth in the hands of the white elite and middle class. Slum clearance, that is, narrowly directs and locks rhythms into uninterrupted repetition. It produces the exact kind of cancerous, invisible spread of devastating motion it attributed to blighted areas. The multifaceted, complex definitions of slums as motionless spaces or as interruptions of the city's normative functions dissimulate the constitutive role that the rhythms of capital and state power play in the life of poor neighborhoods and their inhabitants.

The symphonies of the margins marshal a rhythmanalysis that contests the figure of blight in part by documenting the vital motion that exists in poor neighborhoods. The films not only trace these rhythms, they also indicate the extent to which capital and state power are always already present within such areas, delineating the ways in which these flows of power regulate quotidian itineraries and activities. One of the major tactics the films use to accomplish this is the foregrounding of *dressage*. Henri Lefebvre defines dressage as the ways in which humans discipline the circadian rhythms of the body to the requirements of the relations of production. Lefebvre understands dressage as a consensual, or at least complicit, process that people undergo to be admitted into social structures, groups, and categories. Dressage is a contortion of the self: "Humans break themselves like animals. They learn to hold themselves. Dressage can go a long way: as far as breathing, movements, sex. It bases itself on repetition."[27] This repetition composes rhythms that render the body fit for labor, engendering it with a use-value. To keep that body fit, dressage also allows "a little room" for "education and initiative, for liberty."[28] That little room is given and determined by capital's requirements for the body that receives it. Dressage, that is, describes what rhythmanalysis sets out to uncover: the rules and regulations behind spatial practices.

Slum clearance produces particular holding and breaking rhythms on the individual and collective level that maximizes the use value of residents and the exchange value of the places from which they are ejected. To display the dressage demanded by slum clearance and to assert the existence of the movement and vision that blight denies exists, the symphonies of the margins focus on the rhythms of festive play. The films emphasize forms of play tied to a given neighborhood, only accessible to its residents, and in most instances outside the normative and legal uses of space. They thereby reveal the circumscribed place dressage allots such play. They indicate the role play has in renewing the use value of the bodies engaged in it as well as the exchange value of the spaces in which it occurs. However, because the symphonies of the margins also minimize a time *outside* such play, they force open the "little room" dressage allots for liberty until that time suffuses the diegesis, becoming an archaic pause outside labor, a utopian festival.[29] All the symphonies of the margins reclaim the rhythms of marginal areas and assert their inhabitants' rights to shape them. However, except for *In the Street*, the symphonies of the margins minimize the role racism played in slum clearance and the figure of blight, again indicating this utopian form's horizon of limitation.

Press Here for Secret Passage: *In the Street*

In the Street contests blight's equation of East Harlem, a racially diverse and economically marginal area, to a motionless, lifeless trap. The film instead renders the neighborhood as a viable, functional community. It does so by demonstrating the ways in which performance as a spatial practice infiltrates all aspects of daily life. It also intervenes into the usual function of cinema within urban planning. Instead of positing the camera as "seeing behind" the false front of blighted areas and exposing them, *In the Street* associates the residents of such places with cinematic technologies. It conjoins the street with the screen, the city with the cinema, producing the city-cinema as a place rife with secret passages composed by theatrical spatial practices. These passages exist within and between the rhythms created by dressage and the unintelligible, blighted status it accords places like East Harlem.

Of all Manhattan neighborhoods, East Harlem was the most fully remade by slum clearance. Fully 10 percent of all public housing built by the NYCHA throughout the five boroughs was located in this neighborhood. Erecting this housing demolished the street grid in large sections east of Park Avenue below 120th Street and above 98th Street. These high-rise developments were generally not occupied by former neighborhood residents, who either did not qualify economically for public housing or who were bumped down the waiting list by New Yorkers displaced by earlier clearances in other neighborhoods.[30] The income guidelines of the new public housing resulted in an increase of poverty in the neighborhood. The high rises broke up the street grid and inserted barriers between major streets in the neighborhood. These physical barriers increased racial segregation in what had once been a mixed Italian, Puerto Rican, and Black area. Progressive public servants and several community groups had advocated for major federal intervention into the area, including slum clearance, beginning during the Great Depression. They did so because overpriced, overcrowded, neglected housing had sparked rent riots in the early 1940s. They argued that leveling extant housing stock, ending the hold of slumlords on the local economy, and building affordable, modern housing under the auspices of the federal government would drastically improve residents' quality of life. However, as the true impact of slum clearance became clear, they turned against it.[31]

As East Harlem, and the greater Harlem area, experienced major social upheaval, they became popular subjects for photographic studies. Paula Massood shows how popular magazines like *Look* and *Fortune* commissioned photo essays that used the language of stasis, as well as racist logic, to equate residents to their environment. This included a photographic caption that labeled a group of young black boys as "Five Social Problems," embodying in them dysfunctional schools, elevated crime levels, and an inability to escape Harlem.[32] The boys' race signified their neighborhood as blighted and, in turn, residence in the area as itself an intractable sign of social failure. Traditional Left organizations like the New York Photo League also used the photo essay and the photography book to document social ills in Harlem. These photographers, including Aaron Siskind, Morris Engel, and Gordon Parks, produced images that emphasized togetherness in poverty rather than social abjection. However, such work was still regularly appropriated by conservative and center-right commenters and fitted to the figure of blight, especially when, as they often were, the photographs were accompanied by the text of an

essay.[33] Massood names *In the Street* as a striking exception to these studies, in part because Levitt resists labeling or titling any of her images.[34]

In the Street was shot in 1945–1946 in East Harlem and released in
various versions in 1948 and 1952.[35] The film displays irruptive moments
of encounter in which play coalesces into the striking tableaux of spatial
appropriation typical of Levitt's work. In this film play takes on a specifically ritual flavor, as James Agee intimated in the opening title crawl.

> The streets of the poor quarters of the great cities are, above
> all, a theater and a battleground.
>
> There, unaware and unnoticed, every human being is a
> poet, a masker, a warrior, a dancer: and in his innocent art-
> istry he projects, against the turmoil of the street, an image
> of human existence.
>
> The attempt in this short film is to capture this image.

In the Street emphasizes the actions and gestures of its subjects, who
are drawn from all of East Harlem's major racial and ethnic groups, as
performances that organize encounters and social roles. However, the
film does not position these performances in comparison to any notion
of natural or authentic behavior; they are not consonant with the trained
rhythms of dressage. Neither does *In the Street* suggest that a particular
performance offers evidence of behavior "typical" of a racial or ethnic
group. Rather, the inhabitants' poetry, masking, fights, and dances show
the traces of the body's training while constructing a kind of constant
festival that suspends the systems that demand this training.

Much of the scholarship on Levitt's work, especially her still photography, foregrounds her recording of private behavior, play, and drama
that erupt into the public space of the street.[36] Jan-Christopher Horak
emphasizes the (e)motion of Levitt's images, which spill beyond the
frame. In capturing these rhythms, Horak argues, Levitt troubles the
traditional subject/object relationship in both mainstream documentary
and modernist photography, instead "looking and documenting her own
subjectivity."[37] Horak's analysis suggests that the moments Levitt depicts
are less decisive than they are "impossible," because they uncover or
enable *illicit* rhythms and relations. Levitt's camera produces spaces of
encounter in which tenement dwellers coalesce their own public spaces
outside the demands of exchange value. The street becomes the space
in which multiracial neighborhoods can experience being together with

strangers beyond the racially limited boundaries of community, children "fanaticize a certain kind of freedom," and inhabitants range themselves against the extant social order.[38]

For Levitt, play composes spatial practices that cannot be encompassed by the current production of space. As Agee's epigraph suggests, this includes the dissolution of the space and time among mise-en-scène, photography, and projector. The performances, "the innocent artistry" of the inhabitants' rhythms, are a projector. Stored in and released by that bodily projector is "an image of human existence" visible only against the screen of the street. Here, Levitt and Agee's camera is the last step in the filmmaking process. It records an image of life projected between inhabitant and habitat in an endless rhythmic loop. This model of projector/street performance/camera contests the paradoxically static/infectious nature attributed to East Harlem. It asserts the inhabitable, rhythmic nature of the slum and engenders an empathetic relationship with its residents. As Tom Gunning puts it, *In the Street* inspires "a way of seeing that assumes one's shared vulnerability with the subject of the image, while a moving image allows us to mime the thrill of movement witnessed in the spontaneous action of another."[39] This way of seeing is composed, in part, by the reorganization of camera/projector/subject, and offers an alternative to the photo essays Massood discusses.

In the Street's conjoined camera/projector/subject makes "a space apart," as Horak has it, that is also the opposite of the extant socio-spatial order because it is a space *together*. It produces an encounter between subjects as well as between photographer and subject by opening and connecting spaces outside of or atomized by the current reality. In this way, the film builds on the themes best exemplified by one of Levitt's 1936–43 photographs of children and street life. This image, "N.Y.C (Button to Secret Passage)," (1938) was exhibited in her first solo show at MoMA, "Photographs of Children." It is included as photograph number six in her book *A Way of Seeing* (1965), for which Agee wrote the essay quoted at the beginning of this chapter. The photograph features a scrap of grated doorway or fence on the left side of the frame to provide scale and texture contrast. It otherwise consists of four rectangular brownstone bricks, their shadows, textures, and pockmarks captured with crisp depth of field, and a rag or piece of paper stuffed in the crack between the topmost brick and the one beneath. On this second brick, just above a faint dollar sign, the words "Button to Secret Passage: Press" are chalked next to a dot placed within two concentric circles. This image, lacking any visual contextualization, framed so tightly that it omits the street beyond it, paradoxically suggests a limitless expanse of space and multiple temporal registers. The photograph conjures another world folded, accordion-like, into the very fabric of the mundane stone façade of the street and the dollars that determine its contours. It also redefines the extant space of the street as an otherwise dead end that *needs* to be escaped, putting both spaces, the physical/visible and imaginary/invisible, into the "play" typical of utopian space.

This city written within a city is guided by rhythms that remain invisible to the naked eye because they can't be read through the dressage that otherwise structures the urban quotidian. The normal hegemonic relation between narrative sign and space is overthrown. The significance of the architecture—sturdy, forbiddingly ugly building materials that conjure schools or jails more than a residential brownstone, the wire mesh's ineffectual, fearful division between public and private—is challenged by the whimsical chalk message's communication. The entire dominant signage of the edifice speaks of forcible exclusion; the message extends an impossible invitation. In this still image that features no human figures or poses indicative of motion, Levitt produces a striking arrhythmia, a secret passage that provides otherwise forbidden points of connection, one that defines the center as that which remains out of sight, written invisibly between built structures. Levitt's work not only produces a vital, animated East Harlem that contests slum clearance's rhetoric of deadening blight, but also suggests that its very rhythms produce it as an alternative center. This centrality is not geographic, economic, etc. Rather, East Harlem is central to a city produced according to residents' needs, rather than the use value of their bodies and exchange value of their built environment.

As in Agee's epigraph, *In the Street* constructs such secret passages and the festivals they shelter by jettisoning the city symphony's typical unifying structure. Instead of depicting a composite day, the film articulates rhythms of play that demand and produce their own time. *In the Street* consists of three sections, which are unequal in length and, appropriately, have relatively porous borders. The first section, which begins immediately after Agee's opening text and ends after approximately five minutes, concentrates on intertwined scenes of intergenerational play and caretaking. The second, which runs approximately seven minutes, chronicles Halloween activities. The third, running just over three minutes, depicts children's sustained interaction with the camera in a vacant lot as well as a meditation on adult performance. These sections do not produce the sense of the progression of a constructed "day" in the action. Even the seasons are disarticulated, with the first section featuring footage of both winter and summer, the second limited to the end of October, and the third indistinct.

Understanding *In the Street* as a utopian riposte to the figure of blight and the policy of slum clearance allows us to recognize both the organizational possibilities and the political resonance of play and its rhythms within the film. From its very first image, *In the Street* marshals play to contend against slum clearance. As Agee's text fades to a black screen, the film's first image appears: an East Harlem street, filmed perhaps three feet above the ground and with such depth of field as to capture the entire streetscape. The frame is dominated by a young white boy pedaling madly on his bike, drafting behind a horse-drawn cart filled with milk for delivery. Although two older cars appear at the edges of the frame, they are not the image's focus, nor are they contrasted with either of the other two vehicles. Where slum clearance argues for the removal of the past because it fouls the motions of the present with stasis and congestion, *In the Street* turns the past into play. The open vista of the street with its flowing traffic contests the frequent invocation of the slum as blind and airless. Moreover, the past, as embodied by the bicycle and horse, sets the area into motion in a series of contrasting rhythms that transform a major commercial street into a playground.

This shot's conjoining of past and present is complicated and deepened by the next paired images. These shots measure time in terms of human lifespan and bonds as opposed to technologies of labor and transport, suggesting, perhaps, what the cost of slum clearance's excision of the past would be. The two medium shots feature the sidewalk in front of a brownstone stoop, where older women sit, chatting. From the bottom left of the frame, a toddler flails toward the women, his arms outspread. One of the women rises, duplicates the boy's pose, and sweeps toward him. In this shot, the past and the future embrace one another and caretaking, with all its stratified gender roles, becomes mutual performance. In two successive shots, two middle-aged women greet each other the same way, and young girls playing with a baby carriage face mothers pushing their own carriages. These shots indicate the training of bodies to the performance of femininity, especially the latter shot, which demonstrates how such tutelage is transmitted. Yet the middle shot, which details the "secret passage" of affective bonds between mature women, suggests a kind of play or slack in the reins of dressage, which here spills over into behavior that does not increase the use value of the body. Moreover, these shots depict multiethnic groups in which light-skinned, ethnically ambiguous residents predominate. The film recasts *Time* magazine's invasive, threatening "hordes of Italians, Puerto Ricans, Jews, and Negroes" as an unremarkable, everyday gathering of highly individuated figures, whose racial and ethnic traits do not reduce them to social problems.[40]

The next series of shots further destabilizes the patriarchal organization of space under capital through moments that are even more explicitly performative and playful. In one of the longer takes of the film, a white boy and girl of about four, both wearing somewhat ragged dresses, utilize a single doorway in their play. They transform it into ground to be held, a stage on which to act out a romance, and a bulwark in exhaustion, as they intermittently fight, hug, and sob. Most notably, they perform for one another, dancing energetically. Except for the camera, these children are unsupervised in their play, and they command the entire frame. Adults appear only at the margins, engaged in their own conversations or interactions, but generally unbothered by the children's behavior. Other shots of the street depict similar play, including activities that redefine or contest space: a multiracial group of boys unlock a fire hydrant and leap over the resulting flow intercut with a woman sweeping the sidewalk. The next shot reframes the entire expanse of the street: two women speak to one another, one leaning out of a window at the right top of the frame while the other occupies the lower-left edge of the frame. The street is established as a bounded, policed territory with ragged demarcations of interior and exterior, even as the understanding of play/performance extends to include quotidian conversation, and as that territory is deracialized. Moreover, this polyphony of play, though shaped by the rhythmic contrasts between and within the behavior of adults and that of children, is not structured by an opposition between labor and leisure.

This is not to say that the sequence features no images of labor. It does, and they range from a Puerto Rican woman sweeping her steps, to neighbors returning from the laundromat, to an older white woman walking her dog. But these acts of labor and marks of adulthood, as well as the children's play, are subsumed under a rhythm of caretaking. As the sweeper progresses across her threshold, children running past wave their greetings. As the woman walks her dog, a stray comes up and is allowed to greet the pet. As the neighbors bring their laundry in together, they chat to a neighbor—a woman with noticeably darker skin—overlooking the street from a window in their building. This sequence subverts the claim, central to the logic of slum clearance, that poor neighborhoods are characterized by congestion, fractured social ties, and unusable, unhealthy space. It also contests the idea that slum clearance, public housing, and other forms of urban redevelopment are required to produce racial integration.⁴¹ The film depicts communal structures of mutual caretaking that occur in and are organized by the rhythms of public space. It also helps dramatize the relatively porous nature of the boundaries between the racial and ethnic groups that slum clearance helped segregate.

Although such rhythms are affective and sincere, they are also performances that oscillate between behaviors shaped by dressage and those that, as Horak argues, are fantasies of freedom in opposition to the present moment. The next section, the Halloween sequence, follows children through the preparation, execution, and exhaustion of holiday activity. The sequence makes the film's thesis—that being in the street is a kind of performance—explicit through its focus on costume, role-playing, and theatrical games. However, the Halloween sequence is not clearly demarcated from the prior sequence and does not begin with children. The time of the everyday and the time of prescribed play bleed into each other through a shot in which a Black woman wearing a fur coat and chewing gum stands in front of the stairs to the Third Avenue El. The next shots feature a young Black boy with a cape, Puerto Rican girls watching from windows, pirates and pilgrims of all races walking past corners. Rather than conveying a sense of headlong abandon or speed through editing, the sequence constructs a series of portraits, beginning with a carefully composed medium-long shot of old women waiting on a front stoop. The objects of their anticipation are disclosed in the following portraits of boys eating candy, applying their costumes, and filling nylon stockings with flour for mock attacks on one another.

The use of portraiture in this section removes the neighborhood's inhabitants from the agglomerate of social problems and interruptions of use and exchange value to which slum clearance reduces them. It restores their individuality, cataloging the rhythms of each performance. Black and brown bodies are prominent in this section, their joyful activities and engagement with the camera contrasting the taxonomic function and stasis to which slum clearance reduces them. Moreover, as the tension between the traces of dressage and the performances that defy it continue, the play in the Halloween sequence recalls Marin's understanding of "spatial play" in *Utopics*. The play between negation (dressage and slum clearance) and connection (affective community bonds created through performance) produces the space of the inner city as festival. In the final moments of this section, the flour-filled nylons whirled by the celebrants spill over onto the surface of the street and the sidewalk. These faint trails map the space and time of play, making them manifest through a physical remnant that traces the irruption of utopia, "a sprinkling of instants where each time all of time is uncovered."⁴²

The confusion of time and the omnipresence of performance continues and intensifies in the third and final section. At the end of the Halloween section, the relatively slow pace of cutting increases while the mobile camera gains in speed and fluidity. The transition to the final section begins with a shot of a pirate directly addressing the camera. In this final section, play is halted. For the first time, adults intervene into children's activities, separating brawlers as crying children are picked up by older siblings. Teenagers step tentatively into the street to begin dates, reinforcing the idea that "official" playtime is at an end. Yet play continues and overflows the "little room" dressage gives to leisure periods like Halloween, producing the time associated with utopia: "the only time it knows is the rhythmic circle of rituals, celebrations, and accomplishments."[43] This cyclic time is the same one Agee's opening text evokes and connects to a redefined production process in which the camera's subject is also the projector.

Figure 3.1. Black children playing in a vacant lot at the end of *In the Street* appropriate the camera as a toy. (Helen Levitt, James Agee, Janice Loeb, Dir. *In the Street*. 1948; Washington, DC: The Library of Congress, 2017. Video.)

The final section not only elaborates on the subject as performer, but also makes the camera itself the object and occasion of play. In this footage, shot in 1945–1946 by Agee and Levitt,[44] the pirate's interactive, fourth-wall-breaking close-up unfolds into a series of games with the camera in a vacant lot. First, in one of the rare mobile shots in the film, there is an extended pan over a row of young Black girls waving at the camera. In the next shot, a Black boy of six or seven watches the camera while eating popcorn as though at a movie. These shots pull Agee's metaphor of the performer/street as projector/screen into the diegesis itself. Gunning's claim about solidarity and shared vulnerability with the image takes on additional resonance here. Very young Black children of both genders, absented from or pathologized by other screens and images of the time because of their race, appropriate and challenge the camera itself as a playmate and as a toy (figure 3.1). The film's final shot reinscribes this reversal of power and recapitulates the city-cinema loop produced by the epigraph. Two white women in nuns' habits regard the camera, turn their backs, and walk up the curve of a hill that suggests a studio set. Here, direct address meets the evocation of location shooting, and the location being shot, as simply another kind of set, another kind of play—of film through the camera, of dressage and its refusal, of space itself.

In the Street's focus on the secret passage and, by extension, on the playful revelatory powers of film, form a final riposte to slum clearance. City planners used cinema and photography to visualize and justify slum clearance sites because they believed these technologies could record, with perfect detachment, telling evidence of decay and dysfunction, indicating exactly where and what intervention was needed.[45] *In the Street* appropriates this power by allowing East Harlem to speak for itself as a self-sufficient cinematic apparatus, as needing no external, technological intervention to display its nature. Levitt's film depicts the animating mutual care and performative play that define daily life in East Harlem, while revealing capital's violent shaping of the everyday and its rhythms. Siegfried Kracauer said of *In the Street*: "this film is nothing but reportage pure and simple . . . this reporting job is done with unconcealed compassion for the people depicted: the camera dwells on them tenderly; they are not meant to stand for anything but themselves."[46] For East Harlemites to stand for themselves, rather than their neighborhood, or abstract social problems to be solved, or a threat to the city, is to imagine a city in which the measure of a neighborhood is not its potential exchange value and the measure of its inhabitants is not their contribution to the city's surplus labor force. Kracauer's description of the film's "compassion" for its subjects and the camera that "dwells on them tenderly" similarly evokes a different relationship among inhabitants, cinema, and housing. This tender dwelling, this housing of the inhabitants in the body of the film itself, restores to them the individual identity blight strips from them and, through rhythmanalysis, indicates what a utopian dwelling might encompass.

A River, A Trench: *Under Brooklyn Bridge*

Rudy Burkhardt's *Under Brooklyn Bridge* produces another kind of utopian dwelling and encounter for its subjects, the adolescent boys of Brooklyn's Fulton's Landing neighborhood. Fulton's Landing was named for Robert Fulton's ferry company, which provided service between Manhattan and Brooklyn in the nineteenth century before the construction of the Brooklyn Bridge. In the twentieth century, it was a working-class, mostly white, industrial neighborhood defined by factory and dock work, eventually supplanted by the residential neighborhoods of DUMBO and Williamsburg. By 1912, Fulton's Landing was cast into perpetual twilight by the massive twinned structures of the Brooklyn and Manhattan Bridges as they arced overhead. The Brooklyn and Manhattan Bridges rhetorically and physically erase neighborhoods such as Fulton's Landing by rendering them invisible from most vantage points. This lack of visibility and industrial setting aligns Fulton's Landing with the figure of blight, which consistently describes poor neighborhoods as darkened by the pollution, both social and environmental, of industry.

In discussions of literally darkened spaces like Fulton's Landing, the general sense of pathology and social violence attached to slums sharpens to focus on the physical violence of criminality and delinquency. This can be seen in mid-century depictions of Red Hook, another Brooklyn neighborhood defined by its dependence on dock work, and eventually the presence of high-rise public housing blocks. These depictions focus on the socio-spatial isolation produced by massive infrastructure, as well as a clannish, white-ethnic, working-class criminality that dominates all aspects of inhabitation and whose social structure is impenetrable to outsiders. Late modern cinema and literature like Tom Wolfe's "Only the Dead Know Brooklyn" (1935), Hubert Selby's *Last Exit to Brooklyn* (1957), Arthur Miller's *A View from the Bridge* (1955, filmed by Sidney Lumet in 1962), and the Warner Bros. John Garfield vehicle *Out of the*

Fog (1941) not only dramatize Red Hook as criminal and illegible space, they also represent it as almost sapient and malignant in its socio-spatial incoherence and ethnic and class difference.[47] These and other popular cinematic depictions of tenements and slums in other areas of New York continually fixed on the public space of the street—as opposed to the relations of production that caused poverty—as responsible for social ills in these areas, and sometimes explicitly advocated for their destruction in social problem films like William Wyler's *Dead End* (1937).[48] Such representations heighten the language of blight used in official discourse. They visualize poor areas as housing monstrosity and mindless violence, where residents display an innate criminality they seem to have inherited, and which renders them indistinguishable, from their environment.

This conflation is typical of blight, but in the case of Fulton's Landing and Red Hook, it takes on an additional threatening aspect. One of the usual characteristics attributed to blighted, unintelligible space is its remote nature; geographic distance doubling social difference. Yet monumental works of infrastructure like the Brooklyn Bridge are central to the legibility of the city and also epitomize public space. Under Robert Moses's tenure such massive infrastructure projects became more common and played a key role in suburbanization and commuting. In the postwar period, such infrastructure expanded to include the intra-urban highways and commuter beltways whose completion required the razing of blighted neighborhoods in their path. The possibility that such monuments might house and *cause* blight makes the neighborhoods in their shadows particularly pernicious in the logic of slum clearance.[49]

Under Brooklyn Bridge contests the titular monument's metonymic function as well as Fulton's Landing's association with blight. In their place, the bridge and the neighborhood it shelters emerge as liminal spaces. The Brooklyn Bridge simultaneously foregrounds and mitigates Manhattan and Brooklyn's status as islands. Typical miniaturizing aerial and skyline photography emphasize the bridge's mass and its capacity to naturalize abstract space while effacing the neutral, ambiguous aspects of a structure that stretches over islands and a trench, a classical association with utopia. This suggests Fulton's Landing not as an inherently or uniquely dangerous place, but as an other space that is also the other of space. Fulton's Landing is Manhattan's other when Manhattan becomes the image of the center reduced to exchange value, accumulation, and consumption. The rhythms engendered by the bridge itself and the river underneath it are relentlessly repetitive, resisting the entropic decline associated with blight. They also enact the tidal rhythms of commuting that feed the asymmetrical accumulation of capital on the Manhattan side and thereby engender the very deadening of time that slum clearance facilitates.

Under Brooklyn Bridge draws on the utopian strains inherent in its natural geography to contest the Fulton's Landing of 1953 as a particularly infectious blighted space. Instead, it depicts the bridge as a place of dwelling rather than transience—cradling, rather than erasing, a world—one that belongs to its inhabitants as a festival space of communal encounter. Moreover, the film captures the threat slum clearance poses to the neighborhood through specific omissions and repeated images. While early scenes depict industrial spaces and warehouses by the docks, no activity or human figures are visible in these images, several of which appear to be stills. Instead of the shipping and dock work for which the area was once famous, *Under Brooklyn Bridge* features scenes of demolition, especially of residential areas. The film depicts slum clearance in action. It illuminates the rhythms of an area slum clearance claims is rhythmless and shows how slum clearance interrupts those rhythms. At the same time, the film continually denies the bridge its monumental and metonymic status, rescaling it through forced perspective, composition, and camera angle to make it just another outcropping in the texture of the neighborhood, magnifying the itineraries that play out on, beneath, and around the bridge. This visually raises Fulton's Landing to the status of center and landmark while placing the bridge into its possession as an object of play.

This mutual rescaling is evident from the opening of the film, which places the title card across an image in which the bridge's Brooklyn tower occupies the center background of the shot, peeking from behind the apartment buildings and warehouses that cluster in front of it. The tower is also partially obscured by part of the bridge's span, which cuts across the middle of the shot from screen right to the center. These choices shrink down the highly recognizable tower, defamiliarize the span, and draw the viewer's attention to the residential and industrial buildings from which the bridge seems to emerge. After this title image, a series of close-ups and medium shots provide an extensive study of the doors, architectural details, and sculpted eagles perched on the warehouses and other industrial buildings that provide jobs within the neighborhood. These static shots firmly refute the rhetoric of blight and establish the multiplicity of rhythms and lives made possible by the very physicality and shadow of the bridge. This montage, which holds the bridge offscreen, provides no horizon or human figures for scale. The result is that, by the time the camera finally gains mobility and the frame begins to fill with people, more than ninety seconds into the film, the neighborhood has lost its too-easy legibility as a slum or mere terminus for the bridge. Instead, when the bridge emerges for the first time at the two-minute mark, only one tower is visible, sandwiched between two modestly sized apartment buildings (figure 3.2). The next six shots depict the bridge in piecemeal fashion, from close enough that even in a lengthy panning shot all the viewer sees are anonymous, decontextualized snippets of the span, rather than the typical panoramic view of the entire structure. When the whole bridge is briefly depicted in the following shot, it appears squeezed into the frame, with the buildings that surround it on the Brooklyn side appearing bigger than the Manhattan bridge tower and almost the same size as the towers of Lower Manhattan in the far background. Rather than dwarfing and defining the neighborhood, the bridge is nestled within it.

The next sequence begins abruptly, with a close-up on a sign reading "Must Vacate." The sign could refer to a given building, the bridge,

Figure 3.2. The first shot of the bridge in *Under Brooklyn Bridge* defamiliarizes this iconic structure. (Rudy Burckhardt, Dir. *Under Brooklyn Bridge*. 1953; New York: Microcinema, 2012. DVD.)

or the neighborhood itself. The following sequence, which is slightly undercranked, splits its focus between the automated, repetitive motion required by demolition work and sculptural, erotic reveries on the skin of the workers. The workers stand on the roof of a building level with the elevated approach to the bridge, themselves monumental figures. This sequence, as Scott MacDonald notes, radically telescopes and replays the physical gestures and amount of time required to complete the demolition, recalling early Lumière films and their playfulness with human physicality at work on the physical environment.[50] At the same time, the sequence documents the training capital demands of workers to extract their use value. The shots display the demolition workers' dressage through the precision, repetition, and untiring nature of their movements, which in turn are responsible for imbuing the built environment with increased exchange value. Yet these images of automatic movement are intercut with appreciation of the workers' very human bodies. Their sweat, eccentricities, and weaknesses come to the fore as Burckhardt pans their length and pauses on the detailed play of muscle in arms, clenched effort on faces, and hands wiped on pants. These shots register the camera's desiring look at male bodies, divorcing them from their work and more figurative use value as progenitors of additional surplus labor.[51] They also highlight the mix of races and ethnicities among the workers without distinguishing among or encoding difference within them. This sequence illuminates the way dressage structures slum clearance at its most intimate level. Yet the sequence exists outside the rhythms dressage organizes. The camera's queered gaze valorizes the workers, dwelling on their bodies at rest and, through the play of cinematography, renders those bodies a festival site, a space of pleasure.

The next sequence makes this attention to the festival and amusement literal as it follows a group of adolescent boys. The boys pick their way through scrub brush and construction rubble to a secluded beach under the bridge, swim in the river, and interact with the camera, recalling the children at the end of *In the Street*. Here, the bridge occupies the margins of the frame and provides a staging area for the boys to repeatedly jump and dive into the river and bask in the sun between swims. Like the construction workers, their bodies are magnified by the same false perspective that shrinks the bridge, allowing them to visually dominate their environment. Like the majority of figures in *Under Brooklyn Bridge*, the boys are white, yet their whiteness does not oppose them to the threat of the "five social problems" that their Harlem counterparts allegedly pose. At the time *Under Brooklyn Bridge* was shot, popular culture and Hollywood cinema positioned poor white teenage boys as juvenile delinquents poised to fulfill the dire predictions made in the final moments of *The City*.[52] In *Under Brooklyn Bridge*, the boys become audience surrogates and near avatars of the area, redefining its rhythms as those of the river as the site of a pleasurable festival. Despite being the sequence set most literally "under Brooklyn Bridge," this is also the sequence in which the bridge is least important. Instead, the river occupies most of the screen, asserting its own utopian affiliations as a liminal space.

Fulton's Landing never replaces Brooklyn Bridge as a metonym for New York, nor does *Under Brooklyn Bridge* affirm the dangerous, incomprehensible status blight accords the neighborhood. Instead, occupying the entirety of the frame, redefined through rhythms of leisure and celebration, the neighborhood becomes an alternative center. *Under Brooklyn Bridge* insists that its titular object actually engenders alternate itineraries and spatial practices in its immediate sphere, educating our desire for a world in which monumental structures offer real and rhetorical shelter instead of the threat of displacement.

On the Bowery: Eddies in the Urban River

Of all the areas slated for slum clearance, the Bowery may have been the one most commonly used as a shorthand for blighted neighborhoods. Even in literary essays and progressive sociological studies, the Bowery encapsulated the slum's association with stagnancy, loss of vision, and habitat with inhabitant. E. B. White's essay, "Here Is New York," focuses on the multiple interlocking rhythms that make up the city, from the "pattern of neighborhoods" that circumscribe inhabitants' daily spatial practices to the "tidal pull" of commuters. The one exception to this textural play of motion is the Bowery. White defines other areas through the desires, needs, and connections of their inhabitants, but he characterizes the Bowery as so quiet and lifeless it might be an office building on a summer Saturday evening. The habitat's stillness spreads to its residents, who White reduces to passive tableaux observed and derided by the only sightseers mentioned in the essay. Moreover, while every other space in the essay literally or figuratively borders one another, White associates the Bowery with a literal and figurative "end of the line." He dwells on the dank, noisy conditions imposed by the passage of the Third Avenue El overhead and conflates the neighborhood with the wards in Bellevue where its luckier inhabitants will end.[53] White's depiction of the Bowery as a space of deathly motionlessness that generates a lack of internal differentiation and destroys the possibility of exit was widely shared during late modernity.

Elmer Bendiner, whose sociological study of the area, *The Bowery Men*, was published in 1961, thirteen years after White's essay, closely echoed White's description. According to Bendiner, after its raucous nineteenth-century heyday as the intersection of gangs, political machines, theater, and immigration, the Bowery "became drunk and prim and quiet. Its senescence seems to be sealed."[54] Moreover, Bendiner connected this stillness to the end of intelligibility and knowledge. In the static space devoid of animating rhythms, inhabitant and habitat became indistinguishable from one another; analysis of either became impossible. In the introduction of his book, Bendiner noted the necessity of performing embedded ethnographic research in the Bowery because, despite the plethora of public health and urban affairs literature diagnosing the area and cataloging its ills, it had not been described from an internal perspective. Not even interviews with residents could correct this, as their lack of coherence, combined with the degradations they accepted as their quotidian reality, rendered their responses incomprehensible to the nonresidents Bendiner imagined as his readers. Thus, no one from the outside world was capable of distinguishing the area's component parts and rhythms, and none of its inhabitants were capable of communicating them. In Bendiner's account, as the Bowery subsumed its inhabitants' identities, it also removed these residents from the world.[55] In White and Bendiner's writings, as in those of local housing authorities and slum clearance organizations, the Bowery becomes a space that is monstrous because it reduces residents to extrusions of it.

On the Bowery unbundles the terminal status blight accords the eponymous neighborhood through a doubled rhythm. First, the film produces a strong, repeating rhythm composed of the daily movements of Bowery inhabitants as they shift from flophouse to street to bar to soup kitchen and back again over the course of a day. It uses the classic organization of a city symphony to explore a small area the film depicts as homogenous in terms of class (poor), gender (male), and race (mostly white). Second, the film details the unique, deadline-narrative-like rhythms of Ray, a white railway worker on a weekend binge in the neighborhood. Ray is played by Ray Sayler, a real-life railroad worker and sometime resident of the Bowery, just as other speaking parts in the film are cast with nonprofessionals playing versions of themselves and speaking lines that were developed in part through interviews with them. While Bosley Crowther described *On the Bowery* as a city symphony in his 1956 *New York Times* review, the echoes of Robert Flaherty and John Grierson's work in *On the Bowery*'s production history led other contemporary critics and scholars to discuss it as a proto-observational documentary.[56] I would argue, however, that the film's casting of amateurs for social type, didacticism, and melodramatic aspects align it just as closely with neorealism—a fiction form whose attention to the urban quotidian already connects it to the city symphony.

Developing Ray as a protagonist in the neorealist mode and surrounding him with the vestiges of a deadline narrative structure—Ray must be convinced to leave the Bowery and aided in his exit before he succumbs to the neighborhood's gravitational pull—helps *On the Bowery* challenge the neighborhood's status as the ultimate static, blighted area. The film insists on the circulation of capital and people within the neighborhood and on connections between it and the wider world. Moreover, Ray's job ties the Bowery, usually isolated rhetorically and visually from the rest of New York City, to the regional and national circulation of populace, goods, and trade via the railways. By tracking Ray's circulation within the Bowery, both in concert with and then parted from his money, the film traces his arrhythmic relation to the neighborhood's normal patterns. It thereby both distinguishes inhabitant from habitat and emphasizes the temporary nature of residence in the neighborhood.

Although the Bowery included a sizable Puerto Rican population by the mid-1950s, and its skid row was frequented by people of all races and ethnicities, *On the Bowery* depicts the area's residents, including indigents and workers, major characters like Ray and passersby, as almost entirely white. This deviation from the neighborhood's real demographics are striking given director Lionel Rogosin's interest in racism and European imperialism as key axes of oppression, which he critiqued in later works like *Come Back, Africa* (1959) and *Good Times, Wonderful Times* (1966). *On the Bowery* maintains the New York city symphonies' typical deracializing of whiteness and dissolution of it into a series of ethnic variations. However, it does not center people of color in the frame or accurately depict neighborhood racial demographics. This destabilizes the equation of blight with people of color, yet it also elides the presence of people of color in the Bowery, erasing their daily rhythms and the ways in which these rhythms helped produce it as a neighborhood. *On the Bowery* takes place in a neighborhood that was almost as noticeably racially heterogeneous as East Harlem. Through its presentation of that space

as predominantly white, it affirms that *Under Brooklyn Bridge*'s selection
of a largely white neighborhood and attention to white male bodies is
typical of the New York city symphonies' erasure of the core role race
plays in slum clearance and the unequal burden Black and Latino New
Yorkers were subject to under its auspices.

Even as *On the Bowery*'s treatment of race reinscribes that category
as the New York city symphonies' ideological limitation, its conjunction
of forms and rhythms equally disrupts the relegation of areas like the
Bowery to unnarratable mistakes. Every film in the New York cycle challenges the hegemonic dominance of narrative over space. But because
On the Bowery incorporates a more traditional use of narrative than most
of the other films, its duality resonates especially strongly with theories
of space that emphasize narrative's political potential. Iris Marion Young
argues that urban discourse productive of power relations among various constituencies can take three forms: rhetorical, narrative, and phatic.
Rhetoric is the language of the center and of capital. It functions like
conceptual space to name, define, and encode habitats and inhabitants
by situating the speaker and the subject. Rhetoric compels the acknowl-
edgement and acquiescence of all constituencies through this definitional
work. Often, the only tool marginalized groups can marshal against rhetoric is the phatic, a kind of untranslatable greeting or placeholder that
indicates core social interactions like "hello." The phatic, like experiential
space under the hegemony of conceptual space, marks the space in which
self-articulation and definition is attempted, yet cannot be communicated
or acknowledged. In Young's formulation, narrative offers an alternative
that preserves polyvocality.[57]

Unlike Lefebvre's understanding of narrative as a conceptual displacement of experiential space, narrative in Young's sense enables dialogic understanding among multiple groups when the terms of a conflict
are so differently conceived that constructive argument is impossible. It
does so without compelling agreement and without implying the falsity
of other narratives or constructing them as oppositional. For Young,
narrative is the democratic city's linguistic form, a powerful tool for
protest and the drafting of progressive policy. For Young, narrative is
liminal, a utopian structure that indicates the contradictions on which
the current production of space is founded and points toward space constituted otherwise.[58] *On the Bowery*'s combination of symphonic content
with neorealist fiction functions like Young's narrative. It estranges the
rhetoric of blight while producing a space that narrates the affective
bonds within the Bowery as well as the economic links between that

community's habitat and the surrounding city. Throughout the film, the conjoining of city symphony and neorealism insist on the repeated, daily rhythms of the Bowery and the unique, lost weekend itinerary of Ray as distinct yet unopposed dialogic narratives that belie the conflation of habitat with inhabitant.

On the Bowery opens with both rhythms, beginning with the repeating patterns of the area. The first shots track across wide expanses of sidewalk, pedestrians, and traffic. In these images the camera's attention is continually drawn to the incongruent, unstable tableaux formed by bustling commuters as they brush past the motionless or slowly ambulating forms of the Bowery's drunks and indigents, who are pushed off into gutters and doorways. The street truly does "flow" in the way Kracauer claimed in *Theory of Film*: as a complex stream of current and eddies, crowd and miscreants.[59] By representing other Bowery residents and visitors on their way into or out of it, the opening shots contests the image of the Bowery as a hermetically sealed, socioeconomically homogenous area inhabited only by unmoored social outcasts. More important, these shots insist on linking this marginal space to the urban center and its engines of capital; the crowds flowing through skid row are largely dressed as though on their way to work.

The film thus sets multiple spaces into polyphonic play before Ray and his plot emerge to further complicate the Bowery's circulation. Ray emerges from an extreme long shot of an anonymous crowd making its way down from the steps of the El. As the shot switches to Ray's point of view, it captures the police loading drunks into the van under the trestle. The entrance of the protagonist and the semifictional plot he represents coincides with the unwilling exit of the real people he typifies, as though he has both emerged from them and come to (temporarily) replace them. Yet he does not stand for them, and neither does his more conventional fiction plot rhetorize the space they occupy. Rather, Ray's introduction suggests the character's likely future *and* a dominant but usually invisible daily rhythm in the area. These shots imply that the carceral system, rather than the Bowery, is the true locus of stasis, terminus, and monstrosity.

Like a 1920s city symphony, this overture, which telescopes the entirety of the action, is followed by three "acts" that correspond to the three days Ray spends in the Bowery. Each emphasizes his point of view while insisting on his distinction from the neighborhood's dominant rhythms. The first act remains largely within the confines of one of the neighborhood's bars, focusing on Ray's observations of his peers as well as his conversation with Doc (Gorman Hendricks), an older resident of a local single-room occupancy (SRO) flophouse. The second act expands from this personal focus to illuminate the extent to which the neighborhood's rhythms are delimited by trips to the church mission and soup kitchen, spaces that dramatize the role of state-aligned social agencies in shaping the Bowery. A sequence at the soup kitchen features several highly stylized shots that emphasize the prison-like bars that separate the soup line from the sleeping area (figure 3.3). In one objective shot, Ray is seen standing on line with several other residents as an older man explains the many regulations of the kitchen to him—you must sleep on the floor if you are new, cannot leave and return, must wake up at 6:00 a.m., and may remain for a week. Here, the frontal composition of the shot, profile views of the men, and prominence of the bars recall the aesthetics of the mug shot in particular and the prison in general. The cinematography communicates Ray's perception of the soup kitchen as a place of incarceration, estranging the location of charity so that its function as an engine of dressage is revealed.

Figure 3.3. Ray and other indigent Bowery residents are seen through the prison-like bars at the local mission. (Lionel Rogosin, Dir. *On the Bowery*. 1956; New York: Milestone Films, 2012. DVD.)

In the film's third act, Ray awakens in an alley after having been mugged in a sequence intercut with Doc waking in the SRO; the Bowery, too, has degrees of difference and multiple spatial practices. *On the Bowery*'s articulation of SROs as stable, sought-after housing was especially important given the role they play as putative vectors for social ills in slum clearance policy. For example, in 1950, a nonprofit housing advocacy group connected with Columbia University understood their neighborhood to be in the throes of a "sickness" (blight) that they traced directly to the prevalence of SROs in the area. The group referred to SROs as part of "a vicious cancer of slum housing."[60] In 1962, the University bought one of the only remaining SROs in the area and ejected the mostly African American and Latino tenants. When they returned, it was to new regulations. Each tenant was now required to surrender front door keys, was not permitted guests in rooms or to buzz into the locked building after midnight, and had to accept constant surveillance from both the NYPD and private security forces.[61] As this suggests, part of the anxiety around SROs is that they did not sufficiently enforce dressage or maximize the use value of their inhabitants.

In *On the Bowery*, Doc's SRO residency testifies to his high status and importance within the neighborhood. Immediately after waking, a montage sequence shows Doc using his own long tenure as a Bowery resident—that is, his failure in the context of a larger society—as social currency to secure the return of Ray's belongings, which he in turn sells for more than they are worth. On a thematic level, the sequence shows how a long-standing resident can use his history in the area to protect new arrivals. As Doc approaches Ray with the money, Ray recounts the film's narrative in voiceover, using the third person to describe his own experiences, opening a liminal space that resembles Young's narrative between fiction and documentary. Rogosin here employs the form of an expository documentary to renarrate Ray's fictional experiences as though they happened to someone other than the character—as if Ray speaks for and through the collection of real people who have had similar experiences. Doc eventually hands the money over to Ray with a command to "get off the Bowery and stay off." In this exchange, inhabitant and habitat are forcefully disarticulated, with the implication that Ray's separation will be permanent and that the long-standing residents of the Bowery do not share any of its allegedly innate destructive qualities.

The film ends in the same spot it began, with Ray looking at passersby as he stands at the steps to the El. As he watches, the expected reverse shot fails to materialize. Instead, the camera moves behind him to assume his point of view as Doc, in voiceover, describes the lives of local residents. Thus, the "terminal" aspects of the Bowery are complicated through repetition and the creation of something like a communal point of view: of a narrative in Young's sense of the term. Overlaying Doc's description of the area's daily life with a shot indicative of Ray's point of view distinguishes the inhabitants from their environment, implies their right to encounter one another in it, and suggests the Bowery's function, even for temporary visitors, as a kind of center rather than terminus. *On the Bowery* opens secret passages within the Bowery in the form of affective bonds and communal care. It depicts the Bowery as a festival destination structured by the dressage—in the form of police intervention, disciplinary institutions, poverty, and crime—that limits this festival. The very infrastructure that helped position the area as blighted through its shadowing of the streets, the Third Avenue El, was closed as the film was completing production in 1955, and was demolished over the next two years. This resulted in skyrocketing real estate prices along the Bowery, the removal of most of the indigent and poor population, and the reclamation of even this most blighted area by the textual city.

Little Fugitive and the Dressage of the Nickel Empire

While the history of the Bowery and the production of *On the Bowery* are perhaps the most dramatic examples of the drastic change that befell the allegedly changeless slum neighborhoods, all the neighborhoods featured in the symphonies of the margins were similarly impacted. As Jan-Christopher Horak points out, Helen Levitt's "impossible images" from *In the Street* would become truly impossible a few years after the film's release because they were generated by the social structures that comprehensive slum clearance would erase along with East Harlem's built environment.[62] *Under Brooklyn Bridge*, for its part, actually documents one of the demolition projects that would change the face of Fulton's Ferry. These films foreshadow and critique the depredations of slum clearance. *Little Fugitive*, by contrast, displays the devastation wreaked by slum clearance through the barren spaces that pocket the film. As to be expected of the symphonies of the margins, it deemphasizes the disproportionate impact this devastation had on people of color by focusing on white protagonists and filling its shots with white bodies. This is especially notable because *Little Fugitive* is largely set in Coney Island, such a crucial site for *Weegee's New York*'s production of an alternative center defined by a multiracial assemblage.

Little Fugitive details a weekend in the life of two brothers, Joey
Norton (Richie Andrusco), six, and Lennie Norton (Richard Brewster),
eleven, who are left to care for one another when their mother must leave
them unattended to visit their sick grandmother, breaking her promise to
take them to Coney Island to celebrate Lennie's birthday. Left to their
own devices, Lennie teases Joey until he runs away. Joey spends a day
and a night at Coney Island before Lennie finds him and brings him
home. In relating this plot, *Little Fugitive* estranges Coney Island as a
public, festival space and produces it instead as a bastion of dressage. Its
rhythms teach inhabitants how to inscribe use value into their bodies
and structure their habitat through exchange value. By doing so, the film
shows how the circulation of capital defines even those spaces that slum
clearance policy and its attendant figure of blight produce as stagnant
threats to this circulation. Moreover, although *Little Fugitive* is not the
latest entry chronologically in the symphonies of the margins, it is in
some ways the most inscribed with a sense of finality and loss. This loss
extends from its diegetic spaces to its contested place in film history.

The film was an important influence on the French New Wave,
especially Truffaut's early work. It was also a spiritual precursor to New
American Cinema. Jonas Mekas described it as the film that most contributed "to the growth of low-budget feature production in America."[63]
This casts *Little Fugitive* as a somewhat obscure, or at least singular, link
between more established film movements. For today's viewers, it has an
air of belatedness: made too late (and in the wrong place) to participate
in the first neorealist flowering in Italy and made too early to join fully
in the late 1950s development of American independent cinema in New
York. The aura of anachronism surrounding *Little Fugitive* is compounded
by contemporary critiques of its perceived inexpressiveness. Mid-century
critics like Thalia Selz praised the film for its "naturalness" and "portrait
of innocence," yet ultimately concluded that this artless charm was not
artful. Selz repeatedly describes this fiction feature film as a documentary—much as critics would do three years later with *On the Bowery*.
Selz also points to a lack of urgency in *Little Fugitive*'s presentation and
a lack of sophistication in its form, especially its editing. Ultimately, she
concludes, this "humble" work was significant mainly as proof of concept: that an American film could be made outside Hollywood.[64] Indeed,
even recent reviews of the film on the occasion of its release on DVD
or screening in a repertory theater note its slightness.[65] *Little Fugitive*'s
reception and fitful entry into the canon of New York independent cinema produces it as a kind of dead end, a motionless artifact that captures

and documents a milieu so accurately that it takes on its inert status in an act of imitative fallacy, reproducing the zeugmatic relation between inhabitant and habitat in slum clearance discourse.

While blight always renders its subjects in an eternal present-past, this effect is particularly pronounced in the case of Coney Island, which enjoyed a unique status as the mirror of the urban center, as evidenced in *Weegee's New York*. Yet it also hosted fifteen separate high-rise low- and middle-income housing developments constructed from the post-*Berman* 1950s though the early years of the urban crisis in the late 1960s.[66] More important, the construction of these projects punctuates a hundred-year discourse that describes Coney Island as always already in decline, sometimes via a paradoxical temporality in which a single moment is both the area's height and nadir. Various scholars, ranging from somewhat conservative sociologists like Raymond Weinstein to progressive urban historians like Sharon Zukin, have located this moment everywhere from the burning of Dreamland in 1911,[67] to Coney Island's designation as a blighted area by Robert Moses in 1949,[68] to the highwater attendance mark of the late 1950s,[69] to the urban crisis of the 1970s.[70] Coney Island embodies the "little room" dressage cedes to leisure, but it is always ready to force that space open and intimate the time of the utopian festival. Capital defines Coney Island as inherently anachronistic because it challenges the inscription of use value in the body and the maximization of exchange value in those bodies' habitats. Even otherwise sympathetic recent scholarly work on Coney Island emphasizes its "failure" to fully exploit the potential ground rents generated by its unusually large number of open and unimproved lots and to display "growth as an urban or tourist center."[71] Yet, as captured in *Weegee's New York*, the neighborhood did serve as a center in Lefebvre's sense of the word. It promoted encounters that themselves helped produce the entire area as a collective work of art to which the masses have a right.[72] *Little Fugitive* illuminates this function, even as it also displays Coney Island as an arena for dressage, one in which even the liminal, neutral space of the festival may be recruited to train bodies to hold themselves to use value.

Little Fugitive's place in the cinematic canon, tenuous as it is, is due almost entirely to its use of Coney Island, yet the film does not begin there. *Little Fugitive* opens on the sidewalk outside its protagonists' apartment building. This building is typical of the five- to nine-story art deco structures that dotted the city landscape starting in the 1920s. These buildings represented a step up the economic ladder from the tenements their residents were likely to have occupied a generation prior.[73] While the built environment therefore suggests some measure of economic security, it is contextualized by precarity. Lennie, Joey, and Lennie's friends race up and down a street full of vacant lots, demolition debris, impromptu dumps, and the cattails and grasses fringing a dingy bay. This is not, even by the standards of the time, a blighted area. Rather, the absences that mark the street wall and the traces of recent wrecking balls suggest that this neighborhood has already entered into the first phases of slum clearance through the removal of blighted housing stock.

The strange, half-built children's wonderland that results has the feeling less of a city and more of the frontier that horse-obsessed Joey loves to watch on television. It also prefigures the "urban frontier" that resulted from slum clearance's destruction of housing stock and home value.[74] *Little Fugitive*'s opening scenes display an odd temporality, gesturing simultaneously to the secure lower-middle-class neighborhoods of a generation before and the burned-out ruins of a generation later. They also contain a strange anonymity for a film whose reputation is so tied to the specific and the authentic. While contemporary press for the film and its catalog entries at the American Film Institute list shooting locations in South Brooklyn, Joey and Lennie name a street in Queens as their home address, and Joey's mother leaves the city via the northern Manhattan access point of the 125th Street station in Harlem. These inconsistencies not only speak to the lack of strict script continuity that might be expected for any independent feature but also indicate the extent to which poor neighborhoods were essentially interchangeable in slum clearance discourse. Moreover, they illuminate the extent to which slum clearance rendered such spaces interchangeable as sites of concentrated surplus labor by imposing identical rhythms of razing and rebuilding on them—all the while holding them to be rhythmless.

Coney Island stands in sharp counterpoint to the amalgamated outskirts where *Little Fugitive* begins and ends. While the rest of the film eschews spatial continuity, the Coney Island scenes are shot more conventionally, albeit from a height and angle that mimics a child's point of view, so that the beach and amusement areas are kept in clear relation to one another. Joey's escape to Coney Island is driven by an imagined outlawry—Lennie tricks Joey into thinking he has shot and killed him— that should resonate with the area's association with a time outside of capital. Yet from the moment Joey enters Coney Island, his rhythms are determined by his need to train his body into use value so that he may survive in the economy of the nickel empire. The first thing horse-obsessed Joey does is ride the carousal. The editing of this scene produces a shot/reverse-shot structure between Joey, absorbed in his wooden mount, and the other children, who reach desperately to grasp one of the golden rings suspended over the side of the ride. Joey appreciates the carousel because of its wooden horses, while the other children understand it as a test of their skill and an opportunity for monetizing it, as gold rings may be exchanged for prizes. Joey himself initially constitutes an arrhythmia in Coney Island because he cannot recognize it as a space of consumption. Instead, his presence in Coney Island is predicated on his perceived transgression of the law, social norms, and the representational space of familial ties. Coney Island thus takes on the festival's aspect of liminality as a space outside authority and law. Just as Joey conceptualizes Coney Island as an outlaw space of refuge, his spatial practices enact his refusal to restrain his own body; he seeks out and consumes prodigiously sized junk food that dwarfs him.

Despite his distance from the space's normative rhythms and seeming innocence of its function as exchange value, Joey is equally distant from his fellow inhabitants. Unlike the space of encounter produced by the other marginal symphonies, editing, camera distance, and camera angle all isolate Joey in the frame and deny him interactions except for monetary ones. Soon Joey begins to try his luck at the games of chance and, driven by injured pride and his awareness of his dwindling stock of nickels, sets himself to practicing in an alley so he may win. In a slowed-down, simplified training montage, Joey teaches himself to succeed at the milk jug toss: he learns how to hold himself so that his body may accumulate use value and enter more fully into the rhythms of exchange value that structure Coney Island. Willingly submitting himself to dressage, Joey wins his habitat's acknowledgment through the automated importuning of arcade games and fortune-telling machines, who address the camera directly in a series of frontally composed, low-angle shots that evoke Joey's point of view. Joey's self-education continues as his wanderings bring him into view of the real pony rides. Finding himself out of money, Joey trudges, disconsolate, along the shore—his sneakers and jeans a sharp contrast to the beach attire worn by other beachgoers, who fill the frame nearly as tightly as the million featured in *Weegee's New York*.

Joey's inability to retain or accumulate money sets him into a rhythm at odds with that of his space, producing him as a walking arrhythmia that analyzes this mass festival's duplication of key structures

Figure 3.4. Joey goes on a quest for Pepsi bottles to turn into nickels and pony rides in *Little Fugitive*. (Morris Engel, Ray Ashley, Ruth Orkin, Dir. *Little Fugitive*. 1953; New York: Kino Now, 2003. DVD.)

of capital. The next step of Joey's self-education makes this even more explicit. In order to acquire the quarter needed to ride the pony, Joey learns to collect empty Pepsi bottles for a nickel each, which we see him do in a montage (figure 3.4). These shots recall his earlier training and locate these artifacts of marketing and consumption in the farthest, most private, seemingly natural reaches of the beach. Having contorted his body into increasingly improbable shapes to tweeze soda bottles from between rocky outcroppings and courting couples, Joey then sets out on a cycle of collection and consumption. He builds up his cash reserve over and over, exchanging it for more rides. At the pony ride, match on action shots show him gaining increased skill in holding and riding the pony around the ring and from one side of the screen to the other, transferring his own dressage to another body that, like his own, has been taught to submit to, and even enjoy, repetitive, restricted motion. Here, the film's focus on white working-class masculinity helps

surface the extent to which such training inheres in every segment of
the population, including those that experience privilege on the basis
of race and gender.

Just as *Little Fugitive*'s invocation of the festival diverges from that
of other marginal symphonies, so too does its treatment of recognizable landmarks, foregrounding them rather than absenting them. *Little
Fugitive* not only highlights the familiar sites of Steeplechase Park in its
establishing shots, it also uses them to motivate its conclusion. Lennie,
tipped off by the pony ride operator, arrives in Coney Island to find
Joey, only to be stymied by the sheer density of the crowd. He turns
to the elevated vantage point offered by the Parachute Jump to attempt
to locate his brother. Although he spots him from the apex of the ride,
he is subject to its pace and duration, and cannot exit before he loses
track of Joey. Lennie next uses the same chalk that Joey used to draw
a horse and detached single-family home on their building's sidewalk in
the opening scene to write messages to Joey on the pavement. However,
passersby ignore or deface the messages, and several shots depict them
being obscured when beachgoers congregate over them; Joey never sees
them. These shots exchange the flour trails from *In the Street*, which
demarcated the time of the utopian festival irrupting into the neighborhood and indexed the free movement of an unrelated, racially integrated
group of children, for a failed attempt to resurrect the private space of the
white nuclear family and through it lay claim to the entire public sphere.
Lennie eventually finds Joey because a downpour utterly disrupts Coney
Island's smooth functioning as a space of consumption and disperses its
crowds. The only encounter possible in *Little Fugitive*'s Coney Island
is the reconstruction of the representational space of the white nuclear
family, not the "tolerant mingling" of being together with strangers, as
in Weegee's depiction.[75]

The film's last scene limns the precise threat such limited social
constellations pose to neighborhoods like Joey and Lennie's, as well as to
Coney Island itself. The final images of *Little Fugitive* frame the Nortons'
television set over Joey's shoulder, as he watches a western TV show,
which, one assumes, contain both the horses and single-family dwelling
for which he longs. While the Nortons do not live in the suburbs, the
film's conclusion invokes the increasing privatization and virtualization
of leisure in the postwar period. This trend would eventually produce
the suburbs as a "properly" white space.[76] It would also diminish Coney
Island's crowds even as it concentrated its increasingly Black and Latino
population in high-rise housing projects, the space of leisure leading

irretrievably back into the stagnant circulation of capital demanded by slum clearance policies.

Secret Passage as Cinematic Infrastructure

The symphonies of the margins drew on the festival and the secret passage to recenter the neighborhoods they chronicled. Yet their exhibition yielded infrastructures that would help resist slum clearance and make encounters among their audiences possible only in Greenwich Village, where they were screened, not in the neighborhoods where they were shot. After one rough-cut screening at MoMA in 1947, Cinema 16 laid claim to *In the Street*, exhibiting it multiple times and renting it to other film societies outside New York. Its 1953 and '54 program notes name *In the Street* as one of the most beloved, popular, and best-known titles in its repertoire.[77] In fact, *In the Street* was so successful that Cinema 16 used it to publicize other city symphonies, touting new films like the Scottish *The Singing Street* (1955) in publicity flyers and playing it as the main attraction at repertory showings of city symphonies or discussions of films about the city.[78] *In the Street*'s popularity helped Cinema 16 fulfill the terms of its charter, which was to "advance the appreciation of the motion picture not merely as an art, but as a powerful social force," by creating an audience for "artistically satisfying, socially purposeful" noncommercial cinema and, within the audience it generated, inspire the production of new films.[79] *In the Street*'s popularity helped sustain Cinema 16 as exactly such a space of encounter. Yet *In the Street* never produced such a space in East Harlem, and was not screened in the neighborhood for its subjects.[80] *Under Brooklyn Bridge*, *On the Bowery*, and *Little Fugitive* found similar success within the New American Cinema and its Greenwich Village exhibition venues, yet also failed to make any impact on, or even engage with, the neighborhoods that were their subject.

The symphonies of the margins express their utopian nature through their diagnosis of the capitalist city's dependence on the removal of poor and minority neighborhoods, but they also remain *ideological* critiques of ideology. Lauren Rabinovitz has shown how the New York avant-garde was both dependent on and limited the accomplishments of female directors. The symphonies of the margins demonstrate that race played a similar role, although crucially here people of color are relegated to content and subject matter rather than acting as creators.[81] This absence is especially puzzling given Engel's tenure as head of the

New York Photo League, which emphasized engagement with marginalized populations, Rogosin's interest in civil rights issues, and Burckhardt's
earlier films, which displayed notable racial diversity. Similarly, Engel
and Levitt were aware of, or, in the latter case even participated in,
the contemporary parallel tradition of slum clearance critique through
photo essays undertaken by Black writers and photographers in Harlem.[82]
Moreover, not only did the symphonies of the margins fail to emphasize
the white supremacy underlying slum clearance, their distribution and
exhibition practices testify to their inability to conceive of a space in
which filmmaking could include racial minorities as creative personnel,
or as a primary audience.

   This stands in sharp contrast to the cultural and political role these
films played in defining Greenwich Village, a mostly white neighborhood,
as a collective work of art and encounter. As the symphonies of the
margins screened repeatedly at Cinema 16, filmgoers who met there to
watch them went on to make city symphonies of their own and, in turn,
used the success of those films to build their own alternative screening
venues. Rogosin's success with *On the Bowery* prompted him to start
Bleecker Street Cinema, dedicated to promoting films of social uplift
and protest, which did not run on a subscription model and so reached
larger swaths of the public.[83] Bleecker Street Cinema reinforced the Village's status as an alternative center. It went on to screen *Little Fugitive*
and *On the Bowery* to audiences that, like those of Cinema 16, included
makers of city symphonies, including Stan Brakhage and Shirley Clarke.[84]
Beyond the relatively literal, physical confines of these exhibition sites,
the symphonies of the margins also helped produce the New American
Cinema. Writing in 1962 in *Film Culture*, Jonas Mekas identified not only
Little Fugitive, but also *In the Street* and *On the Bowery* as key precursors
to the movement.[85]

   The New American Cinema, along with Bleecker Street Cinema
and Cinema 16, made Greenwich Village a center of encounter in which
artistic practices indicated an alternative concept of space. Greenwich
Village was often associated with an anachronistic premodernity and
classed as a slum, discussed using the same vocabulary of congestion,
darkness, and stasis as the other neighborhoods in this chapter.[86] Yet it did
not suffer the same fate as East Harlem, Fulton's Landing, the Bowery,
or Coney Island. Instead, the Village became a center of resistance to
slum clearance, one whose residents successfully organized to preserve it.
Members of Cinema 16, Bleecker Street Cinema, and the New American
Cinema were among these activists, and their efforts, discussed in the

next chapter, included the production of city symphonies dedicated to threatened infrastructure.[87] Yet these very city symphonies, which elicited direct action on behalf of Greenwich Village when screened within it, did not rouse their audiences to action on behalf of the neighborhoods in which they were shot. The relationship was not reciprocal, and it is hardly an accident that Greenwich Village had a higher median income and was whiter than the settings of the symphonies of the margins. No city symphonies about Greenwich Village made their way to other marginal areas, and neither were any exhibition spaces erected in neighborhoods like East Harlem, where screening these images might have helped coalesce new groups of symphonic practitioners. Instead, antislum clearance, anti-urban renewal activists promoted Greenwich Village as an alternate center or festival site that sheltered and promoted encounter. As discussed in the next chapter, these opponents justified their arguments with the exact same rhetoric of legibility that slum clearance used to condemn neighborhoods like the Village and demand their removal.

4

Spectacle in Progress

Symphonies of the Center and Advocacy Planning

What is called for is a renewed urban society, a renovated centrality, leaving opportunities for rhythms that would permit full usage of moments and places. . . . Centrality of course does not imply the center of power but the regrouping of differences in relation to each other.

—Eleonore Kofman and Elizabeth Lebas, "Lost in Transposition"

Architecture produces living bodies, each with its own distinct traits. The animating principle of such a body . . . reproduces itself within those who use the space in question, within their lived experience.

—Henri Lefebvre, *The Production of Space*

FIVE MINUTES AND EIGHTEEN seconds into *N.Y., N.Y.: A Day in New York*, everything is quiet. The film's director, Francis Thompson, draws on the optical effects pioneered by Weegee in "New York

Fantasy." He combines them with especially rapid montage, a propulsive jazz score by Gene Forrell, and fractal, cubist images to produce a dizzying impression of a day in Midtown Manhattan. From a gentle predawn beginning, the film accelerates into a headlong commuting sequence whose frantic pace is emphasized by the soundtrack's insistent plucked strings and the endlessly reflected image of subway straps as camera movement and editing increases. Then, all at once, the score drops out, the editing becomes leisurely, the camera limits itself to a slow, stately tilt, and the complex optical effects disappear from the frame for the first and only time in the film. The screen is filled with a nearly desaturated image of white light filtering through the glass panes of a vaulted, arched ceiling suspended above a darkened staircase. We have arrived in McKim, Mead, and White's 1910 Pennsylvania Station (figure 4.1).

N.Y., N.Y. is typical of a group of city symphonies made between 1954 and 1964, slightly after most of the symphonies of the margins. Like the "New York Fantasy" section of *Weegee's New York*, these films use striking visual effects to distort and defamiliarize the built environment. They apply these effects to iconic sites and infrastructure, as well as

Figure 4.1. The first shot of Penn Station in *N.Y., N.Y.* eschews the optical effects for which the film is otherwise known. (Francis Thompson, Dir. *N.Y., N.Y.: A Day in New York* 1957; New York: Museum of Modern Art. 16 mm.)

locations and activities associated with the accumulation of wealth. Like the symphonies of the margins, these films provide a utopian critique of capital's claim to the city as expressed by contemporary urban planning. However, their form varies dramatically from the symphonies of the margins, utilizing experimental rather than documentary techniques and foregrounding architectural entities rather than human bodies. These differences should be understood in light of the kind of space each group of films address and the nature of the urban development and figurative image they contest.

City symphonies like *N.Y., N.Y.* deal with spaces that determine how the differences that make up the urban ensemble relate to one another: the center. These are places where laws are written, investments are made, people are transported to work, and capital is accumulated until it scrapes the sky. They are places that determine how the differences that make up the city—quotidian spatial practices, embodied experience, extraction of capital, hailing by the state apparatus—relate to one another. The are the places that the rules regulating the city's rhythms favor.[1] In addition to *N.Y., N.Y.*—and *Go! Go! Go!*, as discussed in the introduction—the symphonies of the center include *Jazz of Lights*, *Wonder Ring*, *Bridges-Go-Round*, and *Skyscraper*. These films deal with and define the center in a variety of ways. They also locate it in different places. For *Jazz of Lights* the center is Times Square, for *Wonder Ring* it is the East Side leg of the Third Avenue El, for *N.Y., N.Y.* it is Midtown and Downtown Manhattan, for *Bridges-Go Round* it is several Manhattan bridges, and for *Skyscraper* it is the Tishman Building at 666 Fifth Avenue between Fifty-Second and Fifty-Third Streets.

Writing about *Go! Go! Go!*, Angela Joosse argued that the film's striking syncopation and its grinding shifts between time-lapse and stop-motion were in essence posing a question to the audience: "What is the rhythmic presence of modern urban life? What compels us to go go go?"[2] That question is, in some sense, the question all the New York city symphonies ask. In the case of the symphonies of the center, including Menken's film, that question is asked through monuments, architecture, and infrastructure—aspects of the city we usually don't think of as being in motion at all. The symphonies of the center draw on their highly abstract, often unsettling or alienating, forms to excavate the rhythms of the built environment. They demonstrate how, where, and why that environment makes us go go go. The symphonies of the center analyze the ways in which the repetitive, mass rhythms of commuting and office work—which is to say, socioeconomically compulsory activity—produce

the dazzling, monumental spaces with which they are mutually imbricated. The films ultimately demonstrate that such spaces prevent architectural bodies from producing a truly animated, meaningful existence in
the bodies of their users. In *N.Y., N.Y.*, the appearance of Penn Station
throws these qualities into sharp relief by offering a space that produces
a different relationship with its user, one of almost religious awe, its
sheer scale offering an oasis of quiet contemplation. Thompson frames
our first view of Penn Station as a visual joke; although the image is
not treated with the prismatic effects that dominate the rest of the film,
its architecture produces a similar visual impact. It possesses naturally
what Thompson must artificially impose on the rest of the cityscape, but
here a fractal aesthetic is capable of containing multitudes rather than
atomizing them. Penn Station, in this film, suggests what a center that
oriented relations differently—that was based on the needs of its users
for encounter rather than capital's need to maximize exchange value—
would look like.

Thompson's film premiered in 1957. This was three years after
the Pennsylvania Railroad sold the air rights above Penn Station to a
developer. Nineteen fifty-seven was also the year that the Railroad, in
an attempt to update the neoclassical building, built a modernist ticket
stand that Lewis Mumford, among others, decried as ruining the station.
In 1961, plans were announced to demolish Penn Station to build the
current Madison Square Garden. Those plans were met with the largest,
longest-lasting, and most broadly supported protest of any major demolition or construction project in late modern New York.[3] As with so many
other attempts to stop the removal of buildings or neighborhoods, these
protests were ultimately unsuccessful. The demolition of Penn Station,
however, indicated and incited two key shifts in urban planning and in
the imaging of New York. The symphonies of the center engaged and
critiqued both these shifts.

First, the destruction of Penn Station was driven by private capital
rather than a public/private partnership backed by federal funds. It was
an example of capital unrestrained by state power asserting its claim to
the built environment, rather than an instance of urban renewal or slum
clearance.[4] This marked the beginning of the end of the late modern
redevelopment of the city through federal funding; from now on, private equity would largely determine the city's contours and contents.[5]
Second, Penn Station's destruction sparked local and state historic preservation policies that remain in place today. These policies were the
governmental manifestation of a sea change in urban theory, specifically

urban imagery. These new theories understood old buildings as crucial, rather than detrimental, to modern urban life. They focused on users' abilities to orient themselves to, and find their identity within, the built environment.[6] These ideas of the city still fundamentally accepted it as a space of exchange that capital had the right to shape. They did, however, represent an important difference from, even a reversal of, the ways in which urban renewal and slum clearance policies defined and visualized the city and its inhabitants. The symphonies of the center respond to these new policies and figurative images aimed at the urban core. They challenge a new form of urban planning that exists outside the auspices of the state, advocacy planning, and a new figurative image, a cognitive mapping of the spectacle. The name "symphonies of the center" does not only refer to the kinds of places they depict. It also articulates their struggle to lay claim to the center.

The Right to the Center and the Possessive Spectator

Henri Lefebvre argues that one of the key ways the masses assert their right to the city is by taking and remaking the center. For Lefebvre, the center does not refer to an architectural, political, or even necessarily geographic location. Rather, it refers to the ways in which differences of embodied experience and spatial practice relate to one another through the space that determines their collective orientation. To take the center, in this sense, means asserting that people and the built environment relate to one another through the logic of encounter rather than exchange. Exchange value currently determines relations and differences in the city, and therefore its center, from landlord/tenant to planner/developer to supplier/customer. If instead the city is based on encounters that range from mass demonstrations and urban rebellions to performances and mutual enjoyment of public space, then daily life in an urban environment becomes a collective work of art. This life is a shared masterwork, an oeuvre continually in progress and contributed to by everyone in the course of their spatial practices.[7] What, then, does a symphony of the center look like? How can a city symphony depict the everyday and the rhythms that shape it in the spaces that currently cement capital's claim to the urban ensemble? How can images of such locations help us imagine what the center of a city oriented otherwise—that is, to the needs and uses of its inhabitants—might be like? The symphonies of the center used distortion and defamiliarization of familiar, iconic sites to accomplish this. These strategies contested the logic underlying advocacy planning and its figurative image.

Urban renewal projects and slum clearance policies had always faced some opposition. However, until the mid-1950s, opposition was concentrated in those populations directly impacted, who tended to have very limited political power and social capital. For example, in the 1940s, organized labor supported suburbanization and progressive urban politicians supported slum clearance. Opposition to urban renewal and slum clearance was decentralized and led by women, people of color, and the poor.[8] By the mid- and late 1950s, as the site of urban renewal projects shifted to whiter and wealthier neighborhoods—and as the failure of slum clearance to translate into housing reform became evident—organized opposition efforts included public intellectuals, local politicians, the white middle class, and their affiliated media, including the *New York Times*. When the identity of the opposition changed, so too did their efficacy. For example, while tenant activists vociferously protested slum clearance projects in the Lower East Side in 1951 and 1953, they were unsuccessful and their activities garnered little notice and less approval outside their community. In 1959, tenants worked with liberal-left supporters to organize the Metropolitan Council on Housing to advocate for rent control and against urban renewal. By collaborating with middle-class organizations across lower Manhattan, they successfully opposed a large project in Cooper Square.[9]

Moreover, by the early 1960s, the quality of life in the suburbs was beginning to come into question. Suburbanization had always been the shadow setter of many urban renewal and slum clearance policies. This was especially evident in Robert Moses's work, which included the development of suburban amenities outside the city as well as infrastructure—notably elevated highways such as the Cross-Bronx Expressway—that rebuilt New York neighborhoods as a space for commuters to pass through rather than for urban dwellers to live in. When Moses began to be plagued by corruption scandals, loss of political favor, and well-publicized critique from white middle-class women—the very mothers suburbia was supposed to serve—his damaged credibility fed a larger cultural critique of suburbia.[10] This tradition, typified by books like William H. Whyte's *The Organization Man* (1956), tied the suburbs to larger traditions of conformity and intellectual timidity in American life and labor. This conformity was spatialized in the ready-made, identical houses and grids that typified suburban planning and erased any sense of history from the landscape, encouraging anonymity and mediocrity in its residents. Antisuburban sentiment returned positive attention to the urban center in the form of historical preservation, which sought to protect important buildings and areas in order to encourage a sense of continuity and individuality in their users.

Although there are differences of personnel and agenda among the theories and practices outlined above, all of them are anti–urban renewal and anti–slum clearance. They have collectively come to be known as advocacy planning, which became increasingly dominant after the 1960s. Advocacy planning was originally associated with public intellectuals, activists, and authors like Jane Jacobs and Kevin Lynch, who both published influential, iconoclastic books on urban planning at the start of the 1960s. Lynch published *The Image of the City* in 1960. Developed over many years of study with colleagues at MIT, where Lynch taught architecture and urban design, *Image of the City* presented three case studies of how residents oriented themselves to the urban environments of Boston, Jersey City, and Los Angeles. Lynch found that several characteristics of the built environment determined whether or not people were able to find their way around the city, imagine themselves as members of a community, and derive emotional well-being from their environment. These characteristics included the ways different destinations were connected to one another, barriers that enclosed or limited specific features or areas of the city, and large, long-lasting structures that designated the character/function of certain areas and announced entry to them. For Lynch, the optimal arrangement of these characteristics allowed inhabitants, especially when acting as pedestrians or making use of mass transit, to devise a personalized yet coherent mental map of the spaces they moved through. Lynch called this kind of visualization "cognitive mapping," and argued that only Boston's older neighborhoods truly provided arrangements conducive to it. Jersey City functioned as a commuter town and depressed industrial space, resulting in cognitive maps overwhelmed by the figure of New York across the river, and Los Angeles was designed for high-speed car travel through attenuated neighborhoods that lacked clear division and character.[11]

As Fredric Jameson argues, cognitive mapping offers a useful metaphor: Lynch's subject's position in physical space closely resembles the subject's position in ideology. Jameson's version of cognitive mapping can both describe the subject's alienation—in circumstances where ideology inhibits awareness of/orientation to the relations of production—and the ways in which the subject can become aware of how capital has produced this position.[12] Lynch's model, however, does not have this duality. For him, cognitive mapping describes how the subject responds to the built environment *as a given*. When that environment lends itself to navigation, then cognitive mapping is successful, when it does not, cognitive mapping is inhibited. Lynch's model does not admit for a mapping that helps the subject understand the forces that determine the environment's construction or the possibility of the subject taking control of that construction.[13] Although Lynch is alone among advocacy planners in using the term "cognitive mapping," that idea, and its limitations, also informed the thought of other advocacy planners, most notably Jane Jacobs.

Jacobs was a resident of the West Village, a contributor to *Architectural Review* magazine, and a neighborhood activist. From 1957 to 1964, she successfully led or participated in campaigns against two urban renewal projects and one slum clearance project, all headed by Robert Moses. As part of a local advocacy group, she defeated a proposal to raze fourteen "blighted" blocks of the neighborhood. Working with the nascent historic preservationist movement, as well as a surprising coalition that included local activists like Shirley Hays, iconoclastic public intellectuals like Lewis Mumford, and Tammany precinct boss Carmine de Sapio, she ended Moses's bid to construct a four-lane highway through Washington Square Park. With these and other groups, she defeated multiple proposals (Moses advanced versions of the plan on at least three separate occasions) to run the ten-lane Lower Manhattan Expressway through TriBeCa, SoHo, Chinatown, and other downtown areas. Given this background, it is not surprising that her 1961 book, *The Death and Life of Great American Cities*, begins by stating: "This book is an attack on current city planning and rebuilding."[14] Jacobs advocated for maintaining traditional neighborhoods at their current scale, widening sidewalks, shortening blocks, scattering cultural centers throughout the city, and "unslumming" neighborhoods by financially supporting individual homeowners living in poor districts. Like Lynch, she advocated for a city that could be easily negotiated by pedestrians or mass-transit users, and whose built environment helped foster flexible, supportive communal ties. As an activist, she insisted on the populace's role in approving urban planning projects. However, also like Lynch, she did not articulate a right to the city outside the demands of exchange.[15]

Lynch and Jacobs, along with other advocacy planners, directly challenged the logic of regional planning, urban renewal, and slum clearance. They argued that planning should center the lived experiences of urban dwellers and should engage the built environment as something to negotiate rather than remove. Above all, Jacobs and Lynch argued that a city built with regard to these precepts gave its residents the ability to claim their own conceptualizations and images of the space they inhabited. Their advocacy planning shares several connections to the kind of rhythmanalysis that I have linked to utopian, anticapital- ist notions of the city. However, advocacy planning understands itself as diametrically opposed to utopia. Jacobs, in particular, articulated her anti-utopianism as a rejection of planned communities and a top-down model in which only elites had "the right to have plans of any signifi- cance." Her critique included regional planning projects like Greenbelt and depended on the common understanding of utopia as the good place that is no place, rather than the Marinian model of utopia as dialectic I have been using. However, advocacy planning *also* rejects utopia as a Marxist diagnostic tool, a systematic critique of extant social relations and their contradictions.[16]

Advocacy planning is structured by a form of possessive specta- torship. Eric Gordon argues that possessive spectatorship underlies the mutual development of moving image technologies and the American city. Possessives spectatorship is "a way of looking that incorporates immediate experience with the desire for subsequent possession" and that "renders the city knowable, even desirable." It does not assert inhab- itants' right to decide how a city is built and lived in. Instead, it only affirms that inhabitants always already have a right to the city in that they have *the right to consume it* as a series of image-sites.[17] Despite advocacy planning's progressive aspects, it is ultimately founded on the assumption that the ability to draw a mental map of the city, to image it, is to live functionally within the city by possessing it as an image rather than pos- sessing it in terms of having the right to make and remake it. For exam- ple, Lynch's "way finding" in the city requires constantly mapping one's environment to determine the limits of the city, drawing on the (mental) visibility of those limits to recognize patterns and decode symbols.[18] For Jacobs, a functional neighborhood is one whose merchants and residents may accumulate capital and improve property undisturbed.[19] These theo- rists valorize and reproduce the reduction of the city to an image while ignoring this image's mutually constitutive relationship with the urban renewal policies they abjure. Lynch and Jacobs fundamentally accede to the current socio-spatial order. They do not reorient the relations of its differences; they celebrate our ability to way-find within the current relations. In doing so, they continue their predecessors' reproduction of capital's socio-spatial relations.[20]

Advocacy planning's possessive spectatorship and its desire for the city as an image/an imageable city closely aligns it with the figure of the spectacle. The spectacle is capital accumulated to the point at which it becomes an image. By the mid-1950s, due in no small part to the concentration of capital and the visual figures urban renewal and slum clearance promulgated, New York had become such an image. Guy Debord describes the spectacle as the expulsion of history from analysis. In its place, the spectacle proffers an artificial vision unlimited in both time and space that claims nothing lies beyond it: "all it says is all there is."[21] The spectacle denies its own underpinnings in comprehensive social separation and fragmentation by establishing itself as a separate and self-sufficient image that mediates social relations to ensure our lack of consciousness of their nature.[22] The effects of this unconsciousness includes the corruption of scientific fields of inquiry such as sociology, which, in the United States, "began to focus discussion on the living conditions brought about by present development, complied a great deal of empirical data, but could not fathom the truth of its subject because it lacked the critique immanent in this subject."[23] This description encapsulates the research that justified urban renewal and slum clearance as well as the logic of advocacy planning. For example, in one of the concluding passages of *Image of the City*, Lynch identifies his ideal city as a carefully bordered, separated, and distinct space that enables viewers to say "here is my town, there is another."[24]

The symphonies of the center dispel the spectacle's production of a unified image, "a map that exactly covers its territory."[25] They do so by short-circuiting normative cognitive maps of the city, dramatizing the impossibility of truly possessing a right to the center through such an image. In the place of cognitive mapping's images, they substitute a self-reflexive emphasis on the cinematic apparatus as productive of urban space. The symphonies of the center concentrate on the spaces most closely associated with the spectacle and advocacy planning: the infrastructure of and monuments to places of exchange. Their aesthetics foreground the built environment and elide most recognizable human figures, directing viewer attention almost entirely to matters of form. This formalism lavishes attention on the surfaces of the city. By abstracting those surfaces from the relations of production and social relations they house, the symphonies of the center make those very relations visible through the rhythms they generate.

While all of the symphonies of the center represent similar types of sites, the various functions of those sites within the spectacle and in cognitive maps of the city determines how each film is organized: *Jazz of Lights* presents Times Square as the center of the real estate exploitation that generates the city's wealth; *Wonder Ring* produces the

Third Avenue El as an infrastructural subjectivity that maps a time and space beyond the demands of the spectacle's rhythms; *N.Y., N.Y.* depicts the inherent disruption Midtown Manhattan poses to would-be users of the center. Finally, Shirley Clarke's films build on and incorporate all of these tactics to propose architecture as an oeuvre that produces the city as a collaborative work in progress rather than a fixed cognitive map or spectacle. All the symphonies of the center imagine a space in which the masses have a right to encounter one another as fellow artists rather than as consumers, and to which they contribute as a collective work rather than possess as a map. In the place of capital accumulated to the point it becomes an image, the symphonies of the center produce a series of surfaces that can be *inhabited* by the diverse temporalities of architectural bodies and by the differently embodied spatial practices of their users.

Jazz of Lights: The Exploitation of St. Francis

Times Square's flood of neon lights, huge billboards, walking advertisements, tourists, and mass entertainment makes it an especially apt example of the spectacle. These same features, combined with its distinctive topography and importance to mass-transit, render it a key feature in cognitive maps of New York. Yet the area's relationship to the spectacle is deeper and of longer standing than these immediate connections. Originally named Longacre Square, for the oblong shape created by Broadway's intersection with Seventh Avenue as it veers east, Times Square was created by speculation thrice over. First, its contours were laid out by the Commissioners' Plan of 1811, which created Manhattan's grid system and allowed capital to lay exclusive claim to the city as a rationalized space, even as unprepared and unimproved earth. Second, it was renamed by *New York Times* publisher Adolph Ochs in 1904, when his paper took up residence on Forty-Third Street. In 1907, the New Year's Eve ball drop from the Times building further associated the area with mass gatherings and the visual consumption of crowds. Third, from the 1920s on, Times Square was the entertainment capital of the city. It was known as the home of legitimate theater in the 1920s, of movie palaces in the 1930s, and of exploitation and pornographic theaters beginning in the 1940s and 1950s.

In fact, as Themis Chronopoulos argues, Times Square was so central to Americans' image of New York that, by the postwar period, it had come to stand for the city as a whole as "a monument to inauthenticity, to commercialism, to the power of symbol over substance."[26] This reputation nuanced and reinforced late modern New York's utopian position as a metonymy of the nation's future and the embodiment of all its fears.[27] The city government, real estate consortiums, and business associations tried to align this image with more respectable forms of commerce. After the war, local and city leaders sought to repress the area as a working-class public space. While Times Square's status as a location of illicit sex and entertainment (and eventually, sex as entertainment) had inspired police raids and punitive policies since the 1910s, in 1948 and 1954 the city turned to rezoning as a cure-all for a place that seemed to gain prominence in the urban imaginary even as it increased its down-market, working-class, queer, and nonwhite affiliations. To combat this, and to turn Times Square's capital-generating abilities toward the legitimate commerce that would improve the city's image, a 1948 zoning order eliminated all future arcades and honky-tonks. These orders were ineffective, and in 1954 the board of estimate approved proposals to outlaw new construction and new business openings of any kind along Forty-Second Street.[28] The policies hastened the area's economic downturn and allowed for increased inroads by organized crime into local sex trade and protection rackets.

Jazz of Lights challenges the dominant image of Times Square and its function within the spectacle by connecting consumable images/goods with the power structures that the spectacle obscures and indicating how the spectacle appropriates cognitive mapping. *Jazz of Lights* depicts Times Square as an area that is always already reproduced, that has no original materiality, by emphasizing its framing within the cinematic apparatus. Yet this definition of the area as a cinematic image does not insist on its artificiality. Rather, the film surfaces the historical conditions that determine the kind of image Times Square is. *Jazz of Lights* downplays the typical dawn-to-dusk structure characteristic of city symphonies. In fact, its use of gel lenses, superimposition, and optical printing often make it very difficult to determine what time of day it is. This temporal confusion begins to dispel the rhythms of commutation and commerce that structure Times Square. In their place, the film emphasizes the rhythms of those who inhabit the space rather than pass through it. These inhabitants include shoeshine boys and panhandlers as well as the avant-garde composer Moondog and author Anaïs Nin, cast as a St. Francis figure and an Alice in Wonderland *badaud*, respectively. However, the film grants the same subjectivity to the huge billboards and marquees that hover over inhabitants and visitors alike. By giving these advertisements their own point of view, or at least the power of critical commentary, *Jazz of Lights* unravels their function as consumable things. The film instead presents them as architectural presences, capable of interacting with the bodies of their users, inscribing lived experiences at odds with contemporary rezoning justifications and the perception of Times Square as an exceptional space of spectacle.

The film also extends this critical function of image to, and claims it for, itself. Times Square was a common setting for Hollywood film during the late modern period. In backstage dramadies like Joe Mankiewicz's *All About Eve* (1950), its theaters are the locus of impossible dreams, glory, and fame. In noirs like Alexander Mackendrick's *Sweet Smell of Success* (1957), its bars, restaurants, and clubs are where fortunes and reputations are made and broken.[29] But instead of participating in or engaging with these popular cinematic depictions, *Jazz of Lights* foregrounds Times Square's affinity with the materiality of film itself.

Jazz of Lights' first shot features a large theater marquee in the frame's center. On the marquee, the film's title and its director's name are spelled out in the font familiar to any theatergoer. This marquee is doubly framed. First, to either side of it, at extreme screen left and right, two animated strips of celluloid twist and dance. Second, a distorted field of bright, multicolored lights floats over the entire frame—a semitransparent superimposition that connotes the bulbs that illuminate a marquee and the headlights of cars that pass them. This shot suggests that images of Times Square cannot be parsed when encountered directly, but only when viewed through a distorting field cast by the area's most prominent and least palpable commodity: light. At the same time, the film strips frame Times Square itself within the play of that light, by and as a kind of film. By recasting light as constitutive of Times Square's nature and even materiality, *Jazz of Lights* makes a similar claim to combine representation and material reality.

It is worth noting, however, that this filmic bond is not, as in *In the Street*, based on the process of production and the relationship between camera and projector. Rather, the emphasis here is on the space of exhibition, on the theater marquee that describes both the film and the area it depicts. *Jazz of Lights* features several different theater marquees. Each contains the titles of some of the broad array of exploitation and art films typical of Times Square in the 1940s and '50s. Like *Jazz of Lights* itself, these marquees title the action that follows them. They forge ties and force comparisons between images that would otherwise remain atomized within the false unity of the spectacle. One example of this is a cut from the marquee advertising a double bill of Stanley Kubrick's *Fear and Desire* (1953) and Luis Buñuel's *The Male Brute* (1953) to a low-angle shot of cops on horseback. The juxtaposition of the two shots establishes the marquee titles as describing the mounted police (male brutes) as well as the kind of feelings that inspire their presence in Times Square in the first place (fear and desire). Here, the everyday sight that proclaims itself the image of civic order is transformed into a vision of (s)exploitation. As well, by aligning his film about the area with those playing in it—including Stanley Kubrick's ultra-low-budget film and Buñuel's melodrama about eviction—Hugo posits a world where experimental film could attract audiences in Times Square. This pairing also intimates how exploitation exhibition venues threaten the city's image not because of their cheap and tawdry nature but because of their critical faculties. *Jazz of Lights* thus rejoins as social relations what the spectacle artificially isolates as disparate commodities.[30] Moreover, by dwelling on the built environments of the theaters the city insisted were responsible for Times Square's negative image, *Jazz of Lights* places them in relation to the bodies that animate and structure them, making visible the social relationships the area's image otherwise obscures.

One of the key ways *Jazz of Lights* accomplishes this is to combine documentary footage of the area with the fictive personae and stylized performances of Moondog and Nin. This conjunction excavates the rhythms of an area that is largely dominated by tourists and commuters, uncovering the regulations and forces that determine their patterns. It also aligns more permanent inhabitants with the advertisements that define their space, at once making the spectacle visible and challenging it. The shot that introduces Moondog is a long, fluid pan that begins with an astronaut whose suit advertises the Galaxy Diner with the slogan "destination moon" and ends on Moondog. This pun establishes Moondog as alien to his environs, but because he recalls the past rather than the future. A tall white man, Moondog sports long, unwashed brown hair, a tangled beard, a staff, a rough brown Franciscan robe, tied with a white rope, and bare feet (figure 4.2). A common sight in Times Square with his friar's robe and long hair, Moondog appeared to be a particularly eccentric indigent, but was in fact an avant-garde composer well respected in Europe and a popular subject of street photographers in the 1950s and early 1960s.[31] As he wanders past construction sites, advertisements for exploitation films, lunch counters, and crowds headed for the subway, Moondog is often the only portion of the shot in focus. He moves with a markedly steadfast, slow stride at odds with the frantic pace of those around him. The effect of costume and cinematography is to cast him as a kind of anti-flâneur, a St. Francis figure propelled by his own unique internal rhythms, his gait a tacit rebuke to the total monetization of the space through which he moves.

However, editing often juxtaposes Moondog, whose pale skin further sets off his costume, with the mostly Black, elderly, and sometimes disabled beggars that Hugo's camera finds huddled in doorways or pressed to the curb by the passage of the crowd. Their rhythms are determined by the demands of the labor market from which they are excluded, and perhaps also by the slum clearance programs that sometimes reduced former tenants to homelessness. Judged against them, Moondog's unconcerned rhythm and performative asceticism is revealed as an image of white, picturesque poverty that can be branded, commodified, and consumed like the cheap religious icons he resembles, and which, a sign visible over his shoulder announces, are "Sold Here." Moondog indicates what kind

Figure 4.2. The performance artist and composer Moondog plays the role of a modern-day Times Square saint in *Jazz of Lights*. (Ian Hugo, Dir. *Jazz of Lights*. 1954; New York: Anthology Film Archives. 16 mm.)

of poverty can generate an image, can be acknowledged and commodified, and therefore implies the willed invisibility of Times Square's extant poor populations, including many people of color whose existence must be banished from its image if it is to represent a city.

Jazz of Lights makes visible the very bodies and social relations urban renewal wanted removed and advocacy planning rejected. It revalues Times Square as an architecture that houses and creates a critical point of view capable of tracing the social relations the spectacle suppresses. As Anaïs Nin wrote of *Jazz of Lights*, in language highly reminiscent of Lefebvre's distinction between things and presence in his "seeing symphonically" passage from *Rhythmanalysis*: "Hugo manipulates with skill the elements which dislocate or blur objects to reveal new aspects of them as they are revealed in emotional states."[32] That is, *Jazz of Lights* imagines Times Square as an oeuvre, while insisting on cinema as a core aspect of this masterwork. *Jazz of Lights* estranges the spectacle by insisting on mediation as a constitutive part of the built environment. The film produces the built environment and the social relations it houses as cinematic projections, naming the conditions of production the spectacle obscures.

Wonder Ring: The Infrastructure Ballet

Wonder Ring performs a similar rhythmanalysis, but of infrastructure. The film chronicles a trip on the last remaining section of Manhattan's last elevated line, documenting the route of a Third Avenue El train. *Wonder Ring* aligns the built environment with the camera and its disembodied, mobile perception as a perceiving subject. In doing so, *Wonder Ring* departs from advocacy planning's valorization of infrastructure like the El as the embodiment of a nostalgic past and as an iconic component of the urban as spectacle. In its place, *Wonder Ring* picks apart the rhythms composed by the El to ask what a center that moves—one that accompanies its users throughout their day—would look like. Advocacy planning tends to either associate the past with the formation of personal identity and communal ties, as in Lynch's work, or with a kind of habitus and social connection threatened by the atomizing force of slum clearance, as in Jacobs's. Popular coverage of the Third Avenue El's slow demolition from the late 1940s to the mid-1960s shows a shift in public perception toward these views and away from slum clearance's association of the past with blight and moribund growth. This coverage also elucidates the ways in which advocacy planning's valorization of the past obscures the spectacle's manipulation of time and rhythms.

The Third Avenue El dates to 1878, making it older than New York's underground subway system. It was, however, fully integrated into that system and functioned as part of the Interborough Rapid Transit (IRT) portion of it from 1903 on. In 1940, the city assumed control of the IRT, as well as the two other major subway companies, the Brooklyn-Manhattan Transit Company (BMT) and the Independent Transit Company (IND). This assertion of civic control and consolidation contributed to the general rescaling of capital during the postwar period and the investment of government funds in the debt-financed infrastructure that drove it. Almost immediately after the city assumed control of the transit system, it began to decommission and demolish the elevated lines on the grounds of their obsolescence, measured by their comparatively small ridership and contribution to the dimness and congestion associated with blight. More important, the demolition of the Els allowed for a further consolidation of capital within the city government and by real estate interests. Removing the Els opened land for housing developments and corporate real estate, which in turn aided in the eventual eviction of prior low-rent tenants. If these tenants remained, they were assessed heavy fees and increased property taxes for their improved air and light quality, paying for the demolition costs.[33]

Decommission and demolition of the Third Avenue El proceeded in segments, beginning with the Bronx in the mid-1940s, continuing with the Downtown portion in 1951, and concluding with the East Village to Upper East Side leg in 1955. Over this ten-year period, popular coverage of the demolition shifted markedly in a way that speaks to the widening rejection of urban renewal and slum clearance policies. In 1950, the *New York Times* described the decommissioning of the southernmost part of the route, from South Ferry to Fulton Street, as a great achievement for modernizing infrastructure. The paper claimed that residents were jubilant and profiled the head of a mission who regarded the removal of the El as the restoration of uninterrupted sleep. The same article dismissed the residents, riders, and activists who turned out to protest the demolition as uninformed curiosity seekers with a perverse investment in the past.[34] Five years later, in 1955, coverage of the last segment's closure was also quite celebratory, but displayed a more cautious tone while embracing a sense of memorialization. Most of this coverage centered on the ceremonial "last ride" the mayor, Robert Wagner, would take on the train, accompanied by performances given by ethnic and racial groups in their respective neighborhoods along the line.[35] Finally, in 1966, long after demolition was complete and two years after the final assessment taxes were levied, the paper devoted its Christmas column—an occasional feature by a local contributor, usually a fiction writer, celebrating an unusual New York encounter—to the plight of a (fictionalized) Italian immigrant who lived in a stretch of the Lower East Side once shadowed by the El. The column, by novelist Edward Streeter of *Father of the Bride* (1949) fame, describes the comfort its protagonist once derived from the regular passage of the trains, and the community and connections engendered by them. When the immigrant returns to the neighborhood after a thirteen-year sojourn in Italy, he not only finds the train and its tracks gone, but also his old neighbors, with the neighborhood now populated by newcomers living in anonymous high-rise residential towers.[36]

This column combines Kevin Lynch's emphasis on clearly oriented, preferably above-ground mass transport's positive impact on individual orienteering with Jane Jacobs's famous description of the "ballet of the street" and the affective, supportive bonds of her West Village neighborhood.[37] It demonstrates how advocacy planning was integrated into, and well-accepted by, establishment outlets like the *Times* and their readers by the dawn of the urban crisis. It also speaks to the ways in which urban renewal's impact, and protests of it, were deracialized by mainstream coverage. The Lower East Side included more Puerto Rican than Italian residents by the late 1940s, let alone by the mid-1960s, yet the implication of this column is that the protagonist has been replaced by wealthier white Americans who are not ethnically marked and makes no mention of the interracial tensions that characterized the neighborhood by the mid-1960s. Similarly, contemporary infrastructure protests organized by African American leaders on behalf of Black communities in the outer boroughs received markedly less, and more critical, coverage in the white press across the 1950s and early 1960s.[38]

The reception history of the El demolition in particular, and the ascendance of advocacy planning in general, indicates how such models obscure capital's role in cognitive mapping. First, although the Third Avenue El is regularly referred to as "the last elevated train in New York"—including in Cinema 16's programming notes for *Wonder Ring*—multiple subway lines retain elevated portions today, including in Manhattan.[39] These elevated sections are found near infrastructure connecting boroughs across bodies of water or in more geographically peripheral and poorer areas. Rhetorically positioning elevated and underground transport as mutually exclusive bolsters the modernizing rhetoric of urban

renewal and the often nostalgic function of cognitive mapping in advocacy planning. For example, while the Streeter column echoes advocacy
planning's typical intersection with historical preservation rhetoric and
Jacobs's critique of urban renewal projects, it also resonates with Lynch's
preference for elevated trains and discussion of the difficulty of integrat-
ing subways with cognitive maps. Lynch argues that subway stations are
key orientation points in the city but are only effective when they can be
mentally integrated with maps of the skyline, serving as landmarks and
reinforcing the entire street grid as a kind of iconography. When they
are not, they disrupt cognitive mapping.[40] Similarly, coverage of the Third
Avenue El's staggered demolition and the coverage's shifting sympathy to
protestors omits that the trajectory of closure roughly followed neighborhoods' whiteness, economic security, and access to political power.
Engineering principles and ridership figures necessarily determined how
the demolition of the route would proceed. However, accepting these
values as objective denies the ways in which capital and segregationist
policies were spatialized in the differentiation of those neighborhoods in
the first place and determined how they related to the center.

The coverage of the Third Avenue El indicates the flaw in advocacy
planning, which claims transit as a component of cognitive mapping while
ignoring its function as a projection of capital, state, and institutional
power that determines spatial practices for riders and residents. In particular, Lynch's insistence on the primacy of the grid and on the collective
landmark of the skyline as crucial orienteering aids ignores their nature.
The skyline is the epitome of capital accumulated to the point it becomes
an image; in this case that image's iconic status allows the spectacle to
aestheticize itself. The coverage of Mayor Wagner's ceremonial final ride
on the Third Avenue El indicates the limitations of advocacy planning,
which, in celebrating the congealed things of which the spectacle consists, duplicates the spectacle's defining condition: "It aims at nothing but
itself." Advocacy planning valorizes a city that produces a more perfect
image of itself, an image that prohibits the desire for consciousness.[41]

Like the Third Avenue El, *Wonder Ring* has often been recruited to
serve this idealization of the urban as image. Commissioned by Joseph
Cornell in 1954, Brakhage shot *Wonder Ring* as a companion piece to
Nightcats (1956) and *Loving* (1957), part of his new focus on color and
rhythm as a means of personal expression. Yet, by the time it was shown
at Cinema 16 in 1959, the film was described as "a nostalgic look back" at
a missing part of the city's built environment that depicted "an intensively
subjective impression of an El ride,"[42] a subjectivity that the program

notes implied was also imperiled by the loss of its conveyance. Cinema 16's description set the terms of critical response to the film as an "expressive legacy" of riders' perception.[43]

By contrast, I argue that *Wonder Ring* does not eulogize a rider's perspective, but rather presents the *train's* point of view. Within the spectacle, communication is dependent on the images that mediate social relations and is unidirectional, as with the decoding and mapping of images. *Wonder Ring* positions the El as a mediation of a different kind, as the meeting place of the relationships between individuals and the relations of the larger social order, as an art of living in the city that is also the art of history, of desiring consciousness. The film accomplishes this by setting the city into polyrhythmic motion: the train, the station, the apparently motionless buildings on the route all attain their own relative movement. These rhythms cannot be negotiated through a cohesive image, and they do not reinscribe and naturalize the extant center as the first point of orientation. Rather, they produce progress through the city as a constant process of centering, relations that remake themselves in, and produce, each space as a moment of encounter, rather than mapping a preextant image.

Wonder Ring's polyrhythmia begins with its construction of the El as an urban subject that witnesses, retains, and integrates the phenomena it encounters. It evokes the neomodern architect Bernard Tschumi's assertion that "architecture is defined by the actions it witnesses as much as by the enclosure of its walls."[44] The film is marked by a consistent vantage point—most shots originate from inside the car—and by associations of the camera with the train. *Wonder Ring* opens with a three-shot sequence that begins with a static long shot of the covered stairs leading up to the El platform, followed by a cut to a medium handheld shot of the stairs from an acute high angle, and concludes with a close-up of the detailed art nouveau scroll work at the apex of the stairs. The shots' disarticulation subverts a conventional reading of the sequence as a rider's approach to the station. The use of abrupt cuts creates a rhythm even in the first shot, which removes identifying details from the exterior of the station and emphasizes its scalar resemblance to the buildings around it. This establishing shot works the station into the fabric of its surroundings without producing it as a landmark. Similarly, the next two shots suggest an opening of and within the station rather than the commuter's rapid ascendance of the stairs toward the goal of the platform, which is held offscreen. These techniques begin to construct the film's point of view as belonging to a mobile infrastructure. They foreground the station as architecture without allowing it to be defined as a point on a map and make the station a part of the train rather than its opposite. This link between the station and the train continues in the next shot, a pan, which features the doors to the platform, the ticket booth, and latticework on the trestles and support beams. This 360-degree shot is the first "ring" that appears in the film. It anticipates the film's overall structure, which consists of the major ring of the El's run up and down its line as well as the smaller rings produced throughout by mobile shots, editing, and reflections within shots.

The train first appears in close up, seeming to emerge from within the station rather than arrive there. Significantly, the station is not depicted after the train departs it, suggesting that it travels with, or houses, the train, and that the view from the train is the view from the station. Once in the train, a series of skillfully edited shots evoke the ring of a 360-pan and mirror the curvilinear shape of the snaking train tracks in fleeting images of city streets, here freed from the frame of the grid. This uptown journey continually emphasizes the spatial practices of the El itself, rather than its ability to aid in cognitively mapping the relation between two points, by prominently featuring the distortion and grime of the train windows. This also manifests the El's long history as memory, as traces that accumulate on and act on its surface, as with brief images of coal ovens within trains and stations. This insistence on material history, on the architecture of the El as a perceiving, rather than perceived, body, unpacks the bundle of the spectacle's urban image. It restores the rhythm of long-standing social structures that the spectacle absents in favor of a static present. It also connects the shorter loops of a single traversal of the tracks to that history, revealing the spectacle's structuring absence as the banishment of history.

Wonder Ring's final moments open onto the El as a mediation and redefinition of the center that might also renew and restore history. This mediation is visualized through superimposition and reflections within shots, as with images of the tracks superimposed over the platform. Similarly, close-ups of riders with their backs against the windows seem to float on the sides of the buildings behind them with no intervening space, both affirming that the images are from the El's point of view rather than the passengers' and producing the very relationship between architectural bodies and user bodies that the spectacle generally represses. As it travels, the El produces a series of such encounters. This indicates the character of an alternative center that will be characterized by mobility. *Wonder Ring* positions the El as a work that produces its own perception of space and orients the spatial practices of others, instead of as a labor delivery system that facilitates the production of more products. Thus, the film uncovers a collective work within the public work of the El, indicating what a renovated center might encompass.

N.Y., N.Y.: Surface Tension

All of the symphonies of the center depict the surface as the visible skin of the spectacle, but none more so than *N.Y., N.Y.* Francis Thompson revives the structure of the 1920s city symphonies, observing a clear dawn-to-dusk stretch of time and foregrounding topics and areas key to those films, notably industrialization's organization of the working day and the association of an artificially illuminated evening with leisure and entertainment. This classical structure is combined with especially striking, and quite abstract, visual language. Thompson's work, like that of Ian Hugo, Marie Menken, and Shirley Clarke, builds on the optical effects, time-lapse photography, and process editing that Weegee developed to fragment and distort surfaces for the "New York Fantasy" section of *Weegee's New York*. *N.Y., N.Y.* not only participates in this tradition but is remarkable for the consistency with which the film's reception focuses on its use of or its status as surface. This reception included a rapturous recognition from key cultural and artistic institutions around and beyond the city. The symphonies of the center collectively received significantly more institutional support from governmental and elite cultural organizations than the symphonies of the margins. Even given this context, *N.Y., N.Y.* was notable for its immediate embrace beyond the confines of the New York avant-garde.

Although the film was screened at Cinema 16 in 1957, its exposure is indebted to its 1958 screening at the Museum of Modern Art prior to its submission to the 1958 Brussels World Expo as part of its International Experimental Film Festival. In addition to a fairly unusual gala opening at the museum that led to multiple daily screenings over a two-week period, *N.Y., N.Y.* was also championed in the *New York Times* by critic Howard Thompson (no relation to Francis, as far as I know). Howard Thompson expanded his "Of Local Origin" column to twice its usual length for a review of the film that bordered on the hagiographic. This review focused on the improbable, "beautiful," "abstract images" of urban surfaces that came "straight from Mr. Thompson's lens." Thompson claimed that *N.Y., N.Y.* revealed new facets of the "urban canyons" and pushed the boundaries of cinematography because, like the abstract art he compared it to, it refocused the viewer's attention on familiar surfaces and encouraged contemplation of them.[45] Howard Thompson's dual focus on *N.Y., N.Y.*'s optical effects and its revaluation of surface in his review was flattened by subsequent critics and programmers into an increasingly negative sense that the film's optical effects limited its content to surfaces and its concerns to shallow matters of form.[46]

However, the film's play of surfaces is less an abrogation of engagement with the deep structures of the urban environment than it is of utopian liminality. As Giuliana Bruno argues, the surface is the point at which the visual becomes material, an architecture of both partition and habitation.[47] Bruno builds on Jacques Ranciere's understanding that "partition mediates by acting as material configuration of how the visible meets the thinkable as a form of dwelling in the material world" to claim the surface as a visualization of time and clothing of space.[48] Bruno's formulation exchanges a built environment defined through its immutability for one imagined as a wearing (out) of fabric in contact with human bodies, very different from the standard reproduction of architectural bodies in those of their users. *N.Y., N.Y.*'s optical effects remake the center as a series of surfaces in this sense. In its very emptiness the film forces the spectacle to rise to the surface. Through its estrangement and visualization of empty spectacle, the film reworks iconic architecture, domestic objects, and living bodies into a shared surface that is worn as much as seen. It educates our desire for a center in which the relationship between inhabitants and their habitat is one of encounter, with each shaping the other through mutual contact.

N.Y., N.Y. draws attention to the emptiness and atomization of the spectacle from its opening shots. Perhaps surprisingly for a film whose reception turns on its riot of overwhelming images and transformation of the urban scene into a fractal mosaic, *N.Y., N.Y.* begins in complete darkness, the city reduced to a unified black background. First images mimic the opening of *Weegee's New York*. They also gesture to the larger city symphony tradition of beginnings in dark, quiet, and stillness—found in films including *Berlin: Symphony of a Great City*, *Man with a Movie Camera*, and *À propos de Nice*—the better to contrast the frenzy of vision and motion that follows. But where other symphonies introduce light and movement through signifiers of modernity, most notably cars and trains, *N.Y., N.Y.* underlines the city's indebtedness to the natural world and its geography. The blinking lights that eventually cast a weak purple light on the scene belong to ships on the East River, a natural boundary and a much older form of transportation. Similarly, while Gene Forrell's score has been touted for its nearly atonal jazz style, ship horns and lapping waves are more prominent on this opening portion of the soundtrack.[49]

The rest of the film's opening sequence contrasts this floating space of tranquility, where the city's rhythms are set by the physical world rather than by the demands of production, with a series of spaces of labor. These spaces include the domestic sphere, which is depicted as highly automated and alienating. As Scott MacDonald writes, one of *N.Y., N.Y.*'s most striking scenes links the waking of the city to a white-collar worker's morning routine through the film's trademark fragmented surface: an alarm clock going off at 8:00 a.m. "shatters the screen" into still photography.[50] More important, however, is that the alarm ends a sequence as much as it begins one. Rather than proceed from predawn stillness to the beginning of morning commutes, *N.Y., N.Y.* produces a clear itinerary—the only one in the film—far uptown from Midtown East, past the span of High Bridge, and slightly west into a Fort George high rise. Pushing in toward a window does not resolve in an interior shot, or a close-up on a human figure, however. Instead, the next images display a highly distorted low-angle shot of Rockefeller Center that emphasizes the building's setbacks, followed by an image of the state courthouse on Centre Street downtown, before cutting to a residential building that displays the white limestone facade typical of the Upper East Side. Pushing into this facade with the same slightly unsteady tracking shot used to approach the Fort George building, we encounter the ringing alarm clock. Rather than locating a sleeping human whose waking and trajectory would produce a normative cognitive map of the city, *N.Y., N.Y.* shows us the city inside a building.

Fort George, like East Harlem, was subject to sustained slum clearance and the construction of multiple high-rise, low-income public housing. By locating centers of justice and commerce, as well as the city's wealthiest neighborhood, inside an area geographically and socio-economically distant from them, *N.Y., N.Y.* suggests the extent to which marginal neighborhoods are structured toward the center's organization of differences. By this I mean the extent to which the daily, linear rhythms of a neighborhood like Fort George are determined by the center. The residents of this neighborhood awake much closer to 5:00 a.m. than 8:00 a.m. to staff the industries and work in the homes seen in the rest of the sequence. In the unsettling appearance of the courthouse, the sequence also suggests how the longer rhythms of a life are set into motion or cut short by the center, the spectacle that organizes it, and the state power it projects.

Yet if life in Fort George is determined by the demands of the center, then the Upper East Side office-worker's life is equally regimented by the commodities that produce the center as a spectacle. The alarm clock encapsulates Lefebvre's contention that the home as a separate representational space vanished with the standardization of shifts and longer commutes.[51] In addition to the alarm clock, the morning routine inside the brownstone features a juice press, coffee pot, and egg timer. Each of these objects multiplies across the frame in repeating fragments, aligning them with the architectural exteriors seen elsewhere in the film, which receive the same treatment. Just like a building, these domestic objects produce living bodies that reproduce themselves within the bodies of their users. They are a surface that is a habitat, and the characteristics of this habitat—as isolation of body parts within the frame emphasizes—are those of fragmentation of time, self, and consciousness.

While the first half of *N.Y., N.Y.* is characterized by the duplication of, as MacDonald suggests, a "cubist" structure, the second half is much more reminiscent of surrealist images. Here, Thompson uses mylar to bend city surfaces into Escher-like mousetraps with the logic of a Möbius strip. Mylar produces a 3D effect in a 2D image. In doing so, it helps to dissolve the sense of images as being spatialized predominantly through an inside verses an outside, redefining them in terms of connectivity.[52] Thus, the seemingly endless "afternoon" portion of the film occupies roughly a third of the total runtime, and uses a slower editing pace that dilates the viewer's perception of elapsed time. This sequence bends back the FDR Drive on itself so cars continually loop from screen right to screen left, sandwiches the feet and lower legs of office workers on lunch break between two layers of asphalt, and forces a city bus to repeatedly swallow and disgorge itself from the vanishing point at the middle of the screen. By drawing attention to the shared surfaces of the built environment and the automotive and human bodies that traverse it, *N.Y., N.Y.* pulls apart the iterated, unified rhythms of the commute, the lunch hour, and the crosstown trip. In their place, the spectacle's hidden structure of fragmentation becomes visible. The eternal linear flux of commuting is revealed as the static time stolen from and dissolving the border between labor and leisure. The regimented limits of the lunch hour consume the bodies of workers, even as they consume calories to replenish their use-value. The interests of capital that determine the organization of the city grid and the rhythms of its traversal appear as a constant devouring of the potential of public transportation as a space of encounter.

Just as the afternoon section uses mylar to rejoin aspects of social relations that the spectacle fragments, the penultimate movement of the film mounts a literal surfacing of the true nature and limitations of advocacy planning. The sequence begins with an ever-accelerating trip up an elevator shaft that, in one animated shot, distills the building into the load-bearing grid of its curtain wall before emerging into a roof view. Following advocacy planning logic, attaining this elevation through occupation of a landmark building in a central district should produce an encompassing command of our surroundings. Yet all we see, against an impossible, super-saturated sky redolent of technicolor Hollywood musicals, are the characteristic details of beaux arts, gothic revival, and art deco buildings floating in isolation (figure 4.3). In *N.Y., N.Y.*, all that can be apprehended from a privileged vantage point is, in the film's least subtle visual pun, floating capital(s). In the heart of the spectacle, at the center of the image of the city, entire buildings are squeezed until they

Figure 4.3. Floating capital in *N.Y., N.Y.* (Francis Thompson, Dir. *N.Y., N.Y.* 1957; New York: Museum of Modern Art. 16 mm.)

resemble a mere detail at their apex and visualized as scraping the sky, evaporating the urban ensemble. Even as these shots refuse, on a literal level, to depict the social relations the spectacle instantiates, they also manage to display the spectacle's secret—that it is an all-encompassing image of unity founded on emptied fragments—on the surface of the sky.

N.Y., N.Y.'s conclusion reinscribes this magician's flourish by stuffing the film back into itself, much as earlier trick shots did with human and infrastructural bodies. The final three minutes produce a highly self-reflexive city symphony. This includes numerous references to classical city symphonies of the 1920s, especially *Rien que les heures*, as well as to *Weegee's New York*, and to the term "city symphony" itself. In these moments, Forrell exchanges his complex, Miles Davis–influenced cool jazz music for much more popular sounds evocative of big band and be bop. As Forrell introduces each instrument, we see an image of it being tuned and played on screen, until Thompson's montage assembles an orchestra. Yet the final product of this symphonic ensemble is not the symbolic fireworks of *Berlin: Symphony of a Great City*, but rather *N.Y., N.Y.* itself. As the music and pace of editing reach a crescendo, a sudden trumpet flare and cut reveal a black screen onto which the film's title springs in an animated cutout that resembles hundreds of tiny klieg lights piled on one another. The conclusion of the film suggests that the spectacle is finally capable only of producing images of itself, that "its only aim is itself." This conclusion perhaps implicates *N.Y., N.Y.* in the spectacle and its strategies. However, it also positions subsequent symphonies of the center's emphasis on self-reflexivity as a means of estranging the spectacle and educating our desire toward an image that, like Bruno's surface, offers space for habitation.

Shirley Clarke's Subversive Commissions

While all symphonies of the center estrange the spectacle and critique advocacy planning, Shirley Clarke's commissioned films come closest to performing a true renovation of the center and production of it as a collective work. This renovation proceeds not only through the films' texts, but also their relationships to their commissioning institutions. In the second half of the 1950s, Clarke took on commissions from federal agencies as well as private companies. In her production notes for her late 1950s commissions, Clarke evidences a desire to subvert the projects' stated aims, and especially to challenge normative representations of New

York and the United States. In 1956, Willard Van Dyke, codirector of *The City* and founding member of Cinema 16, where he met Clarke, had asked her and other young filmmakers to shoot short films on behalf of the State Department for continuous display as "loops" in the American Pavilion at the 1958 Brussels World Exposition. The assignment was to capture America's natural beauty and high quality of life on screen for world audiences as part of the government's efforts to mount a cultural challenge the Soviet Union. Clarke directed several of the sixteen two-and-a-half-minute films that became known as the *Brussels Loops*, edited the work of collaborators like D. A. Pennebaker, and served as producer for all the loops.[53] Her notes on the project contain maxims like "there is nothing particularly American about Washington DC" and "avoid National Geographic view."[54] They also include reminders to herself and the other directors to feature diverse subjects, integrated spaces, and quotidian locations rather than "Niagara and the Grand Canyon," and to "include at least one horror like Levittown."[55] With these goals in mind, Clarke *detournes* her assignments to produce films that testified to the supreme qualities and comforts of American daily life achieved through mature capitalism. That is, rather than a series of self-contained monumental sites that present a pleasing array of differences and, in doing so claim to represent the social relationships they obscure, Clarke produces the center as a continually renewing spatial practice of construction and self-fashioning that remakes social relations.

In the course of her efforts, she sought out the kind of iconic sites and structures crucial to cognitive mapping and to the spectacle, including Central Park, the George Washington Bridge, and the Woolworth Building. Her interest in approaching these kind of sites through, and contesting their usual depiction in, tourism, civic boosterism, and historic preservation is suggested by a strange object nestled among her reminders to avoid such locations. Clarke owned and annotated an eighty-page pamphlet published by the Circle Line, a company that offers boat tours around Manhattan.[56] The pamphlet, released for the Circle Line's tenth anniversary in 1956, celebrates Manhattan as a series of staggering, monumental views framed by the ship's windows for the enjoyment of its passengers. The pamphlet features and praises urban renewal projects like Stuyvesant Town and landmarks like the Woolworth Building. It encapsulates the typical views and clichéd sites that were so instrumental to the spectacle, the very images Clarke set out to avoid.

Yet Clarke not only featured these sites prominently in several of the Brussels loops, most notably *Melting Pot* and *Bridges-Go-Round*, she had to make a considerable effort to gain access to them. Such locations were not generally open to independent filmmakers, who were without funds for filming permits or equipment. Clarke was able to access these locations with a free permit issued by Robert Moses on behalf of the Parks Department.[57] Willard van Dyke had contacted Moses on September 30, 1957, to request special assistance and consideration for Clarke on the grounds that "Since this project is a non-commercial venture for the government, and since it is in the interests of prestige and good will for the United States abroad, we hope that Mrs. Clarke will receive cooperation in whatever situations she may be filming."[58] Moses responded ten days later granting permission to film in all of the requested sites, the assistance of park employees, and a no-fee permit. His support was predicated on Clarke's providing a copy of all finished films to the Parks Department, granting them screening rights, and an assurance that she would "show our city in a good light to a world audience."[59] Clarke's depiction of New York does place the city in such a light, but not, perhaps, in the way Moses had hoped.

Such is the case in *Melting Pot*, which is largely set in Central Park. Central Park is an entirely artificial construct of the nineteenth century made possible by the eviction of poor communities of color, the wholesale movement and regrading of land, and the implementation of traffic separation and circulation theories that inspired the design for garden cities like Greenbelt. Moreover, Central Park is one of the features that, according to Lynch, helps produce the entirety of Manhattan as a kind of landmark of landmarks.[60] That is, Central Park exemplifies the spectacle's claim to even that which seems to lie outside it or oppose it. In *Melting Pot*, Clarke produces the park as an embodiment of a center defined by encounter. She inscribes racial and ethnic difference into her image of the body politic yet undermines precisely the rhetoric that the term *melting pot* suggests. This is especially notable because, after a series of complaints from southern politicians and American visitors to the Brussels Expo, the State Department removed an exhibit called *Unfinished Business* from the American Pavilion. This exhibit dealt with tensions in American social life, particularly racial segregation and discrimination. After its removal, Clarke's *Loops* were the only depiction of Black Americans in the pavilion.[61] The usual notion of the melting pot is one of hierarchical assimilation that privileges a preextant notion of Americanness as white, straight, male, Christian, and prosperous. In *Melting Pot*, Clarke instead focuses on gestures that preserve and foreground difference and mutuality such as handshakes and throwing/catching. These gestures recall Iris Marion Young's notion of the phatic, the glancing form of urban communication that combines the linguistic with the tactile into a mutual acknowledgment. They are also suggestive of a subversion of the merely imitative, repetitive gestures that Debord argues characterize the spectacle and alienate inhabitants from themselves, the gestures that Menken chronicles and critiques in *Go! Go! Go!*'s college graduation and office work scenes.[62]

Melting Pot begins with a sequence that encapsulates these ideas. It suggests that knowing a space proceeds less from a cognitive map than from a series of meetings and encounters.[63] The first images of the film feature repeated shots of handshakes. These greeting hands belong to people of all ages, genders, and races, and where some seem to grace friendly reunions, others appear to instantiate first encounters. The handshake is a gesture that may denote business dealings, greetings, leave takings, or congratulations, but always connotes a relation of equality and trust between the participants. The handshake thus composes its own short, repeatable rhythm and can be used to indicate other spatial practices and relations of longer duration. Other gestures that share this aspect of the handshake are then featured, with particular attention paid to gesticulation in conversation and the cradling, caring hands of a racially diverse group of children and their adults (figure 4.4). While *Melting Pot*'s second section extends beyond the park, the perception of space it engendered there is maintained. Monumental and neighborhood spaces are intercut and juxtaposed in a series of sometimes pointed equivalences, as when middle-aged white politicians congregating outside City Hall are followed by similarly aged Black numbers men leaning against a nondescript brick wall. The film concludes with multiple portraits of children and their adults in and around the park, again oriented around the use of hands as a means of connection as children are tugged gently across the street, picked up, or wave at departing playmates.

Clarke's work diverges from the other symphonies of the center in its clear representation of identifiable human figures. Clarke also differs from the directors New York city symphonies in general, with the exception of Helen Levitt, in her lavishing of attention on people of color. Her production notes indicate that their presence is intentional and part of her attempt to subvert dominant images of the city. For this Loop, she reminded herself to "get Negro [underlined in the original] mother and child. Get Negro and white kids together."[64] These notes and shots are of a piece with Clarke's assertions that experimental film should address social problems rather than psychological issues. Like Levitt,

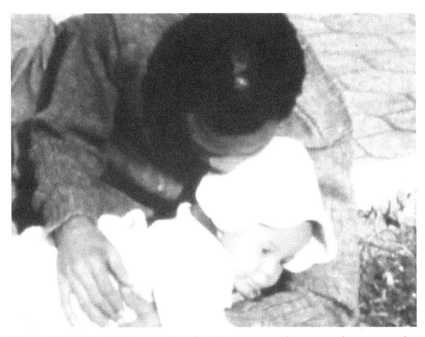

Figure 4.4. Clarke depicts a series of caring, communal gestures that contest the empty movements of the spectacle in *Melting Pot*. (Shirley Clarke, Dir. *Melting Pot*. 1958; New York: Milestone Films, 2016. DVD.)

she translated and displaced her subjectivity and sense of marginalization due to gender, ethnicity, and religion onto other forms of outsider subjectivity.[65] In *Melting Pot* this allowed her to insist that the center as a collective work made through the artful living of its inhabitants must include a multiracial multitude that was not dissolved under the sign of a homogenized American whiteness. This stance was particularly important at a moment in which people of color were increasingly asserting their right to outer-borough minority-majority neighborhoods like Jamaica and Flatbush yet were cut off from financial and service centers by urban renewal infrastructure projects.[66] Clarke's articulation of social issues and marginalized subjectivities was also indebted to her belief that film was a predominantly rhythmic experience that could transform and remake time and space.[67]

One of Clark's loops, *Bridges-Go-Round*, was rejected by the State Department and was not screened in Brussels. However, it was eventually distributed in the US, where its marketing emphasized its similarities to the accepted Loops, particularly in terms of attention to gesture, rhythm, and phenomenological pleasure. This can be seen in the Cinema 16 catalog's description of it as "the sensuous patterns of bridges in space."[68] Yet the film inspires an unsettling, troubling viewing experience as much as it does a pleasurable one. *Bridges-Go-Round*'s camerawork diagnoses the spectacle's co-option of the senses through exactly those components of the built environment crucial to the production of its constrained rhythms and induced sense of cohesion. Clarke's study of the Brooklyn, Manhattan, Queensboro, and George Washington Bridges features very few establishing shots of the bridges, and never includes both their termini at once. Using extreme camera angles, zooms perpendicular to camera movement, superimposition, and image reversal, Clarke engulfs the viewer in a constant traversal of an itinerant space that continually shifts perspective and refuses to reach the solid ground of the other side.

Clarke uses the superimposition of *Wonder Ring* and a variation of *Jazz of Lights*' electronic score by Louis and Bebe Barron—which had been previously expanded and modified for Fred Wilcox's *Forbidden Planet* (1956)—but to very different effect. The electronic notes of the score in Hugo's film always reinforce human action, as when the tempo speeds up as commuters run up the subway steps and slows when the same scene is shot in slow motion. The score naturalizes the surreal imagery and connects it to everyday gestures and behavior, serving an almost soothing function. Clarke's film, by contrast, famously has little connection between the score and the visuals and is often screened twice—once with the Barron score and then with the choral score composed by Teo Mercaro.[69] Mercaro's use of a single note magnified to choral effect and overlaid on a jazz instrumental differs starkly from the Barrons' yet is similarly unnerving. Its unearthliness heightens the discrepancy between the weight of the bridges and the ease of their movement around the screen.

In the Barron score, the repeated electronic beeps played in ascending or descending scales gain and decrease in speed and volume as the bridges rush smoothly onward in a "continuous, fluid sense of motion through camera movement and overlapped images so that each shot dissolves into another."[70] The score functions as the bridges' speech. This anthropomorphism is anything but comforting. From 1958 onward, reviews have focused on the film's "perpetually disorienting effects." I argue that *Bridges-Go-Round*'s disquieting affect is not the product of disorientation at all. That is, viewers are not confused about where they are. Rather, the well-known edifices themselves have been estranged; they are still recognizable, but so unlike themselves that they are discomforting. They recall Nin's description of Hugo's strategies of dislocation in *Jazz of Lights*.[71] Yet where Nin holds that dislocation in *Jazz of Lights* eventually reveals familiar objects remade into presences, in *Bridges-Go-Round* the technique dramatizes the disorienting impact of the spectacle on the viewer. The architecture moves and is mistaken, not the viewer's sense of direction. This shows how the patterns instantiated or corrupted by the spectacle actually orient us to and limit our perceptions of space. Here, things in their "right place" do not orient and help enmesh the viewer in social space, as in cognitive mapping, because the right place is always already determined by, and reinscribes, the spectacle.

By selecting particularly iconic bridges and footage that suggests traversal of them, Clarke whets viewer expectation for the conclusion of the journey, only to deny it, inverting the function of bridges, making them inescapable spaces without origin or end. The bridge thus reveals its true nature, not a passage but a trap for time and the elongation of the commute that helps diminish the home as a separate representational space. The viewer is never disoriented in *Bridges-Go-Round*; one always knows where one is and should be next, and frustrated when deposited back at the point of origin. This communicates the essentially impossible nature of meaningful movement and travel within the spectacle.

The film's final image is shot through a car's windshield as it is finally allowed to complete its suspended traversal of the bridge, only for the road to dead end into the middle floors of the Bank of Manhattan Trust Building (figure 4.5). The Bank looms in the middle of the shot, artificially sutured between the Cities Service Building on the left and the City Bank Farmers Trust Building on the right. This triptych stretches from frame left nearly to frame right, where it blends into a bucolic view of the Hudson River. The pastel filter on the shot lends a continuity to the structures, which appear like a giant steel picket fence, blocking off the city that waits, invisibly, behind them. These buildings are located near one another in Downtown Manhattan, but only look as though they're directly next to one another when see from the Hudson River looking toward the city from just off South Ferry, at the southern apex of the Island. Even then, the Bank of Manhattan should be on the viewer's left, Farmers Trust in the middle, and Cities Service on the right. That geographically accurate view is the subject of one of the photographs used to illustrate Clarke's Circle Line pamphlet, which describes the buildings as "a closeup view of the famous New York Skyline."[72] The Circle Line

Figure 4.5. The final shot of *Bridges-Go-Round* parodies and critiques the touristic views of the city used by Circle Line and other engines of possessive speculation. (Shirley Clarke, Dir. *Bridges-Go-Round*. 1958; New York: Milestone Films, 2016. DVD. Courtesy of the Wisconsin Center for Theater and Film Research.)

deploys the logic of the possessive speculator, offering a special image of the city as a souvenir, a way of possessing the entire skyline—itself a metonym for the city as a space of capital—through the possession of a commodified view. Clarke's shot both evokes and distorts this "famous" view. In doing so, she implies the ways in which the original Circle Line image itself distorted New York, and shows how the spectacle of the city quite literally blocks entrance into the city.

While *Bridges-Go-Round* reveals the alienation underpinning the spectacle's production of a totalizing map of exchange, *Skyscraper* educates our desire for the center as an encounter within a collective work. Clarke, working with Willard van Dyke, was commissioned in 1958 by Tishman Realty & Construction to make a documentary celebrating their new building at 666 Fifth Avenue between Fifty-Second and Fifty-Third Streets, which became known as the Tishman Building.[73] Despite its origins as a corporate vanity film, *Skyscraper*, like its better-pedigreed siblings, testifies to the ways in which the symphonies of the center contributed to the constitution of the international festival circuit as a series of alternative centers. *Skyscraper* competed at a major international festival (Venice) and was marketed after its release with laudatory comments from the Department of Education that urged its use to teach about the virtues of urban renewal and capitalism's democratic qualities.[74]

Despite these misplaced accolades, *Skyscraper* fulfills the potential of the self-reflexivity that characterizes all the symphonies of the center, while also beginning to reconcile them with the symphonies of the margins through the incorporation of documentary. Completing the film two years before Jean Rouch and Edgar Morin's *Chronique d'un été* (1961), Clarke anticipates several of cinéma vérité's key strategies, most notably the interpolation of a film screening for the main subjects into the film itself.[75] But where Morin and Rouch reserve this moment for the final scenes of their film, Clarke returns to the screening room, where her construction workers watch the rapid rise of the building they erected, throughout *Skyscraper*. The film's soundtrack is also organized around the workers' voiceovers as they comment on footage of themselves at work. *Skyscraper*'s proto-vérité qualities inscribe a highly ambivalent, circular temporality that ensures its central work—and its own structure—are never finished.

Skyscraper aligns its own production with that of the Tishman Building, suggesting the construction of both as collective works, in this case undertaken by largely the same personnel. Even as skyscrapers like the Tishman Building reproduce the fixing of the spectacle in the city, they retain traces of diverse historical perceptions and experiences of space, as well as the moment of their construction, thereby producing multiple urban rhythms. *Skyscraper* attends to these qualities while emphasizing the building as a collective effort of creativity and participation. The screening room sequences are intercut with location footage of the construction process. The sequences are bridged by the questions, comments, and answers of the workers and field supervisor, which dominate the soundtrack throughout. Thus, *Skyscraper* assembles a particularly rich matrix of polyrhythmic bodies that continually define the gigantic mass and serialized production of the Tishman Building on a human scale. This prevents a film that depicts a linear construction process with a triumphant conclusion from naturalizing the concept of the city as product and commodity.

However, the bodies in the screening room are uniformly white, male, and working class. In this instance, Clarke's transfer of her subjectivity to other marginalized populations is limited to class. While there are a few Black and Latino construction workers glimpsed in the background of some shots, all of the main subjects narrating the film are white. While this does mutely testify to the continuing segregationist practices of New York unions like the Teamsters and Public Workers, it also excludes people of color and women from the film's evocation of the city as collective work.[76] This depiction is especially notable when contrasted with the presence of Black workers at the demolition sites of *Under Brooklyn Bridge*: even in the utopian realm of the New York city symphonies, people of color can only raze buildings, not produce them. This detail suggests *Skyscraper*'s status as both the apex and limit of the utopian critique mounted by the New York city symphonies, which is borne out by the film as a whole.

Skyscraper begins with a concatenation of various urban spaces that almost suggest a traditional city symphony of the 1920s. These images are accompanied by Teo Mercaro's jazz score and ironic lyrics, which constantly explodes the rhetoric of urban renewal. This overture is essentially a hymn to slum clearance and the compressed time of late modernity, containing lines like: "Old facades must pass away / like the horse they've had their day." The lyrics, however, accompany images of a very much intact wrought iron facade on a SoHo loft and a peddler and horse making their rounds on the Lower East Side. The concept of urban modernity proposed by the lyrics is undercut by the daily spatial practices Clarke captures. This overture ends with the repeated assurance that "It's growing light the city, bright the city"—yet a shadow sweeps over the entire frame before cutting to black. In *Skyscraper*, a true image of the city is impossible to generate because it is constantly in the process of dissolving and renewing itself.

In the next scene, construction workers and their field supervisor view footage of themselves in the act of constructing the Tishman Building. Their comments help create a variety of asynchronous temporalities and subjective impressions of time that contest the relentless, modular construction process chronicled by the image track. For example, one worker remembers the day the foundation was poured as "the day I had the tooth ache." Here, an internal, bodily rhythm that subjectifies space, time, and labor overwrites the unifying power of the construction schedule. It simultaneously documents capital's dominance of labor power and the spectacle's zombie-like control of the body's gestures, which transform a wince of pain into productivity. Clarke's generation of multiple temporalities and rhythms accelerates as construction reaches the twentieth floor. Once the building reaches this height, it begins to command a view of the surrounding area. Clarke shoots through the bare girders to capture

Tishman's neighbors—specifically St. Patrick's Cathedral and MoMA—at oblique and startling angles, so that they seem framed by or to erupt into the iron skeleton (figure 4.6). These shots are accompanied by commentary from the workers, who assert that "St. Pat's has seen three skyscrapers come and go." This comment harkens back to the kind of urban deep time and infrastructural point of view in *Wonder Ring*, while implying that the rhythm of Tishman's construction is ultimately meaningless against the continual witnessing and self-renewal of the urban ensemble as a whole. For its part, MoMA is intercut with images of Tishman's much-derided aluminum siding being attached. The foreman comments, "It's like with anything new, takes time to get used to it." The juxtaposition connects hated prefabricated architecture and valorized modern art. By dwelling on the monumental edifice of the MoMA building, it also shows how quickly innovation can attain the status of tradition.

Figure 4.6. St. Patrick's Cathedral glimpsed through the unfinished floor of the Tishman Building, linking past and future in a single image in *Skyscraper*. (Shirley Clarke, Dir. *Skyscraper*. 1959; New York: Milestone Films, 2016. DVD.)

The film as a whole recasts the supposedly unified, harmonious time of the building's construction as a multifaceted one that includes multiple human and architectural bodies, "symphonic" in Lefebvre's sense. *Skyscraper* redefines the notion of a building "tak[ing] its place in the city," as the foreman declares near the film's end, as an ongoing encounter, a contribution to a work in progress. The Tishman Building takes a place in the city, thereby instituting new spatial practices, bringing a new scale to its surroundings, crafting a new tone for the neighborhood. It also instantiates a new perception of space, both in terms of the ways in which it is perceived by users and the uses it makes possible. Taking a place in the city, the building changes the city, forbidding its reduction to image and its narration as product. At one point in *Skyscraper*, a construction worker watching waste being trucked to Secaucus comments: "This will be a great city if they ever finish building it." This comment recalls the perfect match between the mapping performed by the spectacle and the territory it draws, as well as the absolute closure on which the spectacle and advocacy planning depend. Yet *Skyscraper*, and Clarke's work in general, insists that the city must not be understood as a problem to be solved, a concept or product that can only be grasped in its perfection. Rather, she demonstrates that the city exists as an infinite complexity of rhythms, exchanges, perceptions, behaviors, and itineraries that cannot be reduced to a single image and whose greatness, if any, lies in its imperfections.

The Empty Image and the Abandoned Island

One of the last musical cues in *Skyscraper* is Teo Mercaro's ironic torch song to the city, "My Manhattan." As the new 666 sign on the top of the Tishman Building is illuminated for the first time, the lyrics "My Manhattan, mine tonight" are heard just before the film cuts to black for the last time. With this lyric and one of the only conventional skyline shots in the film, *Skyscraper*'s last shot apparently returns to the logic of possession via viewing that underpins advocacy planning and makes it complicit with the spectacle. Yet *Skyscraper* invokes a contingent temporality that complicates and estranges this image and the policy it undergirds. Manhattan, we are told, is ours tonight, at the present moment, in the here and now that is the place of utopia. Manhattan is ours tonight in the sense that the center's grouping of differences has been renovated; it is now a place of encounter rather than exchange, of collective work rather than legible production—but that state is fleeting, irruptive.[77] As well, *Skyscraper* replaces the triumphant closing fireworks of the 1920s city symphonies and the erotic "fireworks" of *Weegee's New York* with a more prosaic, yet insistent, display. Where earlier films had to depend on frantic montage for their celebratory endings, *Skyscraper* can achieve the same effect with a simple static extreme long shot and a flip of the building's power grid. In that shot, the symphonies of the center's self-reflexive production of the city as the production of themselves is complete. Just as the moment captures the inherently partial, contingent, and temporary nature of the right to the city as collective work of art under capital, it also implies the limitations of the self-reflexive strategies of the symphonies of the center.

The symphonies of the center constantly surface, and play with, emptiness. They make palpable the center's status as an empty image within the spectacle but they also evoke the constitutive emptiness of utopia, the very space advocacy planners reject.[78] *Skyscraper*'s use of this strategy is particularly effective, and is the apex of the symphonies of the center's development of a meta-rhythmanalysis capable of drawing out both kinds of emptiness. However, *Skyscraper* also indicates the limit of this strategy's potential, and in some ways marks the end of the New York city symphony cycle as an utopian critique. Even as the symphonies of the center gained unprecedented exposure for avant-garde cinema and promised that it could, in time, pose a viable alternative to Hollywood film, Shirley Clarke and directors like her increasingly worried that experimental film "as a means to an end rather than an end in itself" had run its course and had become increasingly sterile by the early 1960s.[79] This anxiety and exhaustion resulted in, on the one hand, the production of ambitious feature-length independent fiction films, some of which continued to draw on the city symphony as a central means of expression. On the other, it contributed to the dissolution of the New York avant-garde as concentrated around the city symphony in particular and around social concerns in general.[80]

The fate of the New York city symphonies after *Skyscraper* parallels the fall of urban renewal and the rise of advocacy planning. Their critique of cognitive mapping only seems more prescient and pertinent given the fetishistic status cognitive mapping would soon assume as the late modern city began to pass away into the urban crisis. Advocacy planning not only rejects urban renewal and the dominant role of both the state and capital in planning, it also centers the differing needs of locations and communities.[81] With Jane Jacobs as its symbolic head, this at least potentially progressive school of planning came to be as prominent as urban renewal once was, "yet the revolt against urban renewal ultimately did little to dislodge the power of private real estate developers."[82] Advocacy planning was easily appropriated by the next production of space, the urban crisis, to reinscribe capital in the center and as having the right—now unconstrained by the state—to construct the city to fit its needs.

Just as urban renewal was wedded to the miniature-gigantic image and slum clearance to the figure of blight, the urban crisis's creative destruction criminalized the public presence of the poor and of people of color, especially in the center. The justification for this criminalization was that they threatened the city's imageability.[83] Advocacy planning's complicity with the spectacle and reliance on cognitive mapping forbid the possibility of imagining a radically different world, or even acknowledging the absences that structured this one. Thus, when the urban crisis dawned, it replaced the endlessly legible city with an inescapable abyss. It exchanged a city in which utopia did not need to be imagined for one in which the possibility of utopia was itself a structuring absence. In the next chapter, I will show how the end of the New York city symphony cycle addressed this abyss, its banishing of utopia, and the centrality of racism to its blind view through Shirley Clarke's *The Cool World*.

5

City/Image/Fracture

The Cool World, the Urban Crisis, and Nostalgia for Modernity

> Our cities are terribly unloved—by the people who live in them, I mean. No one seems to feel that the city belongs to him.
>
> —James Baldwin, "Nothing Personal"

A FEW DAYS AFTER THE APRIL 22 opening of the 1964–1965 New York World's Fair, four women, supported by the ACLU and the Congress on Racial Equality (CORE), picketed inside its grounds. They carried signs reading "We Don't Want a World's Fair. We Want a Fair World." Although they were arrested for protesting on private property, their protest did not disturb the teeming crowds flooding once more into General Motors' *Futurama* and other attractions. Built on the site of the 1939–1940 Fair, the 1964–1965 incarnation featured more than six separate exhibits named a variation of *World of Tomorrow/World of the Future.* This included *Futurama II*'s final scene, which revived Bel Geddes's City of 1960 from *Futurama I* and renamed it "The City of Tomorrow."[1] Rather than a eutopian orientation like that of the 1939–1940 World's Fair, these exhibits celebrated the social norms of the quarter-century elapsed since 1939 and the consumption-based cultures of the future they enabled. *Futurama II*, for example, took viewers through new vistas, including an undersea condo and luxury lunar rovers serving a moon base. Its final site, however, closely resembled Le Corbusier's *ville radieuse*, which also served as the climactic City of 1960 model in the 1939 version of *Futurama*. *Futurama II* was typical of the 1964 Fair in its presentation of "the world of tomorrow as the world of the past."[2] Lawrence Samuel argues that attractions at this Fair avoided representation of or engagement with the present's social ills and upheavals.

> The postwar world may have had its anxieties, but, after twenty years, they were known, familiar, and contained, the Fair told visitors, whereas the post-postwar world represented completely uncharted territory that the nation appeared unprepared to navigate. And by bypassing the uninviting near future for a more palatable far-distant one, the Fair offered its millions of visitors hope and confidence that utopia or something like it was not an entirely lost cause.[3]

By drawing on the legacy of the World's Fair of 1939–1940, the 1964 World's Fair assured visitors that social perfection had already been achieved; that a fair world existed in both the urban landscape outside the Fair and the dominance of unfettered corporate spectacle within it.[4]

The 1964–1965 Fair captured the moment when the state ceded the role of urban development to private capital unconstrained by federal power. This is evident even in the case of the protestors, who were arrested by the Pinkerton Detectives that Robert Moses, acting as World's Fair Corporation president, had hired to serve as the Fair's private police and security force instead of relying on the NYPD.[5] Private capital dominated the Fair for several reasons. First, the Fair was imagined and developed by businessmen who sought to maximize their profits. Second, decisions they made in aid of this goal (such as charging rent to foreign exhibitors) brought them into conflict with the Bureau of International Exhibitions, which banned nations like France, the United Kingdom, and the Soviet Union from attending. Third, as private enterprise and coteries of businessmen took up leases for exhibits at the Fair, the planners increasingly began to publicize the Fair as demonstrating the leadership role of business, and particularly the ability of private enterprise to "take up the slack" of national governments they perceived as no longer fostering progress. The emergence of capital as unconstrained by the state is perhaps best encapsulated in Moses's role as president. Moses was in the process of losing his once nigh-omnipotent role as master builder under the new administration of Mayor Robert Wagner. This was partly due to challenges from neighborhood preservation and anticorruption activists as public opinion increasingly turned against urban renewal and slum clearance policies. Moses, however, spun stepping down as the head of the Committee on Slum Clearance and taking up the role of World's Fair Corporation chair as the capstone of his career, and as a service to the free enterprise system and American patriotism he claimed he had always exemplified. As Moses said in a lengthy October 1963 interview with ABC, the Fair would be "an Olympics of progress," "an open competition, where we tell people to come here and exhibit their best products."[6]

The Fair's emphasis on "free enterprise" also manifested as a distinct loss of interest in the city as a site of planning, development, or future habitation. This is palpable even in the site of the Fair itself. Unlike the 1939 Fair, which essentially modeled a regionally planned community, it was not comprehensively planned either in terms of layout or the design of individual pavilions. If the 1939 Fair took on New York as its alter ego and nemesis, then the 1964 Fair relegated it safely to an idealized past and as unimportant to the future. Even the New York State pavilion's dramatic towers and twin viewing platforms were described as "afford[ing] a wonderful view of the Fair," as opposed to the city or the region.[7] The Fair Corporation's publicity materials continually depict the pavilions and their grounds as floating in a black void, with no indication of the neighborhood and highway system that surrounds them or even the Manhattan skyline in the distance (figure 5.1).[8]

This abandonment of the city, and of any cohesive form of urban planning more generally, was one point at which corporate and governmental agendas converged. By the mid-1960s, the state's energies and projection of American progress migrated to the twin alternatives of globalized commerce and the private sphere of the suburbs.[9] The suburbs had solidified as a federal project, subsidized through the 1949 Federal Housing Act, the 1956 Federal Aid Highway Act, and various home owners' loan agencies. The importance of the suburbs to American economic life was only increasing as industry and services abandoned the inner city for the office park. Moreover, the base of organized labor had split. White membership largely resided in the suburbs and drastically

Figure 5.1. The Fair Corporation published many promotional images like this one—a photograph of the diorama exhibited in the American Express pavilion—that erased the city and its environs. (Flushing Meadow Park–World's Fair–Scale Model. Irma and Paul Milstein Division of United States History, Local History and Genealogy, New York Public Library. AZ 05-5469.)

out-earned members who remained in the cities. At the same time, the CIO and other major unions abandoned their support for public housing.[10] The American imaginary increasingly withdrew from the city in parallel with federal funding and civic support.

The 1964–1965 Fair played out this drama as well. In the place of the city as the World of Tomorrow, the 1964–1965 Fair proffered Peace Through Understanding as it inhered in: new environments, as in *Futurama II*; homogenized representations of non-Western cultures that emphasized their anti-urban nature, as with the Mexican and Javanese pavilions; and endless rhapsodies to automobiles, color television, and domestic consumer products. These products collectively allowed their subject to remain cozily ensconced in a detached suburban home—the home that was "the era's chief consumer item"—while aligning this space with economic and social success.[11] The Fair not only projected a corporatist global and suburban future, it also celebrated a highly idealized, whitewashed version of the urban epoch that was now ending. Having achieved its full development and potential, the urban could now be left behind as an organizing principle and planning project, along with its non-white population, who were not represented in the Fair's depiction of the future.

Yet the reminders of at whose expense this urban ideal was achieved, and whose bodies were to be excluded from this future, could not be escaped. On the Fair's opening day, a larger protest organized by the civil rights leaders Bayard Rustin, James Farmer, and CORE inveighed against the Fair's representation of a white future. The protestors condemned the Fair's erasure of police brutality, slum clearance, and economic violence from its celebration of the urban. They criticized the absence of people of color from its planning committee as well as many of the pavilions and exhibits that purported to represent the best of the present and the potential of the future. Their protest, which originally included a mass "stall-in" blocking highway access to the Fair, so threatened the Corporation that Pinkertons and police were dispatched to prevent this tactic and to disrupt the protests—extending the quotidian removal of and violence to Black bodies that structured slum clearance and urban renewal even into the allegedly peaceful, nonurban grounds of the Fair.[12]

Against this backdrop, one of the first scenes from Warren Miller's 1959 novel *The Cool World* comes to seem not only prescient, but also ironic. Miller's novel deals with a few months in the life of Duke Custis, a Black teenager who lives in Harlem, where most of the book is set. Early on, Duke's class takes a field trip to an unnamed museum. At the museum, Duke and his classmates view an exhibit called "the city of the future," in which flying cars and rocket ships feature prominently. In response, Duke says that he isn't fooled, that "it's just a big housing project."[13] Duke's analysis implies the ways in which space exploration and suburbanization *were* housing projects; they received federal funding in the same way that urban public housing did. The scene also acts as an anachronistic riposte to the figurative image that organized the Fair and the new planning policies with which it was mutually constitutive. In addition to abandoning representations of the urban, the 1964 Fair was haunted by the idea that the city could no longer be represented at all and that, contrary to the promises of both urban renewal and advocacy planning, New York resisted visualization and defied logic. These fears were especially attached to the city's black neighborhoods, most notably Harlem. For a Black teenager from Harlem to look at a representation of an anti-urban future and proclaim it a housing project, as Duke does, is to reaffirm the connection between urban and non-urban spaces—undercutting the Fair's premise—and to assert that Harlem, far from resisting visualization, actually authorizes its own distinctive point of view.

Shirley Clarke's 1963–1964 film version of *The Cool World* does not include this scene from Miller's novel. It does, however, perform an important subversion of the figurative image of Harlem as an antivisual space through the use of symphonic tactics. Moreover, by evoking both Duke's subjectivity and the neighborhood's point of view, *The Cool World* relentlessly links Harlem's condition to America's overarching capitalist and racist structures. The leaders of the World's Fair protests, Bayard Rustin and James Farmer, recognized Clarke's film as an important text of the civil rights movement because of these and other qualities. Writing to Clarke in December 1963, Rustin connected *The Cool World* to that August's March on Washington for Civil Rights and Jobs. He stated that the "many Americans who were surprised" by the earlier event would not have been had they seen the film: "These Americans must see *The Cool World*, must see the roots of Negro desperation, and this is what your film unforgettably portrays. I deeply hope that many Americans, black and white, will come and see the face of their grief and conscience: it is the face of a black boy as beautiful as he is condemned."[14] Similarly, in November 1963, James Farmer wrote that *The Cool World* was "an electrifying revelation of the American problem. The dependent marks of segregation will not easily be erased even if every civil rights battle is won for the next ten years. For, as your film clearly shows, the ugly meaning of segregation penetrates to the marrow of a man."[15] Rustin and Farmer perceived Clarke's film as calling for the "fair world" that the Fair protestors demanded, and attributed a great deal of power to that call.

The Cool World mixes the generic tropes of the Harlem crime film with those of the city symphony to relate a summer in the life of Duke Custis (Hampton Clanton). Duke has just finished his freshman year of high school and is a member of a street gang called the Royal Pythons. The film details his attempts to assume the leadership of his gang and become recognized in the wider community by buying a gun and using it to win a brawl with a rival gang. He is unsuccessful in his attempts and is arrested at the end of the film. This synopsis relates a story that does not, at first glance, explain Rustin and Farmer's extremely positive response. Moreover, despite competing at the Venice Film Festival, *The Cool World* did not enjoy the same prominent World's Fair exhibition as prior city symphonies, although its American premiere was on April 20, 1964, just two days before the Fair's. Instead, it opened at Cinema II on the Upper East Side, and never played at Cinema 16, which had closed the year before. *The Cool World* was disconnected from the established critical and political communities and institutions that had nurtured the productions and driven the reception of earlier city symphonies. Cinema II, unlike Cinema 16, was a commercial art theater and one of the first multiscreen theaters in the city. There, *The Cool World* played to overwhelmingly white audiences and critics, many of whom read Duke as a figure of despair, the very reason that America's future was not to be found in its cities. What, then, was the potential Rustin and Farmer saw in this film?

The Cool World expresses the desperation it depicts as a kind of stasis, as the inability to complete meaningful actions or itineraries in space, actions that include the bettering of one's condition and the transformation of one's environment. It articulates this stasis as a symptom of the position to which capital and white supremacy relegate Black lived experience in the city through a dual structure. First, it takes up the same longing for the late modern city that the Fair evidences, but, through the filter of Duke's subjectivity, it turns that nostalgia from a valorization of American consumerism and whiteness to one for Harlem as a center of late modern Black culture. Second, as both Rustin and Farmer intimate, it displays "the roots" of Duke's desperation. Clarke surfaces the ways in which structured flows of power and capital, namely, de facto segregation, economic racial violence, and police brutality, delimit Duke's lived reality. Working in concert, these two tactics puncture the longing for a falsely valorized past and undercut the idea that the American future is threatened by African Americans. One of the film's major political contributions is its insistence that Harlem is not an atypical or alien place, but rather *prototypical* of not only the city, but also the country, as a whole. America's future cannot be secured by outrunning Harlem, because it has created Harlem, and shares its condition. This condition, moreover, is not one of unrelenting misery. Clarke continually contrasts Duke's subjective experiences and desires for the Harlem of the past with lyrical street passages depicting "happy alive kids playing," "a laundress bringing out a chair, people calling to one another, kids dancing," as Clarke described in her production notes, concluding that "Harlem sets the tone."[16] It does so in part through variations of the tactics developed by both the symphonies of the margins and the symphonies of the center. *The Cool World* heavily modifies these tactics to mount a utopian critique of the new era of urban planning and the new figurative image that the Fair ushered in.

This chapter uses the World's Fair and *The Cool World* to explore the destruction of the image of the city as it developed throughout the late modern period and the transformation of the city symphony cycle that critiqued it. *The Cool World* and the Fair occupy the tail end of the late modern period and the onset of the urban crisis. This historical moment was dominated by the absence of a coherent urban planning policy. In its place, the dawn of the urban crisis was characterized by what Mark Shiel has called a "nostalgia for modernity." This nostalgia, this antipolicy, appropriately exchanges the images attending late modern policies like urban renewal, slum clearance, and advocacy planning for an anti-image: the abyss. The abyss, unlike the gigantic, does not correlate to experiential space. The abyss obliterates the urban subject and the city as a social space capable of producing normative subjectivities.[17] Nathan Holmes describes the abyssal qualities of New York in urban crisis crime films like Don Siegel's *Coogan's Bluff* (1968) as "the downtown landscape of the central city, a space of blind corners, soaring ranges of vertical construction, and whirling crowds of strangers."[18] These qualities lend themselves to a lack of image, one that structures the urban crisis through the figure of the city as a blind space, a failed vision. The urban crisis constructs, on the one hand, an intricately detailed fantasy of the city's past (the nostalgia for modernity) and, on the other, the fear that the current city has obliterated subjectivity, social space, and the possibility of the future (the abyss). The World's Fair contained several examples of this logic, particularly in exhibits that use the familiar techniques of the New York city symphony. *The Cool World* responded to these circumstances by developing a new form of rhythmanalysis, one that demonstrates how the nostalgia for modernity and the abyss make meaningful conceptualizations and experiences of space impossible. The film shows how the urban crisis is founded on the negation of Black New Yorkers' right to the city and of the possibility of utopia itself.

Out of Scale: The Appropriated Symphonies of the 1964–1965 World's Fair

The World's Fair of 1964–1965 was, above all, characterized by its refusal to depict the city's present. However, several of its most popular exhibits incorporated the city symphony's iconic aesthetics. The epitome of this contradiction was the Panorama of the City of New York (figure 5.2). The Panorama was commissioned by Robert Moses from Lester

Associates and displayed in the New York City Pavilion at the Fair next to a 1931 model of New Amsterdam circa 1660. The Panorama is 9,335 square feet and uses a one-inch to one hundred-foot scale to reproduce every built structure in the five boroughs, as well as their topography and geographic features. As this description suggests, the Panorama is closely aligned with the transparent, legible, totalizing figurative images that characterized late modern urban planning in New York. It seeks to ally the fears that the city is passing beyond our ability to image—and therefore comprehend—by freezing it into a vivisection, the ultimate naked city.

The exceptions to the Panorama's "photodocumentary" fidelity are threefold. First, the model, constructed between 1961 and 1963, included

Figure 5.2. The Panorama of the City of New York was one of several exhibits that appropriated aspects of the city symphony to communicate a nostalgia for modernity. (Flushing Meadow Park–World's Fair–Panorama. Irma and Paul Milstein Division of United States History, Local History and Genealogy, New York Public Library. AZ 05-5469.)

the World's Fair site as it was projected to be on opening day in 1964, and never included the modifications Moses was forced to make for the 1965 season. Second, all public housing in the Panorama is rendered in bright red, smooth and featureless material. Third, Moses's major infrastructure projects, most notably his bridges and highways, are built larger than scale, and use the only visible metal in the entire Panorama.[19] All three exceptions link the Panorama to a visualization of an idealized past New York. They suggest that the city's apex has been reached, with public-private infrastructure projects and the fruits of slum clearance depicted as though they have been perfected. Furthermore, the larger-than-scale brass replicas of Moses's projects were key to his plans to use the Panorama as a personal branding aid. By 1964, Moses's reputation was suffering and his power was waning; in fact, his mismanagement of and alleged embezzlement from the Fair would accelerate his professional decline. Moses intended to use the Panorama to remind city and business leaders of his past successes.[20]

Yet the Panorama sells more than Moses's résumé. The Panorama was originally viewed from an indoor helicopter ride that circled it in a grand loop, mimicking the full-scale rides that transported the ultra-wealthy from Downtown Manhattan to the fairgrounds. These miniature tours featured detailed narration of the major sites passed, just as on a Circle Line tour. They were enhanced by the illusion of time passing within the Panorama, which repeatedly dimmed and raised the lights in the exhibit room to represent a twenty-four-hour cycle, aided by the appearance of lights within many buildings' windows at dusk. As this description suggests, the Panorama incorporated many aspects of the city symphony into its image of the city. However, just as the original viewing conditions of the Panorama recall the opening of *Naked City*, the Panorama itself advances a view of the city consonant with its reduction to a consumable image rather than performing a critique of it.

The Panorama appropriates the structure of a city symphony to satiate us with a sanitized version of New York that does not have, and does not need, a future. Having been perfected, fully mapped, and real-ized as a unified image, the city cannot be imagined as undergoing or requiring any evolution. Juxtaposing the Panorama with New Amster-dam, 1964 with 1660, while valorizing the infrastructure built under Moses, reinforces the idea that New York has undergone progressive development ever since its colonization as a European settlement and has reached the apex of its potential. Rather than acting as an advertisement for Moses's continued services, the Panorama justifies his retirement;

there is nothing left to plan. The Panorama's idealization of the past, of the urban planning policy and projects that shaped the city between 1939 and 1964, has ensured that the city cannot be otherwise. It remains, as Duke says, one big housing project, a social problem that cannot be solved and a fetish that remains bound to the past. These qualities collectively justify the nation's abandonment of New York in favor of global and suburban fantasies. The Panorama reveals that the obverse of the nostalgia for modernity is the denial of the city's future.

This is even more evident in one of the most beloved attractions at the Fair, the centerpiece of the S. C. Johnson Wax & Co. Pavilion, *To Be Alive!* (1964). Francis Thompson, the director of *N.Y., N.Y.*, was commissioned by the company to make a film for their pavilion at the Fair. He codirected, with Alexander Hammid, a documentary whose use of three screens was an important IMAX precursor. The Johnson Wax Pavilion was singled out by architecture and cultural critics as one of the triumphs of the Fair because of its innovative architecture and "soft sell" of its brand through free exhibits that often did not directly market its products, or even mention the company. *To Be Alive!* was the pavilion's central exhibit, screened in a 600-person theater that looked like a oblong gold egg from the outside, and which was suspended in midair by the rakish, fin-shaped support beams that made up the exterior of the pavilion. The artist's rendering of the pavilion, like the American Express diorama, emphasizes the spatial isolation of the structure, here even removing the rest of the fairgrounds and adding the suggestion of mountains (figure 5.3). Inside this artificially suspended egg, reminiscent of a space capsule or the place of a rebirth, *To Be Alive!* detailed "the joys of living" in a twenty-minute looped documentary that played constantly over the course of the day and often had an hourlong wait to view it. *To Be Alive!* topped many lists of the best exhibits of the Fair, and won several critics and industry awards for its innovative technologies and humanist message.[21]

Anthony Kinik has argued that the film has just in much in common with city symphonies as it does with IMAX experiments or corporate films. He claims that Thompson and Hammid's previous work on city symphonies inspired *To Be Alive!*, as well as other collaborations like *We Are Young!* (1967, made for the Montreal World Expo). For Kinik, these films were "experiments with" or plays on the city symphony form.[22] This connection is born out by *To Be Alive!*, which incorporates footage from *N.Y., N.Y.* However, rather than optical effects, the film relies on the montage between and unification of multiscreen images to immerse

Figure 5.3. The artists' rendering of the exterior of the Johnson Wax Pavilion, in which *To Be Alive!* was screened for more than 8,000 people a day. (Flushing Meadow Park–World's Fair–Johnson's Wax. Irma and Paul Milstein Division of United States History, Local History and Genealogy, New York Public Library. AZ 05-5469.)

the viewer in the narration of childhood and maturation as universal experiences. *To Be Alive!* focuses on children's perceptions, especially the differences between them and those of adults, which the film deems to be less engaged and responsive to stimuli. The film marries *N.Y., N.Y.*'s extreme wide angles to time-lapse reminiscent of *Go! Go! Go!*, depicting the overwhelming repetitive, iterative form of urban life. *To Be Alive!* is structured by the play of scales, oscillating between the depiction of several individuals' development from childhood into adulthood and the metaphoric representation of humanity's development as a species.

N.Y., N.Y. used its fractal aesthetics to critique the current production of the urban center around exchange value and awaken our desire for one based on encounter. By contrast, *To Be Alive!* produces these fractured images as symptoms of a deadened, urbanized *perception*—rather than a real material condition—that can only be renewed by simplifying the image and removing its perceiver from the city. As the film opens, the narrator, Edward Field, characterizes New York much as *The City* once did: "Well, another day. I have to work to live, but is this living?" Field's question accompanies footage reminiscent of and in some cases borrowed directly from *N.Y., N.Y.* As with the opening of that film, optical effects fracture the surface of the screen, iterating partial images of objects across a shot and disarticulating human figures. *To Be Alive!* has a stronger focus on public spaces and collective rhythms in these moments than does the opening of *N.Y., N.Y.* It also uses time lapse, imposing an additional uniformity on the rhythms of crowds and commuting, which are a central concern of this section.

In Thompson's earlier film, this sequence climaxed in the cathedral-like space of Penn Station. By the time *To Be Alive!* was shot, the building had been demolished by the same forces of capital celebrated at the World's Fair. Instead of the hush of Penn Station, the commuters in *To Be Alive!* make their way through an ever more vertiginous, anonymous cityscape where the fracturing of their bodies and iteration of their tasks intrudes even into their offices. Unlike *N.Y., N.Y., To Be Alive!* suggests that escaping this automation of rhythm requires leaving the city for a rewarding life that can only be lived in rural areas, and, metaphorically, in an idealized past. The result is that, rather than a rhythmanalysis of individual and social development, *To Be Alive!* claims that the current socio-spatial order can be appreciated and enjoyed as it is. This enjoyment is made possible by remembering the wondrous perceptions of childhood and renewing our vision through them. The film plays out the collision of the spectacle with the abyss. Life is threatened by a loss of the ability to visualize space, but ultimately redeemed by a vision that experiences, understands, and possesses space as a commodity.

The film makes it clear that such a vision obtains only outside the city. Three minutes into *To Be Alive!*, the cityscape fades to black. The next shot, of a quiet forest, is the first one not to be treated with optical effects and to stretch across all three screens. As the still camera cuts slowly to various forest scenes, the narrator intones, "I remember when I opened my eyes for the very first time; all was new." This statement introduces us to three figures the film returns to several times: a Chinese boy in a wheat field playing with a turtle, an East African boy overlooking a forest, and a white American boy approaching a rowboat in a suburban pond.[23] These three figures embody a renewed sight characterized by innocence. They imply that the only way not to be overwhelmed by the world is to simplify one's knowledge of it. In this sequence, the three figures are presented as equal, representing the general state of childhood. As the film continues, the white boy, and other white male figures, are most closely identified with mental, social, and sexual maturation.

This childlike travel is also tied to the control of perspective and mobility, particularly to forward motion that is an extension of, or powered by, the body. As the narrator breathlessly intones, "we raced off, all the kids of the world," we see a stock car race spread across all three screens from the perspective of the driver in the rear of the car. The film's editing continually creates shots whose denotation of forward motion take on connotative resonances of biological development and human history. For example, the stockcar literally carries the film into the future; the next sequence deals with puberty and marriage. These transitions allow *To Be Alive!* to return the viewer to the same social milieu in which it began but with the "new eyes" of a re-invigorated sight, retaining a newly sensitized, childish perspective that redeems adulthood and even the repetitive labor associated with it. The end of the film can now present the modern world, including New York, as a symbol of humanity's progress and achievement.

Much as with the Panorama of the City of New York, *To Be Alive!* forecloses the future by producing the present as the apex and fulfillment of human potential. In the penultimate scene, the Rockefeller Center ice skating rink stretches across all three screens, followed by scenes of a grandfather and grandson (the boy from the beginning) in a rowboat on a pond. Much as in the opening and closing passages of *The City*, the juxtaposition of old and young intimates repetition rather than a future trajectory. Because we have now reentered the present with a vision made newly innocent, we can experience the present like a child and appreciate the generational improvement that has led to our present achievement, but as adults who are now like children, we cannot see beyond it.

To Be Alive! ultimately evokes the training and breaking of the body to the requirements of a planned corporate economy and service industries as a symptom of a flawed vision of, and relationship to, everyday life, not as its cause. Perhaps even more than the New York city symphonies themselves, *To Be Alive!* thematizes the idea of an alternative, revelatory sight. This is especially evident in a rare midfilm New York scene, in which a Black boy holds a prism up to his eye. In the next shot, which depicts his point of view, the city is suddenly patterned with *N.Y., N.Y.*'s rainbow effects. But that sight uncovers a fulfilled life that is possible only to the extent that one is capable of forgetting the structures that delimit it. To live such a life demands forgetting—or making it impossible to think—any way of being other than the present one. *To Be Alive!* ultimately narrates and enacts the work of ideology rather than utopia's ideological critique of ideology.

The film's politics are evident even in its reception. Critics praised its apparently universal, apolitical message and directly contrasted it to the CORE protests. An anonymous review in the *New York Journal-American* proclaimed that the "annoying sound and fury of civil rights demonstrators at the World's Fair" could not penetrate the Johnson's Wax theater, where "cool, undisturbed visitors" could enjoy "the pure entertainment" of the film.[24] *To Be Alive!* evidences the difficulty of using the rhythmanalysis developed by city symphonies since *The City* to estrange the urban crisis. In this new production of space, a longing for the past and a terror of the blind future has been elevated to an ideal. *To be Alive!*, and the 1964–1965 World's Fair in general, demonstrate that the strategies used to analyze late modern New York could not retain their function within the urban crisis. A new kind of city symphony and a new form of rhythmanalysis was required to do so.

Static City: The Abyss and the Nostalgia for Modernity

During the late modern period, the various forms of urban planning that produced and redeveloped urban space all generated policies and images that tied the success of the city to motion, ranging from the cyclic return of the national day to the interior explorations of cognitive mapping. Even slum clearance, whose discourse described marginal neighborhoods as locked in the past and unable to undertake productive motion, proclaimed that razing and redeveloping such areas would drastically improve capital circulation and ease social ills. The urban crisis, characterized by the lack of a unified planning principle, generated figures of stasis. Longing for an idealized past, as shown by the World's Fair exhibits, means abandoning the city's future and celebrating its development to date as its end point. The abyss, for its part, produces a city that can no longer be imagined or navigated, and is left to sink in upon itself in the dark.

To understand how rhythmanalysis can unpack these static anti-images, and how it modifies the typical structures of the city symphony to do so, it is important to explore how the nostalgia for modernity proliferated in visual culture during the urban crisis. New York's urban crisis was contemporaneous with its transition into a postindustrial economy and characterized by "landscapes of urban decay and deindustrialization, as well as . . . [emerging] realities of gentrification, downtown redevelopment, and global finance."[25] To make sense of these major realignments of the relations of production, popular culture, beginning with the 1964–1965 World's Fair, valorized late modern, industrial, pre-urban crisis New York. This celebration worked in tandem with an excoriation of the postindustrial city as a place of perpetual, incoherent destruction. Even films with progressive aesthetic or political leanings like Martin Scorsese's *New York, New York* (1977) and Sidney Lumet's *Network* (1976) engaged in this discourse.[26] The nostalgia for modernity renders New York's loss of socioeconomic coherence as a loss of the visual transparency that the various images of the city once guaranteed. The resulting crisis-city is an abyss in which the subject cannot envision itself as a social being, and from which the city cannot be imaged or visualized—and therefore cannot be redeemed for the use of white elites. Despairing of this lost city, the discourse surrounding the onset of deindustrialization in New York asserts that the late modern city was livable because it produced itself as a clear, iconic image, and that any future city will only be bearable to the extent that it does the same. In doing so, these texts foreclosed the possibility of producing any truly livable form of urban space or futurity.

This nostalgia was unevenly spatialized and heavily racialized. It concentrated around the core materials of the spectacle: landmarks and infrastructure, including threatened or vanishing places like Penn Station. The nostalgia for modernity did not extend to sites of alternative modernities, such as working-class Coney Island or Black Harlem. These areas had been major cultural sites with at least some middle-class tax base during the late modern period. Due in no small part to the impact of slum clearance programs, as well as the rising cost of housing, Harlem's socioeconomic fortunes fall sharply during deindustrialization, which more than decimated jobs in the area.[27] Harlem, then, would seem to offer itself as a likely object for nostalgia during the urban crisis. Instead, it was produced as an always-already abyssal space at fault for the corruption of the rest of the city; the dire predictions of blight come true.

The Cool World subverts the nostalgia for modernity by having its protagonist practice it. Duke's desire to acquire a gun, defeat the rival gang, and have Harlem recognize him as a "bad man" is ultimately meant to help him secure a position of power, responsibility, and economic comfort. These desires are dependent on Duke's fantasy of his neighborhood's past: they express a longing for *Harlem's* modernity.

Just as with the dominant form, Duke's nostalgia is unreliable, based on an idealized, heavily mediated image of the city's past. *The Cool World* explicitly ties Duke's nostalgia for Harlem's modernity to the conventions and images of the crime genre, particularly 1930s and 1940s cultural productions like race films and photojournalism like Gordon Parks's 1948 profile for *Life*, "Harlem Gang Leader."[28] Through Duke, *The Cool World* evokes a longing for a place that the nostalgia for modernity ignores. At the same time, Duke's understanding of Harlem and his place in the neighborhood are revealed to be fantasies that prevent him from successfully engaging in its life and rhythms. In this way, *The Cool World* mounts an attack against the nostalgia for modernity in general, showing how it makes living in the present city, or imagining a functional future for it, impossible. The disjuncture between Duke's desire for a lost, imagined Harlem and the film's documentary depiction of its present yields the film's second subversion of the nostalgia for modernity. While Duke remains insensible to the city around him, *The Cool World* consistently documents the patterns and regulations that determine daily life in Harlem as well as in New York in general. The film establishes these patterns and regulations as those of white supremacy and a calcified capital. The former restricts and determines the kinds of movement possible in Harlem, while the latter makes meaningful spatial practices impossible in places currently or formerly associated with the center, like Wall Street.

This joint attack on the nostalgia for modernity gives *The Cool World* a distinct aesthetic and plot structure. Throughout the film, space turns back on itself and cannot be navigated. At the end of many of its scenes, a disorienting circular pan deposits Duke and the viewer back at the Pythons clubhouse or his mother's apartment building. Throughout the film, shot/reverse shots and other hallmarks of continuity editing are evoked but later prove to have been impossible given the relative position of characters. Moreover, documentary and fiction footage mingle in uneasy, often illegible ways that suspend the meaning of scenes. This circular, futile world has sometimes been articulated to a politically problematic aesthetic of stasis. In particular, Noël Carroll dismisses the film as an exercise in "black miserabilism" whose documentary footage and montage sequences of street life are "difficult to fit into the story. . . . they seem to almost float into the film, shards of fact related to, but unfettered by, the story."[29]

Recent critiques have been much more favorable than Carroll's, but still find the thematic and aesthetic immobility suspect. For example,

Pamela Robertson Wojcik argues that *The Cool World*'s emphasis on closure and claustrophobia suggest that the "the city is a dead end, offering no future."[30] In this analysis, while *The Cool World* chronicles certain aspects of Duke's lived experience and points out the structural inequalities contributing to that experience's unhappiness, it ultimately "holds out little hope for a better tomorrow."[31] Similarly, Paula Massood characterizes the film as notable for its dramatization of immobility, especially when compared to earlier gangster films set in Harlem, and as a complex entry in a cultural constellation that characterized early 1960s Harlem through "images of violence, destruction, poverty, and decay, the advent of another war, and another wave of urban uprisings."[32] Like Wojcik and Massood, I recognize the film's political limitations, particularly its inability to imagine a future for Black youth. However, reading the film in the context of the urban crisis's figuration of the abyss surfaces the critical power in *The Cool World*'s treatment of stasis.

Like other members of the New American Cinema at the time, Clarke considered feature films a crucial part of cinematic avant-garde practice and a way to cultivate a larger national avant-garde audience, one that could be taught to educate itself about film aesthetics as well as the social issues the films raised.[33] *The Cool World*'s conjoining of the gangster film with the city symphony, and disarticulation of Duke's spatial perspective from the film's, should be understood through this lens. By drawing on popular genre as well as one of the most widespread avant-garde film forms to produce a split subjectivity, *The Cool World* could cultivate a wider audience and teach it how to engage with avant-garde film and its politics.[34] *The Cool World* shows how the popular evocation of Harlem as ahistorical abyss ignores the neighborhood's past social structures. It also traces the deformations of the neighborhood's rhythms to the regulation of space imposed by white supremacy and surfaces the ways in which the nostalgia for modernity renders the city unlivable. The film's symphonic elements grant the viewer an image of Harlem that extends beyond the one Duke offers.[35] *The Cool World* uses these elements to depict an immobility paradoxically produced through a flurry of motion that always returns the characters caught in it to their point of origin. The film thereby subverts the urban crisis's figuration of Harlem as a threatening abyss.

The Cool World's evocation of stasis depends on irrational continuity, a hallmark of false narration. Gilles Deleuze identifies false narration as one of the core components of the time-image. For Deleuze, the time-image replaced the movement-image, where temporality is articulated to, and determined by, progress through space, as in a chase scene. In the normal course of things, motion links space and time together in a rational and causal relation to build audience identification, deadline narrative structure, and recognizable sequences. In the time-image, time emerges as pure duration, decoupled from space to rise "in its pure state" to the surface of the screen. Aesthetics associated with the time-image, like false narration, consistently work to undermine the audience's ability to comprehend or trust the diegesis. False narration destabilizes identity on the level of character, diegesis, and production. In spaces such as those produced by late modernity, narration exists as a system of judgment "according to legal connections in space and chronological relations in time." In spaces such as the city of the urban crisis, however, this is no longer possible, and narrative instead operates according to "the powers of the false." Normative narration establishes a clear path through past, present, and future that results in a coherent subjectivity, but false narration results in the sense that "I is another."[36] This can be expressed by a character's identity seemingly taking on characteristics of their environment or a more general confusion of subjectivity and objectivity, including between character and camera. *The Cool World* performs just such a perforation of categories in its instability of documentary and fictional images, subjective and objective shots, character and city. The film stages the disjunction between characters' ability to witness and act, casting doubt on the existence of a unified present as well as the distinction between subjective and objective points of view. It relentlessly explores the irrational connections between locations, and probes the absolute gaps within them.

These tactics compose a new kind of rhythmanalysis, a falsifying narration that critiques the abyss and the nostalgia for modernity. *The Cool World* demonstrates that the urban crisis, supposedly spread to the rest of New York by places like Harlem, is instead a result of the completely alienated relations of production that always already structure all urban space under capital, including areas regarded as nostalgic icons, like Midtown. The film refuses to produce New York as a perpetual late modern space. Instead, it shows how the desire for total legibility, for the city to exist as an image, actually *causes* social and spatial problems. After all, the nostalgia for modernity is in part a denial that late modern planning policies and their attendant visual culture are proximate causes of the urban crisis. Rather than depicting stasis as an abyss, the film articulates motionlessness as futile repetition, and this repetition, in turn, indicates the liminal space—the future as the other of the present—that the crisis-city must absent.

By critiquing the nostalgia for modernity, rejecting Harlem as abyss, and calling the livability of the city-as-image into question, *The Cool World* shows how the urban crisis expels liminality itself. Nostalgia expels the neutral, the space that is both and neither, by transforming it into an unreachable future-past that makes being otherwise, and therefore utopia, impossible. Duke's desire and the film's diegesis are suffused with a series of constantly collapsing paths, goals, and subjectivities. These impossible itineraries of false narrative render temporality, the built environment, and identity fragile and contingent. They foreground and thematize stasis as the component of the urban crisis that must be estranged for the possibility of another socio-spatial order to exist. *The Cool World*'s opposition to the Fair's spatial fantasies and rhetoric embodies the city symphony's cleavage from popular visual culture. It marks the end of the New York city symphony cycle and provides nascent strategies for analyzing the space of the urban crisis.

False Narrative:
The Cool World and the New Rhythmanalysis

The Cool World opens with an extreme close-up of a street-corner preacher delivering a sermon derived from Black Nationalist and Black Muslim rhetoric on the subject of "the black man as the original man" directly to the camera.[37] This shot is followed by a short establishing sequence in which the rest of the speech, rendered in voice off, is paired with quick glimpses of the surrounding area—117th Street and Madison Avenue—and its inhabitants, including young mothers, older men socializing on stoops and corners, and white police officers. Other than the first shots of the preacher, each shot approaches its subject at a slight angle, with characters glancing up or over their shoulders to meet the camera before looking down or away as the camera quickly pans or cuts to the next face. The exception is the police, the only white figures in the sequence (figure 5.4). They are shot from a lower camera position and stare directly at the camera, in one case mimicking the rightward sweep of its pan as though following the camera out of frame.

The opening sequence ends when the camera approaches Duke (as yet unidentified) from behind. He turns, smiles, and says directly to the

Figure 5.4. The white police officers in *The Cool World* challenge the camera and the African American boys whose perspective it embodies. (Shirley Clarke, Dir. *The Cool World*. 1964; Boston, MA: Zipporah Films. 16 mm.)

camera, "Hey Rod, come here." A reverse shot depicts Rod (Basic Felton), a minor figure in the Pythons and the film. This reverse shot suggests that the preceding moments, apparently recorded by an objective documentary camera, have in fact expressed Rod's point of view. However, the constant volume of the preacher's harangue throughout the sequence complicates this reading. It reminds the viewer not only of the film's constructed status but of a seeming divide between the aural and visual negotiation of space. Similarly, when Clarke finally provides an establishing shot of the street at the start of the next scene, Rod's itinerary should have traced a unidirectional path, but the ceaseless left-right pans constructed a circular one, invoking the alienated, impassable nature of space and the difficulty of individuated, purposeful spatial practices in the abyss of the urban crisis. The police officers' surveilling gaze embodies and races the camera, aligning the viewer's subject position with Rod in particular and Harlem's residents in general as living under an occupying force that sees them as a social problem and threat, and which prevents them from undertaking meaningful movement. The opening sequence establishes

The Cool World's treatment of Harlem as a policed and surveilled space, one in which only futile movement and false narration are possible.

The quick pans, oblique angles, and sense of scanning evoked by the opening sequence as a whole typifies the practiced sleuthing of the urban dweller who must sift through the sensory ensemble of the street to detect their goal, in this case Rod's search for Duke. It equally evokes the rhythmanalyst's attunement to their environment. Yet the sequence documents a failed rhythmanalysis. Whose failure this is, just as the question of whose subjectivity, if any, the camera is aligned with, is suspended during the course of the sequence. The first shot catches the offscreen Rod in midstep, its close-up scale explicable as a redoubling of the preacher's volume. Hearing is the sense extended first and furthest in the urban context,[38] and the loud volume of the preacher's shout represents one of those breaks in self-generated bodily rhythm and focus that can startle any urban pedestrian into a visual encounter with an otherwise overlooked aspect of the street. But here, instead of engaging with the social movements illuminated by the sermon and the possibility of another social order they imply, Rod determinately backs away from them, representing spatially what Duke will spend the rest of the film doing narratively. By disengaging from the calls to action and recognition around them, even as Rod's gaze registers and enacts the dressage to which Black New Yorkers are subject, Rod and Duke become passive witnesses, seeing the world around them without being able to meaningfully engage with it.

At the same time, the opening sequence plays out the ways in which the unequal development and racist production of space in the urban crisis transfixes Harlem as a social space and constrains the spatial practices of its inhabitants. Just as the opening shot disrupts Rod's search, the rest of the sequence details the visual regime and representations of space that determine Rod's spatial practices. The sequence does not fit easily with the narrative, nor is it legible as a simple subjective tracking shot, although it does provide the sense of "typicality" that marks city symphonies. The sequence can be read as presenting a paradigmatic day in the life of Harlem, but it depicts this day in terms of a collectively raced embodiment by positioning the camera as a Harlem resident, with all of the surveillance of the body politic and political bodies this entails.

This critique resonates with James Baldwin's near-contemporary description of Harlem for *Esquire*. In 1960, just after Miller's novel was released, Baldwin argued in "Fifth Avenue, Uptown," that urban renewal had resulted in a "rehabilitation" of the neighborhood that only exacerbated its social problems. Baldwin argues that the vacant lots and brutal high-rises, which "hang over the avenue like a monument to the folly, and the cowardice, of good intentions," articulate a hostile view of Harlem's residents. This hostility is echoed by the the occupying white police force: "both reveal, unbearably, the real attitude of the white world, no matter how many liberal speeches are made, no matter how many lofty editorials are written, no matter how many civil rights commissions are set up."[39] Baldwin also reviewed Miller's original novel version of *The Cool World* and praised it as a revelatory work whose power was bound up in its ability to represent the "strange" aspects of Duke's Harlem, not as exoticized content, but as an alienation and resensitizing of the reader's perception. Baldwin argued that the novel displayed Harlem as a template of the American situation as a whole.[40] For Baldwin, just as urban renewal in Harlem reinscribed the more overt displays of state violence and control over Black citizens, Warren's novel traced the bonds between the neighborhood and the nation that disowned it.

These ties play out in a film structured by the troubled relation between documentary and fiction, city and character. For example, the opening shots enact a literal "search" for the story on Rod's part that records the power relations that determine what kinds of stories can be told, and what their likely outcome will be. The rightward pans that connect shots establish that Rod's attempt to walk down the street, negotiating New York's grid, is continually subverted by the repetitions of Harlem itself as social space within the urban crisis. Because Rod's function is to motivate Duke's verbalization of his wish for a gun (and thus the plot), he almost acts as an extension of space itself. This space enables events, which Massood argues is a hallmark of earlier Harlem films.[41] But where the space Massood describes enables events by contextualizing them in a social order, Clarke's Harlem enables only either boredom or trauma due to its lack of a coherent spatial order. The remainder of the film is structured by the formal characteristics engendered here. Duke occupies an inescapable present in which actions and desire have no impact on space and no ability to craft a future. Quotidian rhythms are limited and constantly repeated, unchanging from day to day. Duke can engage with the city only in the past or in the future, generating false narration marked by "the incompossible." The incompossible is a situation in which "the past may be true without being necessarily true" and in which mutually exclusive presents generated by this past might exist side by side.[42]

Duke exemplifies the incompossible because his desired identity exists only in a contrary to fact future, a future inaccessible not only from his present but also as the future per se; the role he imagines for himself was only possible in an imagined past. For example, Duke's fantasies of leadership and his friendly, protective interactions with other youth figures—particularly a college-bound basketball player—suggest that he longs to be a gangster, enmeshed in an aspirational, only somewhat predatory, entrepreneurial structure that helps weave the community together, rather than a gang member. Such a construction of criminality is aligned with the modern and late modern construction of Harlem as a locus of "change and progress," rather than the urban crisis's construction of the area as a ghetto.[43] At the same time, Duke refuses to articulate the rather depressing, boring, anonymous future his present spatial practices—going to school, selling cigarettes, hanging out in the Python clubhouse—are likely to produce. Instead, he obsessively focuses on the alternative future that will be ensured *if* he acquires a gun.

Like any good rhythmanalyst, Duke is able to view and construct alternative temporal orders and perceive several divergent rhythms at play in the same space, unbundling the connections that lead from his own body's patterns to the built environment and the social order. But Duke's rhythmanalysis of urban crisis New York produces irrational continuities because his analysis is predicated on constantly mistaking the space of the deindustrializing city for an earlier one. His rhythms have been deformed by a nostalgia for modernity. Duke's production of Harlem as a nostalgic image of the city ejects him from the current production of space without estranging that space or diagnosing its structuring absences. He can occupy and act in the space of a fictional past or the space of an impossible future, but not the space of the present. *The Cool World* successfully performs the rhythmanalysis that Duke cannot by staging a collision between the impotent, late modern image of the city Duke dreams of and the abyssal urban crisis he can't quite inhabit. The film questions the "truths" of points of view and spatial relations composed in each sequence through the images of the next. This produces Harlem as a paradigmatic New York location and dismisses nostalgia as an effective tactic for negotiating that space.

One of the key ways the film accomplishes this is by linking Harlem to iconic locations like Midtown, Wall Street, and Coney Island. This linkage occurs through an irrational continuity that includes pans, tracking shots, sound bridges, and graphic matches. The film's casual, picaresque plot further suggests that each location is equivalent to the others, each making meaningful rhythms impossible, each posing a challenge to Duke's future, and each structured by the same relations of production and social relations. For example, after meeting Rod, Duke wanders across 134th Street to seek out local racketeer Priest (Carl Lee, Clarke's partner, who also helped adapt the novel and served as an acting coach during filming) and his white girlfriend (Marilyn Cox), who show Duke and Rod the gun that Duke wants to buy. The boys then walk around the corner to the school bus that will take them on their year-end school trip to Wall Street. The long, fluid tracking shots that connect Duke's progress across space render each stop on their itinerary, each event, as directly related and undifferentiated in terms of import or morality. Hanging out before school leads directly to window-shopping for a gun, which precedes a school trip to the heart of capital. The banal and the extreme are one and the same and begin to redefine each other. The editing renders these events and their connections logical, equivalent, and natural, suppressing the semiotics of genre and morality that usually separate them. The editing simultaneously reveals the power relations and representations of space that organize Duke's particular spatial practices. The film's editing performs the rhythmanalysis its protagonist cannot. In doing so, it estranges his subjectivity and the production of space on which this subjectivity depends, revealing the extent to which both yield impossible, perfected spaces. Such spaces foreclose futures capable of producing a space that is otherwise. *The Cool World* traces a New York in which every neighborhood has been reduced to interchangeable spaces of banality and terror, documenting the impact of ejecting utopia from urban policy and imagination.

As Duke boards the bus, his voiceover—which becomes a crucial aspect of *The Cool World*'s structure—and the shots directed out of the bus window place the audience within Duke's subjectivity. Duke recalls a conversation with his aunt in which he described his plans to work in a liquor store. We hear both participants in the conversation as though from an objective point of audition, even though the discussion is suggested as Duke's recollection and his aunt is not otherwise present in the film. Immediately after recalling the interaction, Duke, still in voiceover, dismisses it as a series of lies on his part: "Shit. Work in a liquor store? Don't she know? What I need and what I want is a gun . . . Duke Custis, leader of the Pythons." Even an interior monologue is not particularly trustworthy. In fact, both halves of Duke's thoughts recount equally phantasmatic futures. The "leader of the pythons" Duke fantasizes about becoming is just as illusory as the employed, upstanding citizen he constructs for his aunt. Furthermore, Duke's voiceover includes not only the memories of conversations but also the fantasy of future interactions.

Just after he names himself leader, anonymous voices interject "There goes Duke, he's cool! Yeah, he's a real cool killer." Duke's identity is entirely dependent on the acceptance and reactions of others.

The street activity the bus passes testifies to the difficult relationship between Duke's identity and his environment. Even as Duke relies on Harlem's acceptance to validate his spatial practices, it remains explicitly indifferent to his desires. Against the sounds of Duke's attempted self-fashioning, the image track records groups of young adults talking with their backs to the street, children waving to their friends on the bus, and older teenage boys pointing and laughing at them. These shots do not display an eye-line match with Duke's point of view, and because we see several shots in succession before cutting back to a shot of Duke, they do not appear to be shot-reverse-shots. Instead, these images of the neighborhood are symphonic in Lefebvre's sense, a series of presences that compose Harlem's multilayered present. This present stands in opposition to the nostalgia for modernity that characterizes both the urban crisis and Duke's subjectivity.

Duke's anachronistic desire reinscribes the urban crisis's conceptualization of Harlem as never occupying New York's present. This sequence's play of indifference and engagement underscores the protagonist's unfulfilled wish for the ability to make the outside match the inside, to make his future flesh through his environment's acknowledgment of him, to construct his identity from this space. It establishes Duke's nostalgia for Harlem's modernity, at once staging Harlem as a space whose past is worth longing for and critiquing the ability of nostalgia for Harlem, or any space, to produce a viable urban future. The film here expresses a subjectivity shown to be not so much unreliable as incompossible: Duke wants a milieu that reacts to what he will be instead of what he is, and which requires the kind of relation between subject and place that no longer exist.

The next sequence shows that Duke is denied a purposeful spatial practice neither because of his criminality nor because of Harlem's inherent lack of imageability but rather because New York as a whole has been swallowed entirely by the spectacle. Reduced to the sign of signs, the city is incapable of granting such a practice. The film's credits finally appear nearly ten minutes in, as the bus passes through Central Park. The diegesis spills over its borders as the credits appear on screen as though seen through the window of the bus, vanishing from sight as the bus passes them and evoking the white light glimpsed between the dark leaves of the trees in the Park. When *The Cool World* exits Central

Park and leaves "the cool world" for the urban financial center, it does so wrapped in, yet critical of, Duke's subjectivity and oriented to the spatial practices of Harlem. The center we emerge into, signified by Radio City Music Hall, Rockefeller Center, and the main branch of the New York Public Library, is just as much an empty play of signs as Duke's Harlem. These spaces and institutions represent the wealthy, white spaces on which the nostalgia for modernity is centered. They also typify the kind of monuments that organize the complementary fantasy of late modern New York as a transparent, legible, unified, and socially coherent city under immanent threat or even already lost. Throughout the sequence, Mr. Shapiro (Jerome Raphael), Duke's white teacher, inadvertently reveals the truth of these sites, describing them in the shallowest of terms, citing their "richness" or trivial aspects. He reduces the New York Public Library to "the largest in the world" and notes that its lion statues have "big wreaths" put around their necks for Christmas, a far cry from the alternate temporality and subjectivity they evoked in *Weegee's New York*. In Mr. Shapiro's account, the urban center is inadvertently revealed as nothing but the signs of products, each interchangeable or encompassed by a whimsical detail, the embodiment of the society of the spectacle. Just like the abyss of the urban crisis, the spectacle is a map that exceeds its territory, allowing for neither critical intervention nor escape. The field trip sequence demonstrates the extent to which Harlem's closure and lack of future is a condition shared by New York as a whole, and is one that spreads from the center to Harlem rather than the reverse.

As Duke and his classmates finally arrive at Wall Street, the vertiginous camera performs a circular pan of Wall Street before a quick, nearly invisible cut spins to a stop in Harlem and a shot of Duke leaning against his mother's front door. This sequence demonstrates the critical power of combining the city symphony with the crime film via false narrative. The iconography of the crime film at once teaches us to read urban surfaces for evidence of illegality and comforts us that crime is to be found in places like Harlem, not Wall Street.[44] Clarke, by contrast, makes Wall Street and Harlem contiguous spaces through irrational continuity. Her symphonic rhythmanalysis reminds us that crimes committed on Wall Street impact Harlem. By blurring the significance and spatial distinctions of these neighborhoods, the sequence shows how the congealing of space in the urban crisis has accelerated past late modernity's false reconciliation of concept and experience to the point that it has become resistant to *any* conceptualization of space, thereby collapsing traditional spatial practices. Wall Street and Harlem become different cells in the same prison, and no amount of movement within the city is capable of freeing Duke from them. This reverses one of the late modern Black gangster film's key tropes, in which success is measured by gaining access to spaces in the city in addition to or outside of one's original neighborhood.[45] The field trip sequence traces the faltering line between self and city. It reinscribes the inescapable nature of the city for Black New Yorkers. After this scene, any trip to another space ends with an unmotivated cut back to Harlem.

In *The Cool World*'s New York, conventional spatial practices are impossible. They exist only as asynchronous signs of the longed-for past or doomed future. The crisis-city produces a space so totally abstract that experiences and concepts of it can no longer be composed, let alone critically estranged. Rhythmanalysis cannot proceed by unbundling spatial practices but must rather excavate this congealed space, demonstrating the irrationalities and impossibilities on which it is founded and which it deflects through nostalgia for modernity and the abyss of Harlem. The field trip sequence demonstrates that, as a blind space in which experience, perception, and conception of space are mutually exclusive, Harlem is not an exceptional space in crisis but rather utterly typical of New York as a whole as a static crisis-city. It is a symptom of this production of space, not the cause of it. *The Cool World* recuperates Harlem as a contiguous part of New York and traces the true flow of corruption and threat between neighborhood and city.

The critical stasis the film builds through false narration helps indicate the liminal, the other space and other of space that the urban crisis makes it impossible to think. The urban crisis systematically erases the idea of borders or ruptures between the past and present and the present and the future through nostalgia for modernity. The abyss, forbidding the envisioning or conception of the city, also foils the production of spatial practices: the abyss relegates the city to the status of an irresolvable crisis that forecloses the future and directs all hope to the past. When the urban crisis removes liminality, it is removing the space of utopia, the place from which the structuring absences of the current production of space can be glimpsed and an alternative to that production can be imagined. Therefore, the urban crisis's structuring absence is liminal space, and the possibility of utopia, itself. *The Cool World* recalls utopia from oblivion by defining it—a space that is not, that is otherwise—as the only experience of space that remains possible within the urban city.

As is only appropriate for a utopian critique, *The Cool World* makes this argument most explicitly in a sequence structured around a series of limits: the horizon and the ocean (figure 5.5). Duke and his girlfriend, Luanne (Yolanda Rodriguez), visit Coney Island to fulfill what Duke interprets as her wish to see the ocean. The sequence begins with the camera following the characters out of the tunnel of the Stillwell Avenue D train stop and onto the Boardwalk. The take continues as one of the film's few extreme long shots reveals a dirty, sparsely populated, decrepit stretch of beach, markedly different from the crowded location seen in *Weegee's New York* and *Little Fugitive*. Duke and Luanne wander the Boardwalk, first encountering and hustling an acquaintance from Harlem and then turning their respective skills as a gangster and a prostitute to their advantage as they effortlessly win each game they play. Unlike Joey in *Little Fugitive*, dressage has already prepared them to triumph in the nickel empire and no onsite training is needed. Here, the skills generated

Figure 5.5. *The Cool World* evokes the utopian aspects of liminality in its Coney Island scenes, particularly in Duke and Luanne's conversation by the ocean. (Shirley Clarke, Dir. *The Cool World*. 1964; Boston, MA: Zipporah Films. 16 mm.)

by the deindustrializing city are no longer exclusively tied to Harlem as a place of perpetual crisis. Instead, they are required to successfully navigate the economically unified space of New York as a whole.[46] "The cool world" of Harlem extends far across 110th street, past the end of the subway, and to the ocean itself.

After these initial establishing shots, filmed objectively, *The Cool World* increasingly presents Coney Island through Duke's subjective point of view. By the time he approaches a quick-draw Western game, the transition is complete. As in earlier sequences, Duke's interior monologue and the film's soundtrack more generally enact fantasies. As always, those fantasies center on his identity as gun-slinging hero, here mediated by the generic semantics of the game. The game consists of a life-sized image of a cowboy who faces the player, gun out, and in a recorded mechanical voice, instructs the player to "draw," addressing the player as a "bad man" when the player wins. The game, then, finally acknowledges the identity Duke wants to construct for himself as a dangerous, competent, admired adult—a bad man. The following shots depict Duke playing and winning other carnival games, but the soundtrack consists of a mix of Luanne's pleased laughter and the cowboy's injunction to "draw" rather than location sound, dialogue, or the audio features of the other games. A shot pushes into a board covered in balloons and then cuts to Duke looking to his side, only to find empty space where he expected Luanne to be. Luanne does not reappear in the remainder of the film. Luanne's disappearance has been discussed as a kind of narrative short circuit, as an implied motive for Duke's self-destructive behavior at the film's conclusion, or even as an instance of *The Cool World*'s refusal of traditional continuity editing.[47] It is also possible to interpret Luanne's laughter, the only evidence of her presence in the film for several minutes before her absence is revealed, as part and parcel of Duke's fantasy of his future self. Having reduced Luanne to the validation of his longed-for identity, Duke loses her real physical presence.

The editing of the sequence implies that Luanne disappears into the irrational relations and disjunctures that pepper both *The Cool World*'s formal structure and the space of the urban crisis. She falls into a gap between cuts, or between the sky and sea, escaping into or consumed by space itself. Earlier city symphonies like *Rien que les heures* and *Berlin: Symphony of a Great City* prominently feature the death or disappearance of women who could not or would not orient themselves and their spatial practices to the dominant representations of space in modernity. Unlike them, Luanne disappears *because* she understands perfectly the nature of the space through which she moves. The trip to Coney Island occurs because of an earlier conversation between Duke and Luanne, one in which critics have claimed Luanne expresses her desire to see the ocean.[48] However, explaining her wish to Duke, she simply says that she wants to "get away," traveling as far as possible, until she gets to the end of America in San Francisco, where "they have an ocean." The ocean is not something Luanne wants to see as such; rather it marks a litmus or limit she wants to approach. Luanne's "away," the end of America, and the ocean all typify what Louis Marin calls "the frontier," the end of known space and a key aspect of utopia.[49] The ocean is completely undifferentiated space and thus not recoverable by the current production of space as either concept or experience. It marks the ends of spatial orders without itself being marked, except as unknowable. The ocean, in its resistance to image, to full conceptualization, and to any kind of typical experience, enacts utopia's ceaseless passage from the known to the unknown.

When Luanne finally reaches the shoreline, she gazes at the horizon and plans her next escape: "What happens when you get to the end? To that line out there?" Duke answers, "Europe." Luanne, however, is not satisfied with the information or location and asks where Africa is without turning to look at Duke, keeping her eyes on the horizon for the remainder of the scene. Luanne's question indicates a different kind of frontier, intimating an Afrocentric origin and social order that harkens back to the preacher's opening monologue. It offers an alternative to America's socio-spatial order and the constitutive role race plays within it. Luanne's desires compose an impossible spatial practice that the film's false narrative is finally able to grant. Wanting only to reach "the end," the line and gap that recedes when approached, the only true experience or concept of space left in the abyss of the urban crisis, she finally slips between another ephemeral line—the one between shots. Unlike Duke, Luanne achieves her goal because she understands the possible spatial practices left in the crisis-city. Luanne and Duke's discussion not only hints that Luanne disappears into utopia, into the space that is the other of the urban crisis, it implies something about the ways in which that space is otherwise. This sequence illuminates the lack of effective spatial practices left to Black people within the urban crisis. It implies that the structuring absence on which the urban crisis is founded is the right of New York's Black inhabitants to the city, their right to develop and dwell within the city according to their needs and constitute its center as a series of encounters between people of color—to make their lives in the city a collective work of Black art.

The ending of the sequence reinforces this absenting and the nature of the space founded on it. Duke, exhausted from his search for Luanne, turns away from the beach, down the empty boardwalk, and disappears at the end of the dark street. He emerges in the next shot, walking from the edge of the lower center of the frame to the front steps of his mother's house. Just as the reveal of Rod's point of view in the opening sequence prompted a revaluation of subjectivity and objectivity, Luanne's vanishing makes Duke's emergence back in Harlem a kind of miracle while simultaneously casting doubt on the veracity of each previous cut. The incompossible present once again produces pasts that are true without being necessarily true, offering a critique of the fantasy of the past on which the nostalgia for modernity depends. These cuts also suggest the existence of spaces beyond the film's capacity to depict. By staging utopia through Luanne's escape to an other space and the other of space, *The Cool World* demonstrates that any alternative to the city of the urban crisis is not located either in an anti-urban future or in a longing for a past that never was. The film insists that the only true city of the future is the city that is otherwise, specifically in its centering of Black experiential space.

Yet the film's indication of utopia and an alternative to the current production of space is not shared by its protagonist. *The Cool World* ends with Duke once again attempting to force Harlem into harmony with his own impossible future self, to conjoin witness and action, a concept of space and its experience. Just before the final fight sequence with the rival gang, immediately after his return from Coney Island, Duke lies on his bed imagining how Harlem will greet and acknowledge him after winning the fight. After an establishing shot of Duke, a cut begins a short montage of street scenes reminiscent of the bus scene at the beginning of the film, but here everyone on the street turns admiringly to look at the camera, and by extension at Duke. However, the loss of Luanne has caused him to lose control of even his own mental space. In voiceover, he says, "I ain't even got the heart for the rumble now," and suddenly the imagined street is full of happy Black families and couples, the life Duke cannot achieve. This sequence depicts a future that only emerges into Duke's consciousness once it exceeds his reach, just as it exists beyond the horizon of thought within the urban crisis, which cannot conceive of Harlem as a functional space.

Finally, the rumble comes, and Duke finds a knife sufficient to kill the leader of the rival gang. Afterward, Duke runs down the street and we finally glimpse Harlem's most iconic spaces—the Apollo Theater and the intersection of Lenox Avenue and 125th Street. Duke's voice is conspicuously absent from the soundtrack, which is filled instead with the horns of Dizzy Gillespie's original jazz score. Duke's flight takes him through spaces that are both hypervisible and easily navigable. They include locations prominent during the modern and late modern periods, but which were never part of urban renewal's image of the city or the nostalgia of the urban crisis. Having finally achieved the act that should trigger his "cool" status, Duke encounters places associated with the Harlem of late modernity that are capable of granting this identity, but he cannot even turn his head to regard them. Duke has entered a vestige of the late modern production of space, but after its dominance has passed, and only once his ability to shape that space with his own spatial practices is lost.

The film's final sequence details Duke's arrest. As he awaits the police, his crime is discussed on the radio, broadcasting his deeds far and wide to an indifferent audience. This audience is not told his name, but only his age and race. The broadcast then excitedly announces plans to bury a copy of the Constitution on the moon, recalling the rocket ships from Duke's city of the future and the lunar base in *Futurama II*. Here the figure of the abyss is even more strongly linked to aspects of race and class as Duke—or at least his projection of his future self—is swallowed by an unknowable space. Duke can no longer visualize a true present or future, even as his image disappears from the screen as he is taken into custody. As the credits roll over the exterior of the patrol car taking Duke downtown, his first voiceover from the class trip is replayed. The film has become a loop in which Duke goes downtown while recounting his future exploits. The final line in the film is Duke reminding us, in voiceover, to "stay cool." This is uttered as the squad car passes into the Upper East Side, the same neighborhood where the film was first screened, reinforcing Harlem's status as the paradigm of, not exception to, New York. The line also issues a command to audience members, reminding them that they too share a part of Duke's fate as occupants of the abyssal crisis-city as long as they share his fantasy of late modern New York as a viable alternative to it.

At the Border

The Cool World is a film about borders, and most of all about the border and boundary embodied in the skin. As a false narrative, the film dissolves the boundaries among camera, director, and character. The space that this dissolution produces yields a story about a city that apparently has no internal borders and can be instantly traversed—as with shots between Harlem and Wall Street—yet is still structured by the irreducible border imposed by white supremacy. *The Cool World* thereby illuminates urban crisis New York's doubly inescapable nature.

The Cool World is also a border in and of itself. As Lauren Rabinovitz has argued, its production, distribution, and exhibition history dramatizes the New American Cinema's increasing marginalization of women and politicized content in favor of an auteurist model of personal expression tied predominantly to straight, white, male directors.[50] If symphonies of the margins like *Little Fugitive* made up the prehistory of that movement, then *The Cool World* marked a rupture within it as its last widely exhibited city symphony and one of its final socially engaged, narrative feature films. The New York city symphony had become unmoored from the popular noncommercial venues and institutional backers that began its cycle in 1939. It also cleaved from its dominant form of production and critical reception. *The Cool World* premiered at the Venice Film Festival like *Little Fugitive*, but in New York it opened at Cinema II, which marked the beginning of multiplex exhibition in New York and the slow mainstreaming and expansion of independent cinema. This expansion did not occur in such a way as to offer direct competition to Hollywood, as Clarke had hoped. Rather, it hastened Clarke's ejection from the New York avant-garde and that movement's adoption, with Hollywood, of an auteurist, canon-based model of "essential cinemas" and film appreciation.[51]

Moreover, *The Cool World* continues the trend seen in earlier city symphonies like *In the Street* of shooting in poor and minority neighborhoods but screening for the creative and middle classes in white neighborhoods. Rabinovitz and Massood have respectively shown that the film played mostly to white audiences and was reviewed predominantly by white critics.[52] This exhibition and reception pattern lends an unpleasant implication to Clarke's statement that "in the two years it took us to make the film, the Negro revolution began, which has been useful in helping us to distribute the film."[53] If the revolution was useful, it appears to have been so in whetting the appetites of white audiences for films centered on African American characters and spaces. Moreover, white critics tended to note the film's "truthfulness" while arguing that it pointed to the characters' own responsibilities for their woes.[54] This undertone of opportunism and appropriation in Clarke's comments, and white critics' incomprehension of the film's structural critique, complicates Bayard Rustin and James Farmer's understanding of the film as useful for advancing civil rights.

Yet, as Farmer and Rustin said it would, the film addressed a national audience and a national issue. This aspect of the film's critique, at least, *was* acknowledged by popular critics. In first run reviews, Harlem's relationship to the nation was discussed as, if not anti-American, then as an abjected part of the country and without reference to New York at all. As *Newsday* put it: "*The Cool World* is the other America."[55] Here, the utopian relationship New York had with America during the late modern period, as both encapsulation of and opposition to national identity, is transferred to Harlem, which the urban crisis had attempted to eject from nation and city alike. As the New American Cinema withdrew from political content and as New York was minimized in the national consciousness, *The Cool World* not only argued the space it depicted was typical of the city, but also of the nation.

The Cool World marks the border between the New York city symphony cycle proper and the city symphonies that came later. These films, such as Hilary Harris's *Organism* (1972), existed within a very different industrial context and, like *To Be Alive!*, without a utopian relationship to the dominant production of space. *The Cool World* does not represent the end of the city symphony or even city symphonies about New York, but rather the end of the New York city symphony as utopian critique. It therefore begs the question of the applications and functions of utopian cinema in general, and city symphonies in particular, as critical tools.

The film shows how these questions can be addressed through the most important of all its borders. *The Cool World*'s ultimate liminality both within and beyond its diegesis is the boundary that rhythmanalysis temporarily dissolves: the skin. Lefebvre understands the body as the first subject of the analyst's pursuit. He presents rhythmanalysis as the sensitizing of the skin, as the deliberate raising of self-awareness of involuntary, internal bodily processes. For Lefebvre, the skin is the boundary between inside and outside, self and world, that the analyst must fully inhabit and marshal like a metronome to both grasp and be grasped by rhythms, to wear "this tissue of the lived, of the everyday."[56] Yet Lefebvre's rhythmanalyst already has a simultaneous advantage and disadvantage when it comes to slipping the skin and exposing the body's nerves and senses to the world. Lefebvre imagines his analyst as himself. Therefore, the analyst possesses a skin that is transparent and unmarked:

straight, white, and male, the skin of the Enlightenment subject.[57] Dressage shapes this skin, too, determines how it holds itself and tugs the body into its training and breaking. The analyst, in his privileged position, has additional work to do in becoming aware of that which is falsely held to be universal. But Lefebvre's skin is not Duke's, and it is not Clarke's, or her camera's. Their skin is always already sensitive, being perpetually grasped by outer rhythms and attuned, for their own survival, to the levers of power that structure the everyday's rhythms.[58]

This is neither to suggest that rhythmanalysis is a tactic reserved for certain bodies nor that *The Cool World* is the first New York city symphony to deal with raced (or gendered, or queered) bodies. Rather, *The Cool World* is an apt end to the New York city symphony cycle because its dramatization of failed rhythmanalysis and tracing of the boundary between late modernity and the urban crisis also points to the frontier of utopia itself. As Marin argues, utopia is "not founded on hope." It is a diagnostic procedure that, as part of its operation, exposes its own inscription in the extant socio-spatial order. It is not a science of space, which is to say it is not a revolutionary undertaking.[59] The New York city symphonies are utopian critiques, but they are not utopian *praxis*. They are the "the narrative figure or pictorial form produced by history in the process of being made."[60] *The Cool World*'s status as a "film of racial impasse" and as one that was read at the time of its release by white critics as critiquing the dysfunction of African American communities is explicable in part because of its utopian nature.[61] *The Cool World* is a trace that history cannot tidy away after itself, one that gives the lie to the urban crisis's claim to resolve the contradictions of late modernity through its longing for it.

Despite these limitations and its ultimate inability to depict or imagine a Black New Yorker exercising their right to the city, *The Cool World* argues that New York is dysfunctional *because* it cannot be claimed by its people, including Black New Yorkers. This is strongly resonant with Baldwin's diagnosis of America's underlying social rot in his 1964 photo essay collaboration with the photographer Richard Avedon, *Nothing Personal*. There, between Avedon's portraits of weddings in New York's city hall and keepers of segregation like Judge Leander Perez, Baldwin wrote: "[T]he country was settled by a desperate, divided, and rapacious horde of people who were determined to forget their pasts and determined to make money . . . this is proven by the spectacular ugliness and hostility of our cities. Our cities are terribly unloved—by the people who live in them, I mean. No one seems to feel that the city belongs to him."⁶² Like Baldwin, *The Cool World* excoriates a city made ugly and hostile because its inhabitants do not have a right to it. It indicates this lack of ownership as the root of a national problem. In struggling with the impossible spaces of the urban crisis, *The Cool World* dramatizes the need for a city, and a socio-spatial order, that is otherwise, one in which, as Baldwin says later in *Nothing Personal*, "human beings are more important than real estate."⁶³ In diagnosing race as the constitutive material of the urban crisis and its abyss, the film not only implies Black New Yorkers' right to the center as a space of encounter but their right to *Harlem* as such a center, a center that regroups differences around their spatial practices. Duke's cool world, seen at this angle, is a reaching out for a city that present practices cannot allow to be imagined.

Coda

Repair

IRESEARCHED AND WROTE PARTS of this book at the New York Public
Library for the Performing Arts. The library holds prints of several of
the New York city symphonies, as well as clippings, interviews, lobby
cards, and other materials related to their exhibition and reception. The
library, tucked between the Metropolitan Opera House and the Vivian
Beaumont Theater, is part of the Lincoln Center for the Performing
Arts complex on Columbus Avenue between Sixty-Second and Sixty-Fifth
Streets. Where the building that holds copies of *The City*, lobby cards
from *Little Fugitive*, and materials from Francis Thompson's production
company now stands, the brownstones and tenements of San Juan Hill
once stood. Lincoln Center was one of the largest urban renewal projects
undertaken in late modern New York, and one of Robert Moses's more
controversial schemes. Years over schedule and massively over budget,
building Lincoln Center required bulldozing San Juan Hill, a working-class Black and Latino neighborhood. Although groundbreaking for
the project began in 1959, the complex was not opened until 1964, and
not completed until 1969. For much of that decade, all that remained of
San Juan Hill and all that had been built of Lincoln Center was a series
of huge holes in an endless construction site, as captured in the opening
sequence of *West Side Story*.[1]

At the time of its construction, Lincoln Center was vociferously
protested by San Juan Hill residents and their allies, especially because
the new construction was not residential; there was no systematic effort
made to rehouse the dispossessed in their old neighborhood. Jane Jacobs,
for her part, decried the project as a catastrophic example of "super-
block" construction that cut off neighboring streets from one another,

destroyed local social fabric, and concentrated elite cultural institutions in a single area instead of spreading them throughout the city.[2] Today, Lincoln Center hosts more than 5 million visitors a year. It is a key component of New York's iconography, a neighborhood landmark, and a beloved institution. The area in which it is situated, Lincoln Square (and, more broadly, the Upper West Side), is one of the most affluent in the city. The case of Lincoln Center and San Juan Hill poses the central premise of New York's late modern redevelopment in especially stark terms: you can have a world-class performing arts center or a place for working-class people of color to live, but you can't have both, and especially not in the same spot.

The New York city symphonies reject this premise. They ask what kinds of relations of production would have to obtain for the arts center and the neighborhood to exist together, instead of as alternatives. Through rhythmanalysis, symphonies of the margins like *In the Street* document an East Harlem caught up in the constant celebrations of its residents; symphonies of the center like *N.Y., N.Y.* conjure a Penn Station worthy of secular worship; and their progenitor, *Weegee's New York*, posits a Coney Island that hosts a democratic assemblage of desires. Tucked away on the third floor of the performing arts library or in the other institutions that house them, like MoMA and the International Center for Photography, the New York city symphonies ask us to imagine a city where Lincoln Center and San Juan Hill cohabit. In that city, what kind of rhythms would delimit people's sleeping and waking, eating and walking, working and playing? What would generate those rhythms, and what kinds of forces and flows of power would be caught up in their strands? This is the utopian work the New York city symphonies do, and this is the other place they help their viewers desire. But in our city, putting up Lincoln Center meant knocking down San Juan Hill, and the average patron of Lincoln Center today is over forty, white, and wealthy.[3] We might ask, then, what the New York city symphonies actually accomplished, and what they are capable of doing now, wrapped in protective cannisters and deposited in elite institutions.

One answer is that the films failed, and failed in ways that are innate to utopia. If we think of the history of film as utopian, as Pavsek argues, as a series of attempts to "take our perception elsewhere" and return us, better able to intervene into the here and now, then "the utopia of film" is a litany of defeat, a succession of failures to achieve what is possible in cinema.[4] As this book has argued, the New York city symphonies participated in this project and were subject to utopian shortcomings. The utopian images produced by the films included an absence or blind spot. They minimized the constitutive role race played in urban redevelopment and could not imagine a Black body with a right to the city, even in a film like *The Cool World*, which implied the need for a body with such a right. Moreover, the New York city symphonies are typical of utopia in that they are not a science or praxis of space; they are not revolutionary films. If they raised their audiences' consciousness as to the limitations of urban redevelopment, they did not occasion a transformation of policy or even of cinema.

The failures of the films as utopia is complicated and amplified by the utopian role late modern New York continues to play in popular cinema. In this case, however, "utopia," far from being a dialectic social critique, regresses to its common meaning of a longed for, impossible, idealized place. This utopian association usually takes the form of a nostalgia for modernity, particularly as mourning for functional social relations that are now lost. Less often, late modernity's utopian association serves as a celebration of activism and policies that developed during the era and are still capable of positive impact today. In any case, however, when popular culture longs for late modern New York, it is wishing for a city that can be imaged, therefore physically and mentally negotiated by its inhabitants, and thus controlled by them.

This impulse is found in films as historically, aesthetically, industrially, and politically different as Martin Scorsese's *Taxi Driver* (1976), Abel Ferrara's *King of New York* (1990), Wayne Wang and Paul Auster's *Blue in the Face* (1995), Matt Tyrnauer's *Citizen Jane* (2016), and Edward Norton's *Motherless Brooklyn* (2019). In *Taxi Driver*, Travis's (Robert De Niro) anxieties are driven by his inability to decode the city, particularly in the sense that he can't tell what kinds of behavior and people belong in which places. Those anxieties are shared by other characters, and many of the older cab drivers and political operatives recall a late modern New York in which that knowledge was automatic, livelihoods were more secure, and social bonds more robust. Travis's attempts to wash the streets clean are an attempt to return to the past.[5] In *King of New York*, the gangster protagonist, Frank (Christopher Walken), seeks to return the city to its late modern glory by funding the restoration of two of that era's civic landmarks, conflating polishing the city's skyline with resuscitating its social fabric. The film also contrasts the unprofessional, rapacious behavior of Frank's criminal competitors, who damage their own communities and the city's reputation, with the care mid-century gangsters lavished on their neighborhoods. In *Blue in the*

Face, a low-budget fiction-documentary hybrid, Brooklyn is still suffering from the psychic and social wound inflicted by the Dodgers' leaving the borough for Los Angeles in 1957. Through scripted scenes, improvised exchanges, and talking head interviews, actors, locals, and celebrities like Lou Reed recount how the Brooklyn Dodgers enabled residents to visualize themselves and their neighbors as belonging to a larger, cross-class, interracial community centered on Ebbets Field. These films all produce late modern New York as a lost Eden that their characters unsuccessfully attempt to recover by restoring the imageability the city one granted its residents. In doing so, they elide and obscure the role imageability played in New York's late modern redevelopment, the constraint it imposed on spatial practices, and the capitalist and racist ideologies it iterated.

This articulation of late modern New York as a nostalgic utopia resonates with the ways in which that epoch has been reduced to the clash of Robert Moses and Jane Jacobs in popular culture. *Citizen Jane* and *Motherless Brooklyn* are part of a larger tradition, including museum exhibits, popular histories, and magazine articles, that attempts to sum up the era as "the fall of New York" or the "transformation of the modern city."[6] One of the reasons Moses and Jacobs are such compelling figures is that their work and precepts can easily be located in some of the most iconic parts of the city. By emphasizing Moses projects like the United Nations and the Verrazano Bridge, or Jacobs's successful preservation of the West Village and Washington Square Park, contemporary New York takes on a visually coherent, compact, iconic image once more, and the association of that image with late modernity is reaffirmed. At the same time, films like *Citizen Jane* and *Motherless Brooklyn*, which utilize these strategies, encourage us to think about urban planning as something undertaken by a handful of charismatic figures, and largely out of the hands of the general public.

The documentary *Citizen Jane* conflates a number of different anti–urban renewal and anti–slum clearance campaigns under Jacobs's persona, downplaying the role of other activists, and particularly the resistance of communities of color to urban renewal throughout the late modern period. It argues that Jacobs succeeded by making New Yorkers aware of the extent to which Moses's decisions were made in secret or without sufficient public input. In *Citizen Jane*, a city that can be imaged by public hearings and guarded by eyes on the street is a democratic one. Similarly, the neo-noir *Motherless Brooklyn* attributes every infrastructural and racial problem suffered by late modern New York to Moses Randolph (Alec Baldwin), its not very fictionalized Robert Moses figure. Moses's perfidy is evidenced by his preference for private, invisible, or underground areas: he gains legislative power in a windowless room in City Hall, he swims in an underground pool closed to the public, and his office is located out of sight underneath the Triborough Bridge (which is historically accurate). Once dedicated sleuthing exposes him, his power to trouble the protagonists is curbed, even as his redevelopment of the city proceeds. Successful detective work is possible in the first place because all of the characters have detailed geographic and social maps of the city in their heads. They can deftly negotiate its streets, mass transit, apartments, and clubs, crossing cultural, class, and racial boundaries as they go. *Citizen Jane* and *Motherless Brooklyn* tie the possessive spectatorship that characterizes advocacy planning directly to progressive urban policies, but their images of the city still do not rise to the level of Jameson's cognitive mapping. In these films, imaging the city is not the first step toward locating oneself within and dispelling ideology, it is the only step needed to decode, and thereby possess, the city—or at least one's personal corner of it.

In this sense, even though many of the films described above critique or condemn urban planning, they are ultimately reinscribing one of its key tenets. As I have argued, the various forms of urban planning that transformed late modern New York all secured capital's claim to the city through their reduction of the city to an image. Roland Barthes captured the enduring appeal of that reduction, as well as its perils, in his 1978 description of the city's grid. The grid makes New York a landmark of landmarks, condensing the five boroughs and especially Manhattan into the kind of iconic lexicon crucial to the late modern production of space and vision.[7] Barthes argues that "the biggest city in the world . . . is also the one we possess in an afternoon, by the most exciting of operations, since here *to possess* is *to understand*: New York exposes itself to intellection, and our familiarity with it comes very quickly. . . . This is the purpose of New York's geometry: that each individual should be *poetically* the owner of the capital of the world."[8] Barthes's emphasis of the poetic nature of this ownership names what popular invocations of imageability as key to identity formation, communal belonging, and understanding of the environment obscure: that to own the city as an image forecloses the desire for the city to be anything else. The image of the city obscures capital's claim to New York and suborns the possibility that its inhabitants could assert a right to their habitat.

If the reduction of the city to an image to be possessed via consumption is the most enduring aspect of New York's redevelopment, then what, ultimately, can the utopian failure of the New York city symphonies offer us? What went right in them, if they could not even dissipate this image?[9] The New York city symphonies offer us an alternative history of the urban. They allow us to glimpse a world where Lincoln Center and San Juan Hill coexist, and they do so solely through images of a reality in which the former destroyed the latter. They change our expectations of postwar American avant-garde cinema by documenting the many different modes included in this movement, demonstrating its popularity with audiences, and orienting us to the political content of films often understood as formalist or institutional cinema. Moreover, they surface aspects of the everyday that usually elude us, and through those aspects they teach us to want another world, one in which the city is a work of art to which the masses have a right. The New York city symphonies achieve these successes within their failure by dismantling the image of the city and locating utopian critique in the depiction of the urban everyday. This success has crucial implications for how we study cinema, the city, and their relation to one another.

The strategies that the New York city symphonies used to break down the image of the city offer new ways of thinking about subsequent entries in the genre and the relationship of cinematic aesthetics to cities in general. Seeing symphonically, awakening to the presence of bodies both human and architectural as they take their time and their place, requires a continual renewal of sight, which is to say, of aesthetics. City symphonies are, after all, always reinventing their genre. As important, city symphonies are, as Laura Marcus argues, how the city and the cinema tell each other's stories.[10] That story is one of rhythmanalysis. If we understand the city symphony in this way, then as we track the transformations of the genre across the increasingly urbanized terrain of the twenty-first century, we will encounter new forms of cinema and new kinds of cities, bound together by the specific contradictions rhythmanalysis makes visible.

Rhythmanalysis exposes those contradictions through some of cinema's core qualities, namely, its ability to dramatize space, time, and perception without using conventional narrative, and to disclose the workings of the everyday through this dramatization.[11] In doing so, city symphonies simultaneously show how rhythmanalysis can act as a cinematic methodology and how formalist avant-garde films enunciate their politics. City symphonies reframe the relationship of film and utopia around a critical aesthetics, and show how a cinematic utopian text can be built solely out of the material of the everyday.

The utopian function of city symphonies ultimately reveals the dangers of reducing the city to an image as well as the potential of the city as a mediation. For Lefebvre, the right to the city is an intervention into mediation.

> The city is a *mediation* among mediations. Containing the *near order*, it supports it; it maintains relations of production and property; it is the place of their reproduction. Contained in the *far order*, it supports it; it incarnates it; it projects it over a terrain (the site) and on a plan, that of immediate life; it inscribes it, prescribes it, *writes* it. A text in a context so vast and ungraspable as such except by reflection. And thus the city is an *oeuvre*, closer to a work of art than to a simple material product.[12]

The city mediates the relationships between individuals and larger social forms like communities or nations. It is the place where capital—in terms of relations of production and the socio-spatial relations that generate them—happens and where it is manifested in the rhythms that make up daily life. The city is not a thing, or an image. It is a collaborative writing, a form of media, a work of art. And what is written can be rewritten. If the city is a mediation, then cinema is not a representation of the city, but rather mutually constitutive with it. Cinema does not depict space but rather produces it. Like a city, it is more than an image. It is a mediation in Lefebvre's sense.

The city symphony, as the matrix through which the city and the cinema tell one another's stories, is a privileged node in this mediation, a place where rewriting that story could be particularly effective. The New York city symphonies use rhythmanalysis to tell a story in which the urban is a collective work whose inhabitants determine its composition and development, promoting artful encounters with one another and with the built environment. The films change the text the city writes and the relations it reproduces; they overwrite the current production of space. This rewriting is not sufficient to remediate New York as a revolutionary site/sight, but it is an example of cinema's potential to contribute to the urban oeuvre. By forcing open the image of the city, the New York city symphonies allow us to glimpse and desire a place where our lives could be a work of art, and where cinema is part of the art of living in the city.

Notes

Introduction

1. Keith Beattie, *Documentary Display: Re-Viewing Nonfiction Film and Video* (New York: Wallflower Press, 2008), 33–35.

2. Henri Lefebvre, *Rhythmanalysis: Space, Time, and Everyday Life*, trans. Stuart Eldon and Gerald Moore (London: Bloomsbury, 2015, 1st ed., 1992), 16.

3. Eleonore Kofman and Elizabeth Lebas, "Lost in Transposition—Time, Space, and the City," in *Writings on Cities: Henri Lefebvre*, trans. Eleonore Kofman and Elizabeth Lebas (London: Blackwell, 1996), 31.

4. Lefebvre, *Rhythmanalysis*, 26.

5. Lefebvre, 19, 37.

6. Lefebvre, 26.

7. Lefebvre, 25.

8. Lefebvre, 41.

9. Lefebvre, 28, 35.

10. For especially useful, detailed definitions of and reflections on the term "city symphony," see Scott MacDonald, *The Garden in the Machine: A Field Guide to Independent Films about Place* (Berkeley: University of California Press, 2001); Steven Jacobs, Anthony Kinik, and Eva Hielscher, *The City Symphony Phenomenon: Cinema, Art, and Urban Modernity Between the Wars* (London: Routledge, 2018).

11. Ruth Levitas, *Utopia as Method: The Imaginary Reconstitution of Society* (London: Palgrave, 2013), 4, 17.

12. Christopher Pavsek, *The Utopia of Film: Cinema and Its Futures in Godard, Kluge, and Tahimik* (New York: Columbia University Press, 2013), 22; Lefebvre, *Rhythmanalysis*, 32–34.

13. Louis Marin, *Utopics: The Semiological Play of Textual Spaces*, trans. Robert Vollrath (New York: Humanity Books, 1st English ed., 1984); Fredric Jameson, *Archaeologies of the Future: The Desire Called Utopia and Other Science Fictions* (London: Verso, 2007); Levitas, *Utopia as Method*.

14. Michel de Certeau, *The Practice of Everyday Life* (Berkeley: University of California Press, 1988), 91.

15. Jennifer Senior, "The Independent Republic of New York," *New York Magazine*, August 9, 2004, http://nymag.com/nymetro/news/rnc/9573/; Brian Rosenthal et al., "How Politics and Bad Decisions Starved New York's Subway," *New York Times*, November 18, 2017; Jonathan Mahler, "The Case for the Subway," *New York Times Magazine*, January 3, 2018.

16. Four of New York City's five boroughs are islands. Manhattan and Staten Island are their own landmasses, while Brooklyn and Queens form the western tip of Long Island. The Bronx is the only borough on the mainland. In addition to the city's physical geography, urban planning and visual culture have intensified a sense of separation that has effectively islanded all five boroughs, even (or especially) the Bronx, from New York state and the United States. The role the city's early-nineteenth-century planning and late-nineteenth-century incorporation played in this islanding is explored in the context of its street grid in Hillary Ballon, ed., *The Greatest Grid: The Master Plan of Manhattan, 1811–2011* (New York: Columbia University Press, 2012). The New York city symphonies I consider were shot and/or exhibited in Manhattan, Brooklyn, and Queens.

17. Jameson, *Archaeologies of the Future*, 5, 29–30.

18. Louis Marin, "Frontiers of Utopia: Past and Present," *Critical Inquiry* 19, no. 3 (Spring 1993): 403–405, 404n19, 405n20, 411, 415.

19. Jameson, *Archaeologies of the Future*, 13.

20. Jacob Javits, "New York, Thy Name's Delirium," *New York Times Magazine*, December 24, 1961, Papers of the 1964–65 New York World's Fair Corporation, Box 589, New York Public Library.

21. Samuel Zipp, *Manhattan Projects: The Rise and Fall of Urban Renewal in New York* (London: Oxford University Press, 2010), 5, 7, 22–25, 28–29.

22. Zipp, 301, 363.

23. Kenneth Jackson, *The Crabgrass Frontier: The Suburbanization of the United States* (Oxford: Oxford University Press, 1985). See also Tom Hanchett, "The Other Subsidized Housing: Federal Aid to Suburbanization, 1940s–1960s," in *From Tenements to Taylor Homes: In Search of Urban Housing Policy in Twentieth Century America*, ed. John Bauman et al. (College Park, PA: Penn State Press, 2000), 163–79.

24. Sonja Dümpelmann, *Flights of Imagination: Aviation, Landscape, Design* (Richmond: University of Virginia Press, 2014); Kevin Lynch, *The Image of the City* (Cambridge, MA: MIT Press, 1960).

25. Lauren Rabinovitz, *Points of Resistance: Women, Power, and Politics in the New York Avant-Garde (1943–71)* (Urbana: University of Illinois Press, 2003), 24.

26. Gilles Deleuze, *Cinema 2: The Time Image*, trans. Hugh Tomlinson and Robert Galeta (Minneapolis: University of Minnesota Press, 1989), 270–81; Gilles Deleuze, "Having an Idea in Cinema," in *Deleuze and Guattari: New Mappings in Politics, Philosophy and Culture*, eds. Eleanor Kaufman and Kevin Jon Heller (Minneapolis: University of Minnesota Press, 1998), 14–22.

27. Pavsek, *Utopia of Film*, 8, 16.

28. Pavsek, 2.

29. David Harvey, *Rebel Cities: From the Right to the City to Urban Revolution* (London: Verso, 2013); Henri Lefebvre, *The Right to the City* in *Writings on Cities*, trans. Eleonore Kofman and Elizabeth Lebas (London: Blackwell, 1996).

30. Lefebvre, *Right to the City*, 19–26, 33–35, 97.

31. Jacobs, Kinik, Hielscher, and their contributors' valuable research expands this canon, identifying city symphonies on four continents, 6–8.

32. MacDonald, *Garden in the Machine*, 152.

33. William Ulricchio, *Ruttmann's* Berlin *and the City Film to 1930* (Unpublished Dissertation, New York: New York University, 1982); Jacobs, Kinik, and Hielscher, *City Symphony Phenomenon*, 4.

34. Jacobs, Kinik, and Hielscher provide a crucial distillation and elaboration of the form's aesthetic and thematic properties, 16–26.

35. Lucy Fischer, "The Shock of the New: Electrification, Illuminated, Urbanization, and the Cinema," in *Cinema and Modernity*, ed. Murray Pomerance (New Brunswick, NJ: Rutgers University Press, 2006), 19–20.

36. Laura Marcus, "A Hymn to Movement: The City Symphony of the 1920s and 1930s," *Modernist Cultures* 5, no. 1 (2010): 32.

37. Marcus, 43–44.

38. Helmut Weishmann, "The City in Twilight: Charting the Genre of the City-Film 1900–1930," in *Cinema and Architecture: Méliès, Mallet-Stevens, Multimedia*, eds. François Penz and Maureen Thomas (London: BFI, 1997), 23.

39. Erica Stein, "Abstract Space, Microcosmic Narrative, and the Disavowal of Modernity in *Berlin: Symphony of a Great City*," *Journal of Film and Video* 65, no. 4 (Winter 2013): 12.

40. Jacobs, Kinik, and Hielscher, *City Symphony Phenomenon*, 4.

41. Malin Whalberg, *Documentary Time: Film and Phenomenology* (Minneapolis: University of Minnesota Press, 2008), 83.

42. My brief gloss here is indebted to Harvey, ix–xv, 4–8 and to Reinhold Martin's "Fundamental #13," *Places Journal* (May 2014). DOI: https://doi.org/10.22269/140512.

43. Edward Dimendberg, *Film Noir and the Spaces of Modernity* (Cambridge, MA: Harvard University Press, 2004), 3.

44. Jacobs, Kinik, and Hielscher, *City Symphony Phenomenon*, 5–7.

45. William Ulricchio, "The City Viewed: The Films of Leyda, Browning, and Weinberg in *Lovers of Cinema: The First American Avant-Garde, 1919–45*, ed. Jan-Christopher Horak (Madison: University of Wisconsin Press, 1995), 287–314.

46. Beattie, *Documentary Display*, 32.

47. Marcus, "Hymn to Movement," 30.

48. Scott Bukatman, "A Day in New York: *On the Town* and *The Clock*," in *The City That Never Sleeps*, ed. Murray Pomerance (New Brunswick, NJ: Rutgers University Press, 2007), 33–47; Scott Bukatman, *Blade Runner* (London: BFI, 2008); Tom Gunning, "Invisible Cities, Visible Cinema: Illuminating Shadows in Late Film Noir," *Comparative Critical Studies* 6, no. 3 (November 2009): 319–32.

49. Chris Barsanti, "Film Review: *Paterson*," *Film Journal International* (January 4, 2017), http://www.filmjournal.com/reviews/film-review-paterson; Richard Brody, "Kenneth Lonergan Discusses *Margaret*," *New Yorker*, https://www.newyorker.com/culture/richard-brody/kenneth-lonergan-discusses-margaret.

50. MacDonald, *The Garden in the Machine*, 151.

51. Jon Gartenberg, "NY, NY: A Century of City Symphony Films," *Framework: The Journal of Cinema and Media* 55, no. 2 (Fall 2014): 248–76.

52. Stavros Alifragkis and François Penz, "Spatial Dialectics: Montage and Spatially Organized Narratives in Films without Human Leads," *Digital Creativity* 17, no. 4 (2006): 221.

53. François Penz and Andong Lu, "What is Urban Cinematics?," in *Urban Cinematics: Understanding Urban Phenomena through the Moving Image*, eds. François Penz and Andong Lu (Bristol: Intellect, 2011), 11.

54. Bosley Crowther, "Down and Outers: *On the Bowery* Looks Candidly at Drunks," *New York Times*, March 31, 1956.

55. Jacobs, Kinik, and Hielscher, *City Symphony Phenomenon*, 7–10, 34.

56. Scott MacDonald, *Cinema 16: Documents Toward a History of the Film Society* (Philadelphia: Temple University Press, 2002), 213; Howard Thompson, "'N.Y.' Top 16mm Entry," *New York Times*, March 30, 1958.

57. Thalia Selz, "Lions on the Lido," *The Quarterly Review of Film and Television* 8, no. 3 (1954): 247; *Little Fugitive* Lobby Cards, Performing Arts Research Collections—Theatre, T-LC, New York Library for the Performing Arts.

58. Jacobs, Kinik, and Hielscher address and complicate this in their study of *Rien que les heures* as the precursor to their discussion of major canon criteria, *City Symphony Phenomenon*, 10–14.

59. Gartenberg, 248, 260.

60. Nathan Holmes, *Welcome to Fear City: Crime Film, Crisis, and the Urban Imagination* (Albany: SUNY Press, 2018), 32.

61. See especially Beattie.

62. Jacobs, Kinik, and Hielscher, 35–36; MacDonald, *Garden in the Machine*, 163–66; Beattie, *Documentary Display*, 45–47.

63. Alexander Graf, "Paris-Berlin-Moscow: On the Montage Aesthetic in the City Symphony Films of the 1920s," in *Avant-Garde Film*, eds. Alexander Graf and Dietrich Scheunemann (Amsterdam and New York: Rodopi, 2007), 77–91.

64. John Grierson, *Grierson on Documentary* (New York: Harcourt, Brace, 1947), 106.

65. Siegfried Kracauer, *From Caligari to Hitler: A Psychological History of the German Film* (Princeton, NJ: Princeton University Press, 1974, 5th paperback printing), 182–88; Siegfried Kracauer, *Theory of Film: The Redemption of Physical Reality* (Princeton, NJ: Princeton University Press, 1997, first paperback edition), 64–65.

66. See especially MacDonald's treatment of *Water and Power* and Eugene Martin's *Invisible Cities* (1990) as major revisions of the city symphony in their critical stances toward the urban, *Garden in the Machine*, 208–21.

67. James Donald, *Imagining the Modern City* (Minneapolis: University of Minnesota Press, 1999), xi, 69.

68. Scott MacDonald, "City as Motion Picture," *Wide Angle* 19, no. 4 (Winter 1997): 111–13 and *Garden in the Machine*, 159–66; Carsten Strathausen, "Uncanny Spaces: The City in Ruttmann and Vertov," in *Screening the City*, eds. Mark Shiel and Tony Fitzmaurice (London: Verso, 2003), 19–22.

69. Gartenberg, 248–50, 64–67; Graf, 77–78, 85–87.

70. Marin, *Utopics*, xiii.

71. Marin, 18.

72. Marin, xxvi.

73. Levitas, *Utopia as Method*, xi–xii.

74. Here, and throughout the book, I am combining Marin's structural mapping of utopia with Levitas's historical and functional analysis of it. See Marin, *Utopics*, xxii and Levitas, *Utopia as Method*, 7, 31 for encapsulations of each author's respective models as they are quoted in this passage.

75. Zipp, *Manhattan Projects*, 268–80.

76. The facts of Moses's career are not in dispute, but his reputation has careened between the authoritarian master builder depicted by Robert Caro in his indelible biography *The Power Broker: Robert Moses and the Fall of New York* (New York: Knopf, 1974) and the unlikely proponent of modernization and mass transit that Hilary Ballon, Kenneth Jackson, and many of their contributors conjure in *Robert Moses and the Modern City: The Transformation of New York*, eds. Hillary Ballon and Kenneth Jackson (New York: Norton, 2007).

77. Hilary Ballon and Kenneth Jackson, "Introduction," 66.

78. Susan Stewart, *On Longing: Narratives of the Miniature, the Gigantic, the Souvenir, the Collection* (Durham, NC: Duke University Press, 1992).

79. Levitas, *Utopia as Method*, 6–9. Ruth Levitas, *The Concept of Utopia* (Oxford: Peter Lang Oxford, 2011), 172–78.

80. Anthony Fontenot, "Notes Toward a History of Non-Planning: On Design, the Market, and the State," *Places Journal* (January 2015), DOI: https://doi.org/10.22269/150112.

Chapter 1

1. E. B. White, "The World of Tomorrow," in *The Essays of E. B. White* (New York: Harper Perennial, 1999), 139–40.

2. White, 145.

3. White, 144.

4. Hanchett, 163–67.

5. Jeongsuk Joo, "The Roots and Development of Suburbanization in America in the 1950s," *International Area Review* 12, no. 1 (2009): 65–79.

6. Lefebvre, *Right to the City*, 76–82.

7. Adnan Morshed, "The Aesthetics of Ascension in Norman Bel Geddes's *Futurama*," *Journal of the Society of Architectural Historians* 63, no. 1 (March 2004): 75–78.

8. Robert Wojtowicz, *Lewis Mumford and American Modernism: Eutopian Theories for Architecture and Urban Planning* (Cambridge, UK: Cambridge University Press, 1998).

9. Kenneth Frampton, *Modern Architecture: A Critical History*, 4th ed. (London: Thames & Hudson, 2007), 42–46.

10. See especially Lewis Mumford, *The Story of Utopias* (New York: Broni & Liverlight, 1922) and Levitas's contextualization of Mumford's thought in historical and theoretical terms in *The Concept of Utopia*, 90–106.

11. Marco Duranti, "Utopia, Nostalgia, and World War at the 1939–40 New York World's Fair," *Journal of Contemporary History* 41, no. 4 (October 2006): 663.

12. Duranti, 667.

13. Lewis Mumford, "The Skyline in Flushing: Genuine Bootleg," *New Yorker*, July 29, 1939, 38.

14. Henry Dreyfuss, "Preliminary Appearance Specifications on Presentation of the Fundamental Design," New York World's Fair 1939–1940 Incorporated Records, MssCol 2233, Box 137, Folder 7, Manuscripts and Archives Division, New York Public Library.

15. Anonymous memo, "Narration of Democracity," April 29, 1937, New York World's Fair 1939–40 Records, Box 137, Folder 7.

16. Memo from Phillip McConnell to Robert Kohn, September 27, 1937, New York World's Fair 1939–40 Records, Box 138, Folder 1.

17. Anne Friedberg, *Window Shopping: Cinema and the Postmodern* (Berkeley: University of California Press), 15–41.

18. Dümpelmann, *Flights of Imagination*, 92.

19. Henri Lefebvre, *Everyday Life in the Modern World* (New Brunswick, NJ: Transaction Publishers, 1984), 58–66. See also Frampton, *Modern Architecture*, 27.

20. For Lefebvre's description and critique see *Right to the City*, 72–74, 95–100.

21. Paul Fotsch, "The Building of a Superhighway Future at the New York World's Fair," *Culture Critique* 48 (Spring 2001), 69.

22. Fotsch, 70.

23. Morshed, "Aesthetics of Ascension," 94.

24. Morshed, 74.

25. Morshed, 77.

26. Morshed, 91.

27. Mumford, "The Skyline in Flushing," 38–39.

28. Alexander Von Hoffman, "Housing and Planning: A Century of Social Reform and Social Power," *Journal of the American Planning Association* 75, no. 2 (2009): 234.

29. Theophilus Lewis, "Harlem Sketchbook: Negro Garden Cities," *New York Amsterdam News*, October 25, 1933, 6.

30. Von Hoffman, "Housing and Planning," 232, 236–38.

31. Mumford, "Skyline in Flushing," 38.

32. Rem Koolhaas, *Delirious New York: A Retrospective Manifesto for Manhattan* (New York: Monicelli Press, 1994), 275.

33. This discrepancy in reception was due in part to the disjunction between the utopian future promised at the Fair and the fall of Central and Eastern European countries to German forces at the start of World War Two. Duranti, "Utopia, Nostalgia," 670–73.

34. "Fair Presents Its Film About City Planning," *New York Herald Tribune*, June 15, 1939, New York World's Fair 1939–40 Records, Box 2107, Folder 3.

35. Anke Gleber, "Female Flânerie and the Symphony of the City," in *Women of the Metropolis*, ed. Katherina von Ankum (Berkeley: University of California Press, 1997), 68–88.

36. Clarence Stein, Memo to Robert Kohn, August 8, 1938, New York World's Fair 1939–40 Records, Box 145, Folder 7.

37. Mumford deals with this modified structure in several works, notably *The Golden Day* (New York: Broni & Liverlight, 1927), in which he articulates the high point of American civilization to the Transcendental tradition in mid-1800s New England and calls for its renewal; *Technics and Civilization* (New York: Broni & Liverlight, 1934), his multivolume work that concludes by advocating for a reorientation of electricity and Fordism to the common good; *The Culture of Cities* (New York: Broni & Liverlight, 1938), which unspools a story of general decline from the compact, living architecture of the Medieval walled town only to imagine its rebirth in the garden city; and his script for *The City* itself, which draws on these works as well as *The Story of Utopias*. For an unpacking of how the national day developed in Mumford's thought, particularly in relationship to his theory of the usable past, which sometimes complicated the American exceptionalist tendencies in his thought, see Wojtowicz, 99–110.

38. White, "World of Tomorrow," 206.

39. Mumford, "Skyline in Flushing," 38.

40. Archer Winsten, "*The City* Opens Saturday at the World's Fair," *New York Post*, May 23, 1939.

41. Howard Barnes, "The Moving Picture's Part in the World's Fair," *The New York Herald Tribune*, May 27, 1939, New York World's Fair 1939–40 Records, Box 2107, Folder 3.

42. William Alexander, *Film on the Left: American Documentary film from 1931 to 1942* (Princeton, NJ: Princeton University Press, 1981); Vojislava Fiopcevic, "Urban Planning and the Space of Democracy: New York of the

Great Depression in *42nd Street, Dead End,* and *The City,*" *Culture, Theory, and Critique* 51, no. 1 (March 2010): 65–91.

43. Lefebvre, *Rhythmanalysis,* 41, 19.

44. Marin, *Utopics,* xiii; Levitas, *Utopia as Method,* xi; Lefebvre, *Rhythmanalysis,* 26.

45. Mumford, *Stories of Utopia,* 194.

46. Lefebvre, "Right to the City," 97.

47. Grierson, *Grierson on Documentary,* 104.

48. Grierson, 104.

49. Grierson, 105.

50. Grierson, 106.

51. Lefebvre, *Right to the City,* 117.

52. De Certeau, *Practice of Everyday Life,* 107.

53. De Certeau, 108.

54. Bernard Tschumi extrapolates the consequences of this stratification through the figures of the pyramid and the labyrinth in *Architecture and Disjunction* (Cambridge, MA: MIT Press, 1996).

55. Tschumi, 27–32.

56. Frampton, *Modern Architecture,* 183.

57. Morshed, "Aesthetics of Ascension," 82–83.

58. Lefebvre, *Right to the City,* 149.

59. Morshed, "Aesthetics of Ascension," 82.

60. Lefebvre, *Rhythmanalysis,* 40.

61. Marin, *Utopics,* 275–76.

62. Marin, 28–43.

63. See Medhurst and Benson, Alexander, and Grierson.

64. I have not been able to ascertain if this particular shot is from Homestead or Pittsburgh, although the section as a whole is commonly called the "Pittsburgh section" by critics writing about the film.

65. Alexander, *Film on the Left,* 250.

66. The viewer is directly addressed in the film's final moments in the second person as well: "You take your choice. The gutter or the playground . . ." In this case, however, "you" is not only granted an agency distinctly lacking in the industrial scenes but also connotes an individual. By contrast, the use in the Pittsburgh section connotes a plural second-person, an atomized "you" not quite deserving the formality of "one" and incapable of integration into the democracy of "we."

67. Max Kozloff, *New York: Capital of Photography* (New Haven, CT: Yale University Press, 2003), 3–4, 14.

68. Kristin Perkins, "Roosevelt and Rexford: Resettlement and Its Results," *Berkeley Planning Journal* 20, no. 1 (2007): 28, 34–35.

69. Von Hoffman, "Housing and Planning," 236.

70. Lefebvre, *The Production of Space,* 99, 138–39.

71. Lefebvre articulates his theory to a meeting of, living with, and knowing relationship to space (*connaître*) rather than the kind of controlled, definitional, knowledge (*savoir*) of space exemplified by current sociological theories, which he wishes to dispel. *The Production of Space*, 10.

72. Hanchett, "Other Subsidized Housing," 64.

73. Stewart, *On Longing*, 1.

74. Guy Debord, *The Society of the Spectacle* (Detroit: Black & Red Press, 2000 edition), 68–71.

75. Deleuze, *Cinema 2*, 44.

76. Grierson, *Grierson on Documentary*, 76.

77. Jameson, *Archeologies of the Future*, 6, 29.

78. Rudy Burckhardt's films *The Pursuit of Happiness* (1940) and *Up and Down the Waterfront* (1946) display many traits of the New York city symphonies but were produced more in the tradition of photodocumentaries than those of cinematic avant-gardes. These films did, however, provide an important precedent for the city symphonies of the postwar avant-garde. *Garden in the Machine*, 154–57.

Chapter 2

1. "Of Local Origin," *New York Times*, March 11, 1948.

2. Dümpelmann, *Flights of Imagination*, 211.

3. Dümpelmann, 212.

4. Sarah Kozloff, "Humanizing the Voice of God: Narration in The Naked City," *Cinema Journal* 23, no. 4 (Summer 1984): 41–43.

5. Scott MacDonald, *Cinema 16: Documents Toward a History of the Film Society* (Philadelphia, PA: Temple University Press, 2002), 52.

6. Ling Zhang, "Rhythmic Movement, Metaphoric Sound, and Transcultural Transmediality: Liu Na'ou and *The Man Who Has a Camera* (1933)," in *Kaleidoscopic Histories: Early Film Culture in Hong Kong, Taiwan, and Republican China*, ed. Emilie Yueh-yu Yeh (Ann Arbor: University of Michigan Press, 2018), 277–301.

7. Zipp, *Manhattan Projects*, 36–37.

8. Zipp, 56–57, 76–77, 104.

9. Dümpelmann, *Flights of Imagination*, 211.

10. Percival and Paul Goodman, *Communitas: Means of Livelihood and Ways of Life* (Chicago, IL: University of Chicago Press, 1947).

11. Goodman and Goodman, 213.

12. Stewart, *On Longing*, x–xiii, 9–14.

13. Zipp, *Manhattan Projects*, 112.

14. Zipp, 82, 98.

15. Martha Biondi, "Robert Moses, Race, and the Limits of an Activist State," in *Robert Moses and the Modern City: The Transformation of New York*, eds. Hilary Ballon and Kenneth Jackson (New York: Norton, 2007), 117.

16. Zipp, *Manhattan Projects*, 76–77.

17. Zipp, 112.

18. Stewart, *On Longing*, 23–27.

19. Stewart, 48–54.

20. Stewart, 72–74.

21. Zipp, *Manhattan Projects*, 48.

22. Stewart, *On Longing*, 56–57.

23. White, "Here Is New York," 168. For an extended discussion of this metaphor and its implications, see Zipp, *Manhattan Projects*, 33–35.

24. White, "Here Is New York," 167–70.

25. White, 148.

26. Dümpelmann, *Flights of Imagination*, 92–95.

27. Dümpelmann, 58.

28. Dimendberg, *Film Noir*, 43.

29. Dimendberg, 45.

30. James Sanders, *Celluloid Skyline: New York and the Movies* (New York: Knopf, 2003), 330–32.

31. Jennifer Fay, *Inhospitable World: Cinema in the Time of the Anthropocene* (Oxford and New York: Oxford University Press, 2018), 97–126.

32. Jonathan Culler, *The Pursuit of Signs* (Ithaca, NY: Cornell University Press, 2002).

33. Walter Benjamin, "On Some Motifs in Baudelaire" in *Illuminations* (New York: Schocken Books, 2007), 155–200; Tom Gunning, "The X-Ray and the Kaleidoscope," *Wide Angle* 19, no. 4 (Winter 1998): 25–61.

34. Though there have been countless fictional female detectives, the detective's function remains phallocentric and supportive of patriarchal structures.

35. Holmes, *Welcome to Fear City*, 16.

36. Marin, *Utopics*, 9–10, 37–47; Levitas, *Utopia as Method*, xiv.

37. Sanders, *Celluloid Skyline*, 88.

38. Castro, "Cinematic Cartographies," 59–60; Dimendberg, *Film Noir*, 42–47.

39. Gunning, "Invisible Cities," 319–23; Dimendberg, *Film Noir*, 17, 121.

40. Dimendberg, *Film Noir*, 64–65.

41. Dimendberg, 70.

42. I am indebted to Edward Dimendberg's reading of this scene, *Film Noir*, 71–72.

43. Rick Altman, A *Theory of Narrative* (New York: Columbia University Press, 2008), 162–70.

44. Donald, *Imagining*, 63–95.

45. Gunning, "Invisible Cities," 320.

46. Marin, *Utopics*, 38–39.

47. Marin, 57, 113.

48. Kozloff, *Capital of Photography*, 33.

49. Kozloff, 35.

50. Eric Lackey, "The Films of Lionel Rogosin, volume 1," *Moving Image* 15, no. 1 (Spring 2018): 129; Rabinovitz, *Points of Resistance*, 9, 98, 132–36. The development of Cinema 16's successors was in part driven by some members' dissatisfaction with Cinema 16's structure and priorities, and particularly founder Amos Vogel's somewhat dictatorial management of programming. Jonas Mekas and Stan Brakhage in particular understood their later endeavors as rebellions against Vogel. See MacDonald's *Cinema 16* for details.

51. MacDonald, *Cinema 16*, 10. Cinema 16 was one of the primary exhibitors of both New York city symphonies and their European predecessors in the United States during the mid-century.

52. Barbara Willinsky, *Sure Seaters: The Emergence of Art House Cinema* (Minneapolis: University of Minnesota Press, 2001), 60–61; Rabinovitz, *Points of Resistance*, 160–61.

53. MacDonald, *Cinema 16*, 263.

54. MacDonald, 103.

55. Fischer, "Shock," 27, 35–36.

56. Dimendberg, *Film Noir*, 49.

57. See especially Miles Orvell, "Weegee's Voyeurism and the Mastery of Urban Disorder," *American Art* 6, no. 1 (Winter, 1992): 18–41.

58. Jacob Deschin, "Distortion in Color," *New York Times*, March 14, 1948.

59. MacDonald places great importance on the film's soundtrack, arguing that its place in the avant-garde canon depends in part on its pioneering inclusion of popular music. I agree with MacDonald that, at points, the soundtrack helps enunciate a commentary on or analysis of the image, but I generally find it less important to either the film's meaning or its social critique. As well, the soundtrack was Vogel's creation and not attached to the film for the first four years of its exhibition. Therefore, I do not discuss it. For a full analysis of the soundtrack, see MacDonald, *Garden in the Machine*, 160–63.

60. Altman, *Theory of Narrative*, 171–75.

61. Lefebvre, *Everyday Life* (vol. 2), 53–58.

62. Betsy Blackmar, "Uptown Real Estate and the Creation of Times Square," in *Inventing Times Square: Commerce and Culture at the Crossroads of the World*, ed. William Taylor (Baltimore, MD: Johns Hopkins University Press, 1996), 51–65.

63. Caro, *Power Broker*, 690–98.

64. Fischer, "Shock," 31–33.

65. Turtles were a fad pet in late modern New York, seen as cheap, hardier alternatives to fish. The turtle and the city, of course, also suggests Benjamin and Baudelaire's famous example of a typical flaneurist practice. Cindy Perman, *New York Curiosities: Quirky Characters, Roadside Oddities, and Other Offbeat Stuff* (New York: Globe Pequot Press, 2013); Benjamin, *Illuminations*, 178.

66. Kozloff, *Capital of Photography*, 35.

67. Zipp, *Manhattan Projects*, 40–41.

68. For further discussion of Coney Island's function in modernity and late modernity, see Koolhaas, *Delirious New York*, 29–81; Michael Immerso, *Coney Island: The People's Playground* (New Brunswick, NJ: Rutgers University Press, 2002).

69. Bukatman, "A Day in New York," 38–39.

70. Fischer, "Shock," 31.

71. Charles Musser and Joshua Glick, "Cinema by the Seashore," in *Coney Island: Visions of an American Dreamland*, eds. Susan Talbott and Robin Frank (Hartford, CT: Wadsworth Museum of Art and Yale University, 2015), 203–60.

72. Biondi, "Robert Moses," 116, 118.

73. Dimendberg, *Film Noir*, 56–62.

74. MacDonald, *Garden*, 162.

75. Max Kozloff, *Capital of Photography*, 32–34.

76. Judy Lopatin, "Retrospective on Weegee," *Mississippi Review* 8, no. 1 (Winter 1979), 63–78; Christopher Bonanos, *Flash: The Making of Weegee the Famous* (New York: Holt, 2018).

77. MacDonald, *Garden*, 162.

78. Bonanos, *Flash*, 182–83.

79. Lefebvre, *Production of Space*, 353.

80. Iris Marion Young, "City Life and Difference," in *Metropolis: Center and Symbol of Our Times*, ed. Philip Kasinitz (New York: New York University Press, 1995), 250–79.

Chapter 3

1. Kozloff, *Capital of Photography*, 40–41, 75.

2. James Agee and Helen Levitt, *A Way of Seeing* (Durham, NC: Duke University Press, third edition 1989), x, xiii.

3. Kozloff, *Capital of Photography*, 28.

4. MacDonald, *Garden*, 412n35.

5. Jacobs, Kinik, Hielscher, *City Symphony Phenomenon*, 223–24, 279–80.

6. Selz, "Lions," 247.

7. Zipp, *Manhattan Projects*, 62, 249–55.

8. Dümpelmann, *Flights*, 213.

9. Zipp, *Manhattan Projects*, 266.

10. Zipp, 88.

11. Zipp, 207–14.

12. Scott Greer, *Urban Renewal and American Cities: The Dilemma of Democratic Intervention* (Indianapolis, IN: Bobbs-Merrill, 1965), 31.

13. Herbert Gans, "The Failure of Urban Renewal: A Critique and Some Proposals," *Commentary* (April 1965), 31–34.

14. Zipp, *Manhattan Projects*, 255–58.

15. Samuel Zipp and Michael Carriere, "Thinking through Urban Renewal," *Journal of Urban History* 39, no. 3 (2012): 359–65.

16. Dümpelmann, *Flights*, 214–15.

17. Zipp, *Manhattan Projects*, 254, 284, 324.

18. Zipp, 21.

19. "Coney," *New York Times*, April 11, 1953; Emanuel Perlmutter, "Steeplechase Park Welcomes Heat and Added Throngs," *New York Times*, July 29, 1963; "Only Elbow Room on Coney Island Boardwalk Yesterday," *New York Times*, March 19, 1945.

20. George Streater, "Growing Burdens Harlem Hospital," *New York Times*, March 9, 1949.

21. Elmer Bendiner, "Immovable Obstacle in the Way of a New Bowery," *New York Times*, January 21, 1962; Homer Bigart, "Grim Problems of Bowery and Its Derelicts Complicate City's New Clean-Up," *New York Times*, November 20, 1961; "The Bowery's Challenge," *New York Times*, May 1, 1953.

22. Wendell Pritchett, "The Public Menace of Blight: Urban Renewal and the Private Uses of Eminent Domain," *Yale Law & Policy Review* 21, no. 1 (Winter 2003): 1–52.

23. Elvin Wyley et al., "Displacing New York," *Environment and Planning A*, 42 (2010): 2602–23. The University of Richmond's Mapping Inequality project is also useful for tracing displacement trends during this period, although the majority of their holdings concentrate on the 1930s to the mid-1940s, https://dsl.richmond.edu/panorama/redlining/#loc=5/36.704/-96.965&opacity=0.8.

24. Zipp, *Manhattan Projects*, 287.

25. Zipp, 370.

26. Zipp, 269–75.

27. Lefebvre, *Rhythmanalysis*, 48.

28. Lefebvre, 49.

29. Lefebvre, *Right to the City*, 88.

30. Zipp, *Manhattan Projects*, 306–7.

31. Zipp, 259–64.

32. Paula Massood, *Making a Promised Land: Harlem in Twentieth-Century Photography and Film* (New Brunswick, NJ: Rutgers University Press, 2013), 95–97.

33. Kozloff, *Capital of Photography*, 28–29.

34. Massood, *Promised Lands*, 94–95.

35. Jan-Christopher Horak describe the film as a shot in 1945–1996 and released in 1953 after a brief preview at MoMA in 1947 or 1948. Jonas Mekas describes the film as shot in 1948 and edited in 1951 in "Notes on a New American Cinema," *Film Culture* 24 (Spring 1962): 7–8. Screenings at Cinema 16 date from September 1952.

36. This view of Levitt's photography also extends to discussion of her film work. See Roy Arden, "Useless Reportage: Notes on *In the Street*," *Afterall* 6 (2002): 100–5 and Elizabeth Gand, "Helen Levitt and the Camera," *American*

Art 23, no. 3 (Fall 2009): 98–102. Alison Dean complicates this figuration and understanding of Levitt in "The Invisible Helen Levitt," *Performance Matters* 2, no. 2 (2016): 23–42.

37. Jan-Christopher Horak, "Seeing with One's Own Eyes," *Yale Journal of Criticism* 8, no. 2 (1995): 69.

38. Jan-Christopher Horak, 74–77.

39. Gunning, "Invisible Cities," 330–31.

40. Zipp, *Manhattan Projects*, 268.

41. Zipp, 310–21.

42. Marin, *Utopics*, xxv.

43. Marin, xxiii.

44. Horak, "Seeing With," 76.

45. Dümpelmann, *Flights*, 95–98, 215–18.

46. Kracauer, *Theory of Film*, 203.

47. Tony Williams, "A Fantasy Straight Out of Brooklyn: From The Gentle People to Out of the Fog," in *The Brooklyn Film*, eds. John Manbeck and Robert Singer (London: MacFarland, 2003), 33–50.

48. Sanders, *Celluloid Skyline*, 162–65.

49. Daniel Waqar, "The End of the Road: The State of Urban Elevated Expressways in the United States," *Brookings Mountain West Publications* (2016): 5–7.

50. MacDonald, *Garden*, 157.

51. Burckhardt was twice married but also had a long-term romantic and artistic partnership with the poet and dance critic Edwin Denby. Anita Haldemann and Hannes Schüpbach, *Rudy Burckhardt: New York Moments* (Basel, Switzerland: Kunstmuseum, 2005), 5–8, 78–83; MacDonald, *Garden*, 158.

52. Juan Antonio Suárez Sánchez connects this trend to independent film culture and avant-garde cinema's production of a queer male subject in the mid-century. *Bike Boys, Drag Queens, and Superstars: Avant-Garde, Mass Culture, and Gay Identities in the 1960s Underground Cinema* (Bloomington: Indiana University Press, 1996).

53. White, "Here Is New York," 150–58.

54. Elmer Bendiner, *The Bowery Men* (New York: Thomas Nelson & Sons, 1961), 90.

55. Bendiner, ix.

56. Bosley Crowther, "Down and Outers: *On the Bowery* Looks Candidly at Drunks," *New York Times*, March 31, 1956; R. M. Blumenberg, "Documentary Films and the Problem of Truth," *Journal of the University Film Association* 4, no. 1 (1977): 19–32; Ntongela Masilela, "Lionel Rogosin: Making Reality Exciting and Beautiful," *Jump Cut* 36 (May 1991): 61–65; Peter Davis, "Remembering Rogosin," *Black Camera* 17, no. 1 (Spring/Summer 2002): 10–15.

57. Iris Marion Young, *Inclusion and Democracy* (London: Oxford University Press, 2002), 53–59.

58. Young, 55.

59. Kracauer, *Theory of Film*, 260.

60. Michael Carriere, "Fighting the War Against Blight: Columbia University, Morningside Heights, Inc, and Counterinsurgent Urban Renewal," *Journal of Planning History* 10, no. 1 (2011): 12.

61. Carriere, 12–13.

62. Horak, "Seeing With," 74–75.

63. Mekas, "Notes," 55.

64. Selz, "Lions," 245–46.

65. Joseph Jon Lanthier, "Little Fugitive," *Slant Magazine*, January 27, 2013, https://www.slantmagazine.com/film/review/little-fugitive; Michael Sragow, "Little Fugitive," *New Yorker*, September 4, 2013, 21; Mark Feeney, "How the French New Wave Got Its Start at Coney Island, *Boston Globe*, March 4, 2013, https://www.boston.com/uncategorized/noprimarytagmatch/2013/03/04/how-the-french-new-wave-got-its-start-at-coney-island.

66. Sharon Zukin et al., "From Coney Island to Las Vegas in the Urban Imaginary," *Urban Affairs Review* 30, no. 5 (1998): 639.

67. Zukin et al., 632.

68. Zukin et al., 637.

69. Raymond Weinstein, "Succession and Renewal in Urban Neighborhoods: The Case of Coney Island," *Sociation Today* 5, no. 2 (2007): 6.

70. Juan Rivero, "Saving Coney Island: The Constructive of Heritage Value," *Environment and Planning A* 49, no. 1 (2017): 179.

71. Rivero, 179.

72. Rivero, 183–87.

73. Wojcik, *Apartment Plot*, 19–24, 43.

74. Neil Smith, *The New Urban Frontier: Gentrification and the Revanchist City* (London and New York: Routledge, 1996).

75. One of Rivero's interview subjects explicitly invokes the photograph that inspired the opening shot of "Coney Island" in *Weegee's New York* as embodying the area's democratic potential and ability to "dissolve" tensions that otherwise exist between different ethnic and racial groups. "Saving Coney Island," 185.

76. Millington, *Race, Culture*, 183.

77. MacDonald, *Cinema 16*, 213.

78. MacDonald, 198.

79. MacDonald, 86.

80. After the last of the theaters showing race films shut down in the late 1930s, or converted to showing Hollywood films, the greater Harlem area lacked an independent theatrical space until filmmaker Jesse Maple opened one in the 1980s. Ina Archer, "Archival News," *Black Camera* 21, no. 1 (2009): 197–201.

81. Rabinovitz, *Points*, 1–13.

82. Helen Levitt is an important exception to this isolation, but her collaboration with the writer Richard Wright was never completed, and her later cinematic depictions of Harlem retreated into the cliché of social problems. Massood, *Promised Land*, 99–107.

83. Ben Davis, *Repertory Movie Theaters of New York City: Havens for Revivals, Indies, and the Avant-Garde, 1960–1994* (New York: McFarland, 2017).

84. MacDonald, *Cinema 16*, 124–32.

85. Mekas, "Notes," 14.

86. Dimendberg, *Film Noir*, 94.

87. MacDonald, *Cinema 16*, 81.

Chapter 4

1. Lefebvre, *Production of Space*, 112, 330–35; Lefebvre, *Right to the City*, 67–82.

2. Angela Joosse, "The Irrepressible Rush of Marie Menken's *Go! Go! Go!*" *CineAction* 93 (June 2013): 25.

3. Eric Plosky, *The Rise and Fall of Penn Station: Changing Attitudes toward Historic Preservation in New York City*, unpublished thesis, master's in city planning at MIT (Cambridge, MA, 2000), 21, 23, 43.

4. Plosky, 29.

5. Fontenot, "History of Non-Planning."

6. John Weiss, "Protecting Buildings from Demolition by Neglect: New York City's Experience" *Widener Law Review* 18, no. 2 (2012): 309–10. See also the New York City Landmarks Preservation Commission website, which positions the fate of Penn Station as central to its current mission, https://www1.nyc.gov/site/lpc/about/about-lpc.page (accessed December 5, 2019).

7. Lefebvre begins developing the idea of the center in *Right to the City* and expands on it in *Production of Space*. It's worth noting that, at times, particularly when Lefebvre is responding to the May 1968 uprisings and other mass actions, his idea of the center becomes more specific and linked to historical, established geographic centers, such as the Les Halles market in Paris. As this example demonstrates, Lefebvre's remade center does include sites of exchange, and interpersonal friction. What changes is the function of such spaces and the way they constitute differences as a result. *Right to the City*, 67, 88, 106–107; *Production of Space*, 112, 351, 356.

8. Parson, "Other Subsidized Housing," 75–80.

9. Zipp, *Manhattan Projects*, 208–9, 354–56, 367.

10. Ballon and Jackson, "Introduction," 66; Robert Fishman, "The Regional Plan and the Transformation of the Industrial Metropolis," in *The Landscape of Modernity: New York 1900–1940*, ed. Olivier Zunz and David Ward (Baltimore, MD: Johns Hopkins University Press, 1997), 123–27.

11. Lynch, *Image of the City*, 2–7, 104–12.

12. Frederic Jameson, "Cognitive Mapping," in *Marxism and the Interpretation of Culture*, ed. Cary Nelson and Lawrence Grossberg (Chicago: University of Illinois Press), 347–60.

13. Lynch, *Image of the City*, 60–61, 71–73, 112–17.

14. Jane Jacobs, *The Death and Life of Great American Cities* (New York: Random House, 1961), 1.

15. It is worth noting that Jacobs's later scholarly work and activism, undertaken after she moved to Toronto in 1968 to help her sons avoid the draft, does somewhat critique capital, for example in books like *Systems of Survival: A Dialogue on the Moral Foundations of Commerce and Politics* (New York: Random House, 1992).

16. Fontenot, "History of Non-Planning."

17. Eric Gordon, *The Urban Spectator: American Concept Cities from Kodak to Google* (Hanover, NH: Dartmouth University Press, 2010), 2, 16.

18. Lynch, *Image of the City*, 33–40, 104, 117.

19. Jacobs, *Death and Life*, 41, 73, 130–32.

20. Miriam Greenberg argues that the onset of the urban crisis marks the beginning of a modern branding campaign built around the city. This attempt to brand what Greenberg calls "a city in crisis" turned on reproducing New York as an iconic image for marketing purposes and, in so doing, privileging the needs of the market over those of the collective. *Branding New York: How a City in Crisis Was Sold to the World* (London: Routledge, 2008).

21. Debord, *Spectacle*, 105.

22. Debord's analysis in *Society of the Spectacle*, especially his emphasis on falsifying unification, is reminiscent of Lefebvre's work in both *Right to the City* and *Production of Space*. However, Debord also explicitly condemns utopian thinkers of the enlightenment period as part of his larger intervention into Marxist orthodoxy. This position can be understood as part of the break with and condemnation of Lefebvre for his embrace of an irruptive model of utopia and as typical of Marxist historiography's treatment of utopian projects prior to Marin's revaluation of utopia in relation to Marxism in *Utopics*. Without wishing to obscure these complexities, I position Debord's analysis of the spectacle as utopian because of his understanding of it as the limitation of the said/thought.

23. Debord, 197.

24. Lynch, *Image of the City*, 94.

25. Lynch, 31.

26. Themis Chronopoulos, "Morality, Social Disorder, and the Working Class in Times Square, 1892–1954," *Australasian Journal of American Studies* 30, no. 1 (July 2011): 1–19.

27. Benjamin Chesluk, *Money Jungle: Imagining the New Times Square* (New Brunswick, NJ: Rutgers University Press, 2007), 37.

28. Chesluk, 32–35; Chronopoulos, "Morality," 14–16.

29. Sanders, *Celluloid Skyline*, 315–17.

30. It also anticipates New American Cinema's interest in exploitation as generic intertext in the work of Jack Smith, Andy Warhol, and others.

31. Kozloff, *Capital of Photography*, 57.

32. Anaïs Nin, *The Diary of Anaïs Nin. Vol. 5, 1947–1955* (New York: Harcourt & Brace, 1974), 253.

33. William Robbins, "Assessments Stir Anger on 3rd Ave.," *New York Times*, July 13, 1966.

34. Richard Parke, "Old El Link Ends Its 72-Year Uproar," *New York Times*, December 23, 1950.

35. Murray Schumach, "Quill, Pickets, and Profit Motive Disturb Third Avenue El Wake," *New York Times*, March 28, 1952, 29; "Polyglot Wake to Be Held for El," *New York Times*, July 24, 1955.

36. Edward Streeter, "In Search of the Third Avenue El," *New York Times*, December 21, 1966.

37. Lynch, *Image of the City*, 74–77; Jacobs, *Death and Life*, 41.

38. Von Hoffman, "Housing and Planning," 238–39; Simon Anekwe, "Charge City Bias in Urban Renewal," *New York Amsterdam News*, July 14, 1962; "Rally So Urban Renewal Is Not Negro Removal," *New York Amsterdam News*, June 23, 1962.

39. MacDonald, *Cinema 16*, 14, 347.

40. Lynch, *Image of the City*, 74.

41. Lynch, 15, 43.

42. MacDonald, *Cinema 16*, 313, 347.

43. Gartenberg, "A Century," 261.

44. Tschumi, *Architecture and Disjuncture*, 100.

45. Thompson, "'N.Y.' Top 16mm Entry."

46. MacDonald, *Garden*, 164.

47. Bruno, *Surface*, 3.

48. Bruno, 13.

49. Martin Norden, "The Use of Sound in Francis Thompson's *N.Y., N.Y.*," *Millennium Film Journal* 10–11 (Winter 1981–Spring 1982): 219–22.

50. MacDonald, *Garden*, 163.

51. Lefebvre, *Production of Space*, 120.

52. Bruno, *Surface*, 98.

53. Rabinovitz, *Points of Resistance*, 100–101.

54. Undated Production Notes for Brussels Loops, Shirley Clarke Papers, Box 3, Folder 6, Wisconsin Center for Film and Theater Research, University of Wisconsin, Madison.

55. Shirley Clarke, letter to Bernard Rudofsky, July 1957, Clarke Papers, Box 3, Folder 6.

56. The Circle Line LTD, "Circumnavigating Manhattan Island with the Circle Line," 1955, 83 pages, Clarke Papers, Box 3, Folder 7.

57. Robert Moses, Letter to Willard Van Dyke, October 10, 1957, Clarke Papers, Box 3, Folder 6.

58. Letter from Willard Van Dyke, September 30, Clarke Papers, Box 3, Folder 6.

59. Letter from Robert Moses, October 10, 1957, Clarke Papers, Box 3, Folder 6; note from Thorald Dickinson (Head of UN Film Services) to Shirley Clarke, March 17, 1959, Clarke Papers, Box 3, Folder 6.

60. Lynch, *Image of the City*, 100.

61. Sarah Nilsen, *Projecting America, 1958: Film and Cultural Diplomacy at the Brussels World's Fair* (Jefferson, NC: MacFarland, 2011), 24.

62. Debord, *Spectacle*, 30.

63. Lefebvre, *Production of Space*, 10–11.

64. Clarke's production notes for *Melting Pot* on unlined scrap paper, Clarke Papers (n.p.), Box 3, Folder 6.

65. Rabinovitz, *Points of Resistance*, 8, 93.

66. Zipp, *Manhattan Projects*, 302–3.

67. Rabinovitz, *Points of Resistance*, 98; David Steritt, "Film Ode to Sax Player Ornette Coleman," *Christian Science Monitor*, March 14, 1986, page 27, Performing Arts Research Collections—Theatre, T-CLP, New York Public Library for the Performing Arts.

68. MacDonald, *Cinema 16*, 364.

69. Rabinovitz notes that this decision was driven by fear of a copyright claim against the film by MGM, *Forbidden Planet*'s distributor, if the Barron score was used, *Points of Resistance*, 102.

70. Rabinovitz.

71. Rabinovitz.

72. Circle Line, 15.

73. Van Dyke is credited as codirector of the film, but production documents show that his role was much more that of a producer, as he considered the project an important one for Filmmakers Inc., a production company he founded with Clarke, Pennebaker, and other Loops alums in 1958. Clarke's production notes also point to tension between her and Van Dyke on several aesthetic and structural issues; their entire correspondence has not survived but does suggest that these disputes resolved in Clarke's favor. See Rabinovitz, *Points of Resistance*, 109–10 and Clarke, undated note to Van Dyke: "I know the last few days were trying for you," Clarke Papers, Box 3, Folder 8.

74. Press Book for Skyscraper by Trident Releasing (n.p.), Clarke Papers, Box 3, Folder 8.

75. Rabinovitz, *Points of Resistance*, 109.

76. Robert Korstad and Nelson Lichtenstein, "Opportunities Found and Lost: Labor, Radicals, and the Early Civil Rights Movement," *Journal of American History* 75, no. 3 (December 1988): 786–811.

77. Lefebvre, *Production of Space*, 385, 392.

78. Marin, *Utopics*, 276–79.

79. Rabinovitz, *Points of Resistance*, 108.

80. Rabinovitz, 9–18. See also John Adams's *Film Quarterly* interview with Clarke, Lionel Rogosin, and Amos Vogel, "Expensive Art," 19–34.

81. Zipp, *Manhattan Projects*, 10–11, 348.
82. Zipp, 370.
83. Smith, *Urban Frontier*, 7–21. See also Sharon Zukin, *Naked City: The Death and Life of Authentic Urban Places* (Oxford and New York: Oxford University Press, 2009), 125–59.

Chapter 5

1. Lawrence Samuel discusses many of the Fair's exhibits and attractions as featuring cities of the future and "world of tomorrow" scenes or conclusions. *The End of the Innocence: The 1964–65 World's Fair* (Syracuse, NY: Syracuse University Press, 2007).
2. Samuel, xv.
3. Samuel, xvii.
4. Magdalena Sabat, "Panorama: Robert Moses' Modern City and the New York World's Fairs," in *Meet Me at the Fair: A World's Fair Reader*, eds. Lauren Hollengreen et al. (New York: ETC Press, 2014), 282.
5. Minutes of the World's Fair Corporation, March 6, 1964, 14, New York World's Fair 1964–65 Corporation Records, Box 555, MssCol 2234, Manuscripts and Archives Division, New York Public Library.
6. For the 1964–65 World's Fair's origins and its conflicts with other member states, see Samuel, *End of the Innocence*, xx, 5–17. For Moses's precarious status, see Samuel 11–13 and Zipp, *Manhattan Projects*, 354–60. For Moses's own attempt to frame his biography and the role of the Fair in his life's work, see the ABC News Bill Beutel report, "The Fair Face of Robert Moses," 1964–65 Papers, Film 00639–40.
7. "The Fair Face of Robert Moses."
8. "Diorama of the Fair," Box 661, Folder 1, 1964–65 World's Fair Papers; Publicity images of the Fair, Box 675, Folders 18–19. See also "Let's Cover the Waterfront," the Circle Line, 1964, 1, 26–28, 40–44.
9. Zipp, *Manhattan Projects*, 27.
10. Joo, "Roots and Development," 67; Parson, "Organized Labor and the Housing Question," 79.
11. Zipp, *Manhattan Projects*, 293.
12. Samuel, *End of the Innocence*, xvi–xvii, 34–37. The CORE protest was not the first held in the far reaches of Queens. Two years before the Fair opened, large protests over public housing in the Rockaways and in Jamaica pitted African American and Puerto Rican protestors and organizations like the Commission against Discrimination in Housing against real estate interests, members of the Board of Estimate, and the Queens Borough President. "Wagner Supporting Negroes Over Clancy's Stern Protests," *New York Amsterdam News*, September 1, 1962.

13. Warren Miller, *The Cool World* (New York: Little, Brown, 1959), 15; I am indebted to Pamela Wojcik's analysis of this scene in *Fantasies of Neglect: Imagining the Urban Child in American Film and Fiction* (New Brunswick, NJ: Rutgers University Press, 2016), 152.

14. Bayard Rustin, Letter to the Producers of The Cool World, December 1963, Clarke Papers, Box 4, Folder 5.

15. James Farmer, Letter to Shirley Clarke, November 21, 1963, Clarke Papers, Box 4, Folder 5.

16. Undated production notes, Box 4, Folder 6, Clarke Papers.

17. Mark Shiel, "A Nostalgia for Modernity: New York, Los Angeles, and the American Cinema of the 1970s," in *Screening the City*, eds. Mark Shiel and Tony Fitzmaurice (London: Verso, 2003).

18. Holmes, *Fear City*, 12, 25.

19. Blagovasta Momchedjikova, "My Heart's in the Small Lands: Touring the Miniature City in the Museum," *Tourist Studies* 2, no. 3 (2002): 267–69. The Panorama's uniform representation of public housing obscures major changes in footprint and building material that chart the downward slide of urban renewal. Initially, public housing was constructed on a cruciform pattern in red brick to facilitate airflow and insulation. In the 1950s, this was changed to slab construction and prefabricated siding. Zipp, *Manhattan Projects*, 288–91.

20. Sabat, "Panorama," 280; Zipp, 358.

21. "Johnson's Wax Groundbreaking, 1962," audiotape 11037; Archer Winsten, "Rages and Outrages," *New York Post*, April 13, 1964, 20; Radie Harris, "On the Town," *Newsday*, May 8, 1964, page 2C; "Fair Film Fascinates Thousands," *Long Island Press*, August 5, 1965, 21, all 1964–65 World's Fair Papers, Box 591.

22. Anthony Kinik, introductory remarks to the program "Films for the Fair: Expansive Exhibition, Multi-Screen Cinema at the World's Fair," Anthology Film Archives, New York, May 11, 2019.

23. Production information for the film is contradictory, which makes determining the source of the African footage and its precise location difficult. The geography, topography, and dress suggest East Africa, specifically Kenya, but it is worth noting that the film strips out more specific identifying information, especially compared to the iconic images of American and European locations elsewhere in the diegesis.

24. "Fair's Wax Pavilion: The Insulation Shines," *New York Journal-American*, April 24, 1964, 1964–65 World's Fair Papers, 20, Box 591.

25. Shiel, "A Nostalgia for Modernity," 163.

26. Shiel, 165.

27. Massood, *Promised Land*, 125.

28. Massood, 113–15.

29. Noël Carroll, "*Nothing but a Man* and *The Cool World*," in *The American New Wave, 1958–67*, eds. Melinda Ward and Bruce Jenkins (Buffalo, NY: Walker Art Center, 1982), 45.

30. Wojcik, *Fantasies of Neglect*, 153.

31. Wojcik, 159.

32. Massood, *Promised Land*, 94.

33. Adams, "Expensive Art," 23, 25–26.

34. Albert Johnson, "The Negro in American Films: Some Recent Works," *Film Quarterly* 18, no. 4 (Summer 1965): 30–31.

35. Massood, *Promised Land*, 119.

36. Deleuze, *Cinema 2*, 129–37.

37. Deleuze, 122.

38. Lefebvre, *Production of Space*, 138–39.

39. James Baldwin, "Fifth Avenue, Uptown," *Esquire*, July 1960, https://www.esquire.com/news-politics/a3638/fifth-avenue-uptown/.

40. James Baldwin, "War Lord of the Crocadiles [*sic*]," *New York Times*, June 21, 1959.

41. Massood, *Promised Land*, 8.

42. Deleuze, *Cinema 2*, 131.

43. Massood, *Promised Land*, 118–19.

44. Holmes, *Fear City*, 7–8.

45. Holmes, 13.

46. Here I differ from Massood's reading in *Promised Land*, which argues that at Coney Island the characters shed the more adult and criminal aspects of their roles and instead act as children, 121.

47. Rabinovitz, *Points of Resistance*, 127; Massood, *Promised Land*, 121; Carroll, "Cool World," 46.

48. Carroll, 44; Rabinovitz, 127.

49. Marin, "The Frontiers of Utopia," 399–402.

50. Rabinovitz, *Points of Resistance*, 132–35, 138–43.

51. Rabinovitz, 17, 25, 140–41.

52. Rabinovitz, 128–31; Massood, *Promised Land*, 123–24.

53. Shirley Clarke, "Whys and Wherefores of The Cool World," *Jeune Cinema*, 1964, 3, Clarke Papers, Box 5, Folder 1.

54. Bosley Crowther, "Review: The Cool World," *New York Times*, April 21, 1964.

55. "Review: The Cool World," *Newsday*, April 21, 1964, Clarke Papers, Box 5, Folder 5.

56. Lefebvre, *Rhythmanalysis*, 31, 37; *Production of Space*, 205–7.

57. Lefebvre does, at a few points, vary the pronouns used for his rhythmanalyst, but in the famous "Seen From the Window" chapter the pronoun remains male and the window remains Lefebvre's. *Rhythmanalysis*, 37–47.

58. This is actually how Albert Johnson, *The Cool World*'s only major first-run African American reviewer, interprets the title, as the constant need to "stay cool" despite the outrages and deprivations inflicted by the white world. "The Negro in American Films," 28.

59. Marin, *Utopics*, 275–76.

60. Marin, 274.

61. Wojcik, *Fantasies of Neglect*, 159.

62. James Baldwin and Richard Avedon, *Nothing Personal* (Cologne: Taschen, 2nd ed., 2002), 2.

63. Baldwin and Avedon, 14.

Coda

1. Zipp, *Manhattan Projects*, 197–253.

2. Jacobs, *Death and Life*, 115, 155.

3. The Broadway League, "Report on the Demographics of the Broadway Audience, 2017–2018," https://www.broadwayleague.com. Lincoln Center also keeps records of its patrons' demographics, but as it uses them to study new patrons and members brought in through new members/young members drives, they are somewhat less complete. They do reveal, however, the average age, race, and income ($222,120) of its members.

4. Pavsek, *Utopia of Film*, 1–2.

5. Haenni, "Geographies of Desire," 67–69, 73–75.

6. Caro, *Power Broker*, 1–12; Ballon and Jackson, *Robert Moses*, 65–67. See also Anthony Flint, *Wrestling with Moses: How Jane Jacobs Took on New York's Master Builder and Transformed the American City* (New York: Random House, 2009) and Robert Kanigel, *Eyes on the Street: The Life of Jane Jacobs* (New York: Knopf, 2016).

7. Lynch, *Image of the City*, 5, 8–9, 71.

8. Roland Barthes, "Buffet Finishes Off New York," in *A Barthes Reader*, ed. Susan Sontag (New York: Hill & Wang, 1982), 160.

9. Pavsek, *Utopia of Film*, 2, 16, 22.

10. Marcus, "Hymn to Rhythm," 45.

11. Adrian Piotrovski, "Toward a Theory of Cine-Genres," in *Russian Formalist Film Theory*, ed. Herbert Eagle (Ann Arbor: University of Michigan Press, 1981), 133–36.

12. Lefebvre, *Right to the City*, 101.

Bibliography

"9 Brussels Films Here: City Museum to Show US Fair Entries Tuesday." *New York Times*, May 24, 1958.

Adams, John. "The Expensive Art: A Discussion of Film Distribution and Exhibition in the US." *Film Quarterly* 13, no. 4 (Summer 1960): 19–34.

Agee, James, and Helen Levitt. *A Way of Seeing*. Durham, NC: Duke University Press, 3rd ed., 1989.

Alexander, William. *Film on the Left: American Documentary Film from 1931 to 1942*. Princeton, NJ: Princeton University Press, 1981.

Alifragkis, Stavros, and François Penz. "Spatial Dialectics: Montage and Spatially Organized Narratives in Films without Human Leads." *Digital Creativity* 17, no. 4 (2006): 221–33.

Altman, Rick. *A Theory of Narrative*. New York: Columbia University Press, 2008.

Amos Vogel Papers. MCHC81-068. Wisconsin Center for Film and Theater Research, University of Wisconsin, Madison.

Anekwe, Simon. "Charge City Bias in Urban Renewal." *New York Amsterdam News*, July 14, 1962.

Archer, Ina. "Archival News." *Black Camera* 1, no. 1 (2009): 197–201.

Arden, Roy. "Useless Reportage: Notes on *In the Street*." *Afterall* 6 (2002): 100–5.

Baldwin, James. "Fifth Avenue, Uptown." *Esquire*, July 1960.

———. "War Lord of the Crocadiles [*sic*]." *New York Times*, June 21, 1959.

Baldwin, James, and Richard Avedon. *Nothing Personal*. 2nd ed. Cologne, Germany: Taschen, 2002.

Ballon, Hilary. *The Greatest Grid: The Master Plan of Manhattan, 1811–2011*. New York: Columbia University Press, 2012.

Ballon, Hilary, and Kenneth Jackson. "Introduction." In *Robert Moses and the Modern City: The Transformation of New York*, edited by Hilary Ballon and Kenneth Jackson, 65–79. New York: Norton, 2007.

Barthes, Roland. "Buffet Finishes Off New York." In *A Barthes Reader*, edited by Susan Sontag, 158–62. New York: Hill & Wang, 1982.

Beattie, Keith. *Documentary Display: Re-Viewing Nonfiction Film and Video*. New York: Wallflower Press, 2008.

Bendiner, Elmer. "Immovable Obstacle in the Way of a New Bowery." *New York Times*, January 21, 1962.

———. *The Bowery Men*. New York: Thomas Nelson & Sons, 1961.

Benjamin, Walter. "On Some Motifs in Baudelaire." In *Illuminations: Essays and Reflections*, 155–200. Translated by Harry Zohn. New York: Schocken Books, 2007.

Berger, Meyer. "The Bowery Blinks in the Sunlight." *New York Times*, May 20, 1956.

Bigart, Homer. "Grim Problems of Bowery and Its Derelicts Complicate City's New Clean-Up." *New York Times*, November 20, 1961.

Biondi, Martha. "Robert Moses, Race, and the Limits of an Activist State." In *Robert Moses and the Modern City: The Transformation of New York*, edited by Hilary Ballon and Kenneth Jackson, 115–28. New York: Norton, 2007.

Blackmar, Betsy. "Uptown Real Estate and the Creation of Times Square." In *Inventing Times Square: Commerce and Culture at the Crossroads of the World*, edited by William Taylor, 51–65. Baltimore, MD: Johns Hopkins University Press, 1996.

Blumenberg, R. M. "Documentary Films and the Problem of Truth." *Journal of the University Film Association* 4, no. 1 (1977): 19–32.

Bonanos, Christopher. *Flash: The Making of Weegee the Famous*. New York: Holt, 2018.

Bruno, Giuliana. *Surface: Matters of Aesthetics, Materiality, and Media*. Chicago: University of Chicago Press, 2014.

Bukatman, Scott. "A Day in New York: *On the Town* and *The Clock*." In *The City That Never Sleeps*, edited by Murray Pomerance, 33–47. New Brunswick, NJ: Rutgers University Press, 2007.

———. *Blade Runner*. London: BFI, 2008.

Caro, Robert. *The Power Broker: Robert Moses and the Fall of New York*. New York: Knopf, 1974.

Carriere, Michael. "Fighting the War against Blight: Columbia University, Morningside Heights, Inc., and Counterinsurgent Urban Renewal." *Journal of Planning History* 10, no. 1 (2011): 5–29.

Carroll, Noël. "*Nothing but a Man* and *The Cool World*." In *The American New Wave, 1958–67*, edited by Melinda Ward and Bruce Jenkins, 40–47. Buffalo, NY: Walker Art Center, 1982.

Castro, Teresa. "Cinematic Cartographies of Urban Space and the Descriptive Spectacle of Aerial Views (1898–1948)." In *Cinematic Urban Geographies*, edited by François Penz and Richard Koeck, 47–63. New York: Palgrave Macmillan, 2017.

Chesluk, Benjamin. *Money Jungle: Imagining the New Times Square*, 23–47. New Brunswick, NJ: Rutgers University Press, 2007.

Chronopoulos, Themis. "Morality, Social Disorder, and the Working Class in Times Square, 1892–1954." *Australasian Journal of American Studies* 30, no. 1 (July 2011): 1–19.

"Coney." *New York Times*, April 11, 1953.

Crowther, Bosley. "Down and Outers: *On the Bowery* Looks Candidly at Drunks." *New York Times*, March 31, 1956.

———. "Review: *The Cool World.*" *New York Times*, April 21, 1964.

Culler, Jonathan. *The Pursuit of Signs*. Ithaca, NY: Cornell University Press, 2002.

Davis, Ben. *Repertory Movie Theaters of New York City: Havens for Revivals, Indies, and the Avant-Garde, 1960–1994*. New York: McFarland, 2017.

Davis, Peter. "Remembering Rogosin." *Black Camera* 17 no. 1 (Spring/Summer 2002): 10–15.

Dean, Allison. "The Invisible Helen Levitt." *Performance Matters* 2, no. 2 (2016): 23–42.

Debord, Guy. *The Society of the Spectacle*. Detroit: Black & Red Press, 2000.

De Certeau, Michel. *The Practice of Everyday Life*. Translated by Steven Rendall. Berkeley: University of California Press, 1988.

Deleuze, Gilles. *Cinema 2: The Time Image*. Translated by Hugh Thomlison and Robert Galeta. Minneapolis: University of Minnesota Press, 1989.

———. "Having an Idea in Cinema." In *Deleuze and Guattari: New Mappings in Politics, Philosophy and Culture*, edited by Eleanor Kaufman and Kevin Jon Heller, 14–22. Minneapolis: University of Minnesota Press, 1998.

Deschin, Jacob. "Distortion in Color." *New York Times*, March 14, 1948.

Dimendberg, Edward. *Film Noir and the Spaces of Modernity*. Cambridge, MA: Harvard University Press, 2004.

Donald, James. *Imagining the Modern City*. Minneapolis: University of Minnesota Press, 1999.

Dümpelmann, Sonja. *Flights of Imagination: Aviation, Landscape, Design*. Richmond: University of Virginia Press, 2014.

Duranti, Marco. "Utopia, Nostalgia, and World War at the 1939–40 New York World's Fair." *Journal of Contemporary History* 41, no. 4 (October 2006): 663–83.

Fay, Jennifer. *Inhospitable World: Cinema in the Time of the Anthropocene*. Oxford and New York: Oxford University Press, 2018.

Fiopcevic, Vojislava. "Urban Planning and the Space of Democracy: New York of the Great Depression in *42nd Street, Dead End*, and *The City.*" *Culture, Theory, and Critique* 51, no. 1 (March 2010): 65–91.

Fischer, Lucy. "The Shock of the New: Electrification, Illumination, Urbanization, and the Cinema." In *Cinema and Modernity*, edited by Murray Pomerance, 19–37. New Brunswick, NJ: Rutgers University Press, 2006.

Fishman, Robert. "The Regional Plan and the Transformation of the Industrial Metropolis." In *The Landscape of Modernity: New York 1900–1940*, edited by Olivier Zunz and David Ward, 106–25. Baltimore, MD: Johns Hopkins University Press, 1997.

Flint, Anthony. *Wrestling with Moses: How Jane Jacobs Took on New York's Master Builder and Transformed the American City*. New York: Random House, 2009.

Fontenot, Anthony. "Notes Toward a History of Non-Planning: On Design, the Market, and the State." *Places Journal* (January 2015). DOI: https://doi.org/10.22269/150112.

Fotsch, Paul. "The Building of a Superhighway Future at the New York World's Fair." *Cultural Critique* 28 (Spring 2001): 65–97.

Foucault, Michel. "Of Other Spaces." *Diacritics* 16, no. 1 (Spring 1986): 22–27.

Frampton, Kenneth. *Modern Architecture: A Critical History*, 4th ed. London: Thames & Hudson, 2007.

Friedberg, Anne. *Window Shopping: Cinema and the Postmodern*. Berkeley: University of California Press, 1994.

Gand, Elizabeth. "Helen Levitt and the Camera." *American Art* 23, no. 3 (Fall 2009): 98–102.

Gans, Herbert. "The Failure of Urban Renewal: A Critique and Some Proposals." *Commentary* (April 1965): 31–37.

Graf, Alexander. "Paris-Berlin-Moscow: On the Montage Aesthetic in the City Symphony Films of the 1920s." In *Avant-Garde Film*, edited by Alexander Graf and Dietrich Scheunemann, 77–91. Amsterdam and New York: Rodopi, 2007.

Gartenberg, Jon. "NY, NY: A Century of City Symphony Films." *Framework: The Journal of Cinema and Media* 55, no. 2 (Fall 2014): 248–76.

Gleber, Anke. "Female Flânerie and the Symphony of the City." In *Women of the Metropolis*, edited by Katherina von Ankum, 66–88. Berkeley: University of California Press, 1997.

Gordon, Eric. *The Urban Spectator: American Concept Cities from Kodak to Google*. Hanover, NH: Dartmouth University Press, 2010.

Greenberg, Miriam. *Branding New York: How a City in Crisis Was Sold to the World*. London: Routledge, 2008.

Greer, Scott. *Urban Renewal and American Cities: The Dilemma of Democratic Intervention*. Indianapolis, IN: Bobbs-Merrill, 1965.

Grierson, John. *Grierson on Documentary*. New York: Harcourt, Brace, 1947.

Gunning, Tom. "Invisible Cities, Visible Cinema: Illuminating Shadows in Late Film Noir." *Comparative Critical Studies* 6, no. 3 (November 2009): 319–32.

———. "The X-Ray and the Kaleidoscope." *Wide Angle* 19, no. 4 (Winter 1998): 25–61.

Haenni, Sabine. "Geographies of Desire: Postsocial Urban Space and Historical Revision in the Films of Martin Scorsese." *Journal of Film and Video* 62, no. 1–2 (Spring/Summer 2010): 67–85.

Haldemann, Anita, and Hannes Schüpbach. *Rudy Burckhardt: New York Moments*. Basel, Switzerland: Kunstmuseum, 2005.

Hanchett, Tom. "The Other Subsidized Housing: Federal Aid to Suburbanization, 1940s–1960s." In *From Tenements to Taylor Homes: In Search of Urban Housing Policy in Twentieth Century America*, edited by John Bauman, Roger Biles, and Kristin Szylvian, 163–79. College Park, PA: Penn State Press, 2000.

Harvey, David. *Rebel Cities: From the Right to the City to the Urban Revolution.* London, Verso, 2013.

Holmes, Nathan. *Welcome to Fear City: Crime Film, Crisis, and the Urban Imagination.* Albany: SUNY Press, 2018.

Horak, Jan-Christopher. "Seeing with One's Own Eyes: Helen Levitt's Films." *Yale Journal of Criticism* 8, no. 2 (1995): 69–85.

Immerso, Michael. *Coney Island: The People's Playground.* New Brunswick, NJ: Rutgers University Press, 2002.

Jacobs, Jane. *Death and Life of Great American Cities.* New York: Random House, 1961.

Jacobs, Steven, Anthony Kinik, and Eva Hielscher. *The City Symphony Phenomenon: Cinema, Art, and Urban Modernity Between the Wars.* London: Routledge, 2018.

Jackson, Kenneth. *The Crabgrass Frontier: The Suburbanization of the United States.* Oxford and New York: Oxford University Press, 1985.

Jameson, Fredric. *Archaeologies of the Future: The Desire Called Utopia and Other Science Fictions.* London: Verso, 2007.

———. "Cognitive Mapping." In *Marxism and the Interpretation of Culture*, edited by Cary Nelson and Lawrence Grossberg, 347–60. Chicago: University of Illinois Press, 1988.

Johnson, Albert. "The Negro in American Films: Some Recent Works." *Film Quarterly* 18, no. 4 (Summer 1965): 14–30.

Joo, Jeongsuk. "The Roots and Development of Suburbanization in America in the 1950s." *International Area Review* 12, no. 1 (2009): 65–79.

Joosse, Angela. "The Irrepressible Rush of Marie Menken's *Go! Go! Go!*" *Cine-Action* 93 (June 2013): 23–28.

Kanigel, Robert. *Eyes on the Street: The Life of Jane Jacobs.* New York: Knopf, 2016.

Kinik, Anthony. "Steiner and Van Dyke's *The City.*" In *The City Symphony Phenomenon*, edited by Steven Jacobs, Anthony Kinik, and Eva Hielscher, 197–210. London: Routledge, 2018.

Kofman, Eleonore, and Elizabeth Lebas. Introduction to *Writings on Cities* by Henri Lefebvre, 3–62. Translated by Eleonore Kofman and Elizabeth Lebas. London: Blackwell, 1996.

Koolhaas, Rem. *Delirious New York: A Retrospective Manifesto for Manhattan.* New York: Monicelli Press, 1994.

Korstad, Robert, and Nelson Lichtenstein. "Opportunities Found and Lost: Labor, Radicals, and the Early Civil Rights Movement." *Journal of American History* 75, no. 3 (December 1988): 786–811.

Kozloff, Max. *New York: Capital of Photography.* New Haven, CT: Yale University Press, 2003.

Kozloff, Sarah. "Humanizing the Voice of God: Narration in *The Naked City.*" *Cinema Journal* 23, no. 4 (Summer 1984): 41–53.

Kracauer, Siegfried. *From Caligari to Hitler: A Psychological History of the German Film.* Princeton, NJ: Princeton University Press, 1974, 5th printing.

———. *Theory of Film: The Redemption of Physical Reality*. Princeton, NJ: Princeton University Press, 1997, 1st paperback ed.

Lackey, Eric. "The Films of Lionel Rogosin, Volume 1," *Moving Image* 15, no. 1 (Spring 2018): 128–30.

Lefebvre, Henri. *Everyday Life in the Modern World*. Translated by Phillip Wander. New Brunswick, NJ: Transaction Publishers, 1984.

———. *Rhythmanalysis: Space, Time, and Everyday Life*. 2nd ed. Translated by Stuart Eldon and Gerald Moore. London, Bloomsbury, 2015.

———. *Right to the City*. In *Writings on Cities*, edited and translated by Eleonore Kofman and Elizabeth Lebas, 63–185. London: Blackwell, 1996.

———. *The Production of Space*. Translated by Donald Nicholson-Smith. London: Blackwell, 1991.

Levitas, Ruth. *The Concept of Utopia*. Oxford: Peter Lang Oxford, 2011.

———. *Utopia as Method: The Imaginary Reconstitution of Society*. London: Palgrave, 2013.

Lewis, Theophilus. "Harlem Sketchbook: Negro Garden Cities." *New York Amsterdam News*, October 25, 1933.

Lopatin, Judy. "Retrospective on Weegee." *Mississippi Review* 8, no. 1 (Winter 1979): 63–78.

Kevin Lynch. *The Image of the City*. Cambridge, MA: MIT Press, 1960.

MacDonald, Scott. *Cinema 16: Documents Toward a History of the Film Society*. Philadelphia: Temple University Press, 2002.

———. "City as Motion Picture." *Wide Angle* 19, no. 4 (Winter 1997): 109–28.

———. *The Garden in the Machine: A Field Guide to Independent Films about Place*. Berkeley: University of California Press, 2001.

Marcus, Laura. "A Hymn to Movement: The City Symphony of the 1920s and 1930." *Modernist Cultures* 5, no. 1 (2010): 30–46.

Marin, Louis. "Frontiers of Utopia: Past and Present." *Critical Inquiry* 19, no. 3 (Spring 1993): 397–420.

———. *Utopics: The Semiological Play of Textual Spaces*. Translated by Robert Vollrath. New York: Humanity Books, 1st English ed., 1984.

Masilela, Ntongela. "Lionel Rogosin: Making Reality Exciting and Beautiful." *Jump Cut* 36 (May 1991): 61–65.

Massood, Paula. *Making a Promised Land: Harlem in Twentieth-Century Photography and Film*. New Brunswick, NJ: Rutgers University Press, 2013.

Martin, Reinhold. "Fundamental #13." *Places Journal* (May 2014). DOI: https://doi.org/10.22269/140512.

Medhurst, Martin, and Thomas Benson. "*The City*: The Rhetoric of Rhythm." *Communication Monographs* 48, no. 1 (March 1981): 54–72.

Mekas, Jonas. "Notes on a New American Cinema." *Film Culture* 24 (Spring 1962): 6–16.

Metzger, John. "Planned Abandonment: The Neighborhood Life-Cycle Theory and Planned Urban Policy." *Housing Policy Debate* 11, no. 1 (2000): 7–40.

Miller, Warren. *The Cool World*. New York: Little, Brown, 1959.

Millington, Gareth. *Race, Culture, and the Right to the City*. London: Palgrave, 2011.

Momchedjikova, Blagovasta. "My Heart's in the Small Lands: Touring the Miniature City in the Museum." *Tourist Studies* 2, no. 3 (2002): 267–81.

Morshed, Adnan. "The Aesthetics of Ascension in Norman Bel Geddes's Futurama." *Journal of the Society of Architectural Historians* 63, no. 1 (March 2004): 74–99.

Mumford, Lewis. *The Culture of Cities*. New York: Broni & Liverlight, 1938.

———. *The Golden Day*. New York: Broni & Liverlight, 1933.

———. "The Skyline in Flushing: Genuine Bootleg." *New Yorker*, July 1939.

———. *The Story of Utopias*. New York: Broni & Liverlight, 1922.

Musser, Charles, and Joshua Glick. "Cinema by the Seashore." In *Coney Island: Visions of an American Dreamland*, edited by Susan Talbott and Robin Frank, 203–69. Hartford, CT: Wadsworth Museum of Art and Yale University, 2015.

New York World's Fair 1939–1940 Incorporated Records. MssCol 2233. Manuscripts and Archives Division, New York Public Library.

New York World's Fair 1964–65 Corporation Records. MssCol 2234. Manuscripts and Archives Division, New York Public Library.

Nilsen, Sarah. *Projecting America, 1958: Film and Cultural Diplomacy at the Brussels World's Fair*. Jefferson, NC: MacFarland, 2011.

Nin, Anaïs. *The Diary of Anaïs Nin. Vol 5, 1947–1955*. New York: Harcourt & Brace, 1974.

Norden, Martin. "The Use of Sound in Francis Thompson's *N.Y., N.Y.*" *Millennium Film Journal* 10–11 (Winter 1981–Spring 1982): 219–22.

"Of Local Origin." *New York Times*, March 11, 1948.

"Only Elbow Room on Coney Island Boardwalk Yesterday." *New York Times*, March 19, 1945.

Orvell, Miles. "Weegee's Voyeurism and the Mastery of Urban Disorder." *American Art* 6, no. 1 (Winter 1992): 18–41.

Parke, Richard. "Old El Link Ends Its 72-Year Uproar." *New York Times*, December 23, 1950.

Parson, David. "Organized Labor and the Housing Question: Public Housing, Suburbanization, and Urban Renewal." *Environment and Planning D* 1 (1984): 75–86.

Pavsek, Christopher. *The Utopia of Film: Cinema and Its Futures in Godard, Kluge, and Tahimik*. New York: Columbia University Press, 2013.

Penz, François and Andong Lu. "What Is Urban Cinematics?" In *Urban Cinematics: Understanding Urban Phenomena through the Moving Image*, edited by François Penz and Andong Lu, 7–20. Bristol, UK: Intellect, 2011.

Performing Arts Research Collections—Theatre, T-LC, T-Pho-B, T-CLP, New York Public Library for the Performing Arts.

Perkins, Kristin. "Roosevelt and Rexford: Resettlement and Its Results." *Berkeley Planning Journal* 20, no. 1 (2007): 25–42.

Perlmutter, Emanuel. "Steeplechase Park Welcomes Heat and Added Throngs." *New York Times*, July 29, 1963.

Perman, Cindy. *New York Curiosities: Quirky Characters, Roadside Oddities, and Other Offbeat Stuff.* New York: Globe Pequot Press, 2013.

Phillips, Wayne. "3 Slum Projects Delayed by City." *New York Times*, October 26, 1959.

Plosky, Eric. *The Rise and Fall of Penn Station: Changing Attitudes toward Historic Preservation in New York City.* Unpublished master's thesis. Cambridge, MA: MIT, 2000.

Piotrovski, Adrian. "Toward a Theory of Cine-Genres." In *Russian Formalist Film Theory*, edited by Herbert Eagle, 131–46. Ann Arbor: University of Michigan Press, 1981.

"Polyglot Wake to Be Held for El." *New York Times*, July 24, 1955.

Pritchett, Wendell. "The Public Menace of Blight: Urban Renewal and the Private Uses of Eminent Domain." *Yale Law & Policy Review* 21, no. 1 (Winter 2003): 1–52.

Rabinovitz, Lauren. *Points of Resistance: Women, Power, and Politics in the New York Avant-Garde (1943–71).* 2nd ed. Urbana: University of Illinois Press, 2003.

"Rally So Urban Renewal Is Not Negro Removal." *New York Amsterdam News*, June 23, 1962.

Rivero, Juan. "Saving Coney Island: The Constructive of Heritage Value." *Environment and Planning A: Economy and Space* 49, no. 1 (2017): 174–96.

Robbins, William. "Assessments Stir Anger on 3rd Ave." *New York Times*, July 13, 1966.

Sabat, Magdalena. "Panorama: Robert Moses' Modern City and the New York World's Fairs." In *Meet Me at the Fair: A World's Fair Reader*, edited by Lauren Hollengreen, Celia Pearce, Rebecca Rouse, and Bobby Schweizer, 281–88. New York: ETC Press, 2014.

Samuel, Lawrence. *The End of the Innocence: The 1964–65 World's Fair.* Syracuse, NY: Syracuse University Press, 2007.

Sanders, James. *Celluloid Skyline: New York and the Movies.* New York: Knopf, 2003.

Schumach, Murray. "Quill, Pickets, and Profit Motive Disturb Third Avenue El Wake." *New York Times*, March 28, 1952.

Selz, Thalia. "Lions on the Lido." *Quarterly Review of Film and Television* 8, no. 3 (1954): 243–53.

Senior, Jennifer. "The Independent Republic of New York." *New York Magazine*, August 2004.

Shiel, Mark. "A Nostalgia for Modernity: New York, Los Angeles, and the American Cinema of the 1970s." In *Screening the City*, edited by Mark Shiel and Tony Fitzmaurice, 160–79. London: Verso, 2003.

Shirley Clarke Papers 1936–83. US MSS 145AN, 3M37. Wisconsin Center for Film and Theater Research, University of Wisconsin, Madison.

Smith, Neil. *The New Urban Frontier: Gentrification and the Revanchist City.* London and New York: Routledge, 1996.

Stein, Erica. "Abstract Space, Microcosmic Narrative, and the Disavowal of Modernity in *Berlin: Symphony of a Great City*." *Journal of Film and Video* 65, no. 4 (Winter 2013): 3–16.

Stewart, Susan. *On Longing: Narratives of the Miniature, the Gigantic, the Souvenir, the Collection*. Durham, NC: Duke University Press, 1992.

Strathausen, Carsten. "Uncanny Spaces: The City in Ruttmann and Vertov." In *Screening the City*, edited by Mark Shiel and Tony Fitzmaurice, 15–40. London: Verso, 2003.

Streater, George. "Growing Burdens Harlem Hospital." *New York Times*, March 9, 1949.

Streeter, Edward. "In Search of the Third Avenue El." *New York Times*, December 21, 1966.

Suárez Sánchez, Juan Antonio. *Bike Boys, Drag Queens, and Superstars: Avant-Garde, Mass Culture, and Gay Identities in the 1960s Underground Cinema*. Bloomington: Indiana University Press, 1996.

Teaford, Jon. "Urban Renewal and Its Aftermath." *Housing Policy Debate* 11, no. 2 (2000): 443–65.

Thompson, Howard. " 'N.Y.' Top 16mm Entry." *New York Times*, March 30, 1958.

Tschumi, Bernard. *Architecture and Disjunction*. Cambridge, MA: MIT Press, 1996.

Ulricchio, William. *Ruttmann's* Berlin *and the City Film to 1930*. Unpublished dissertation, New York: New York University, 1982.

———. "The City Viewed: The Films of Leyda, Browning, and Weinberg. In *Lovers of Cinema: The First American Avant-Garde, 1919–45*, edited by Jan-Christopher Horak, 287–314. Madison: University of Wisconsin Press, 1995.

Von Hoffman, Alexander. "Housing and Planning: A Century of Social Reform and Social Power." *Journal of the American Planning Association* 75, no. 2 (2009): 231–44.

"Wagner Supporting Negroes over Clancy's Stern Protests." *New York Amsterdam News*, September 1, 1962.

Waqar, Daniel. "The End of the Road: The State of Urban Elevated Expressways in the United States." *Brookings Mountain West Publications* (2016).

Weinstein, Raymond. "Succession and Renewal in Urban Neighborhoods: The Case of Coney Island." *Sociation Today* 5, no. 2 (2007).

Weishmann, Helmut. "The City in Twilight: Charting the Genre of the City-Film 1900–1930." In *Cinema and Architecture: Méliès, Mallet-Stevens, Multimedia*, edited by François Penz and Maureen Thomas, 8–27. London: BFI, 1997.

Weiss, John. "Protecting Buildings from Demolition by Neglect: New York City's Experience." *Widener Law Review* 18, no. 2 (2012): 309–22.

Whalberg, Malin. *Documentary Time: Film and Phenomenology*. Minneapolis: University of Minnesota Press, 2008.

White, E. B. "Here Is New York." In *The Essays of E. B. White*, 148–70. New York: Harper Perennial, 1999.

———. "The World of Tomorrow." In *The Essays of E. B. White*, 139–47. New York: Harper Perennial, 1999.

Williams, Tony. "A Fantasy Straight Out of Brooklyn: From *The Gentle People* to *Out of the Fog*." In *The Brooklyn Film*, edited by John Manbeck and Robert Singer, 33–50. London: MacFarland, 2003.

Willinsky, Barbara. *Sure Seaters: The Emergence of Art House Cinema*. Minneapolis: University of Minnesota Press, 2001.

Winsten, Archer. "*The City* Opens Saturday at the World's Fair." *New York Post*, May 23, 1939.

Wojcik, Pamela Robertson. *Fantasies of Neglect: Imagining the Urban Child in American Film and Fiction*. New Brunswick, NJ: Rutgers University Press, 2016.

———. *The Apartment Plot: Urban Living in American Film and Popular Culture, 1945–75*. Durham, NC: Duke University Press, 2010.

Wojtowicz, Robert. *Lewis Mumford and American Modernism: Eutopian Theories for Architecture and Urban Planning*. London: Cambridge University Press, 1998.

Wyley, Elvin, Kathe Newman, Alex Schafran, and Elizabeth Lee. "Displacing New York." *Environment and Planning A*, 42 (2010): 2602–23.

Young, Iris Marion. "City Life and Difference." In *Metropolis: Center and Symbol of Our Times*, edited by Philip Kasinitz, 250–79. New York: New York University Press, 1995.

———. *Inclusion and Democracy*. Oxford and New York: Oxford University Press, 2002.

Zhang, Ling. "Rhythmic Movement, Metaphoric Sound, and Transcultural Transmediality: Liu Na'ou and *The Man Who Has a Camera* (1933)." In *Kaleidoscopic Histories: Early Film Culture in Hong Kong, Taiwan, and Republican China*, edited by Emilie Yueh-yu Yeh, 277–301. Ann Arbor: University of Michigan Press, 2018.

Zipp, Samuel. *Manhattan Projects: The Rise and Fall of Urban Renewal in New York*. Oxford and New York: Oxford University Press, 2010.

Zipp, Samuel, and Michael Carriere. "Thinking through Urban Renewal." *Journal of Urban History* 39, no. 3 (2012): 359–65.

Zukin, Sharon, Robert Baskerville, Miriam Greenberg, Courtney Guthreau, Jean Halley, Mark Halling, Kristin Lawler, Ron Nerio, Rebecca Stack, Alex Vitalie, and Betsy Wissinger. "From Coney Island to Las Vegas in the Urban Imaginary." *Urban Affairs Review* 30, no. 5 (1998): 627–54.

Zukin, Sharon. *Naked City: The Death and Life of Authentic Urban Places*. Oxford and New York: Oxford University Press, 2009.

Index

abyss, 200, 207–12, 225
advocacy planning, 153–57, 159–63,
    168–71, 178, 190, 191–92, 235
aerial photography, 36, 39–40, 43, 53,
    66–67, 83–84, 90, 132
Agee, James, 113–14, 123, 124, 129,
    130
Alexander, William, 57
Alifragkis, Stavros, 18
Alley, The, 75
American Council to Improve our
    Neighborhoods, 115
Angerame, Dominic, 17
antislum clearance activism, 152,
    158–61
anti-urban renewal activism, 152,
    158–61
arrhythmia, 5, 97, 120, 125, 147–48
Ashley, Ray, 114
Auster, Paul, 233–34
Avedon, Richard, 228

Baillie, Bruce, 17
Baldwin, James, 193, 214–15, 228–
    29
Ballon, Hilary, 27
Barnes, Howard, 44
Barron, Louis and Bebe, 184
Barthes, Roland, 235
Bauer, Catherine, 42, 118
"being together with strangers," 110

Bel Geddes, Norman, 39, 40, 81. See
    also *Futurama*
belonging, and social and spatial
    marginalization, 113–14
Bendiner, Elmer, 111, 137
Benjamin, Walter, 101
Berlin: Symphony of a Great City, 6,
    14–15, 23–24, 47, 95, 101
Berman v. Parker (1954), 118–19
Bleecker Street Cinema, 151–52
blight, 117–21
    and *On the Bowery*, 136–43
    and *Under Brooklyn Bridge*, 131–
    36
    and *Little Fugitive*, 143–50
    and *In the Street*, 121–31
Blue in the Face, 233–34
bodies, in *Weegee's New York*, 104–8
Bonanos, Christopher, 108
borders, in *The Cool World*, 225–29
Bowery, 119, 136–43. See also *On the
    Bowery*
Bowery Men, The, 137
Brakhage, Stan, 151, 171, 249n50
Bridges-Go-Round, 16, 155, 183–86,
    257n73
Bronx Morning, A, 114
Brooklyn Bridge, 1–2, 131. See also
    Under Brooklyn Bridge
Bruno, Giuliana, 175
Brussels Loops, 180–85

Brussels World Exposition (1958),
180, 181
Burckhardt, Rudy, *Under Brooklyn
Bridge*, 16, 114, 117, 131–36, 143,
150, 151, 188, 247n78, 252n51

Cao Fei, 17, 20
capital and capitalism
and African Americans' lived
experience in *The Cool World*, 199
in Clarke films, 180
and destruction of Penn Station,
156
New York 1964–1965 World's Fair
as dominated by, 194–95
and production of space, 49, 50, 79
public transportation and rescaling
of, 169, 170
and reduction of New York to
image, 235
and right to the city, 12, 44, 50, 79,
155, 157, 235
and shaping of New York, 4
and slum clearance, 116, 120, 144
and spectacle, 161–62
and suburbanization, 9–10, 26
and Times Square, 163–64
and urban development, 5, 6, 26, 80
Carnovsky, Morris, 43, 54, 56, 60, 65,
66, 67–68
Carroll, Noël, 209
Cartier-Bresson, Henri, 113
Castro, Teresa, 84
Castro Street, 17
center
Lefebvre on, 157, 254n7
neighborhood rhythms determined
by, 176
renovation of, in Clarke's
commissioned films, 179–90
as series of surfaces in *N.Y., N.Y.*,
175
as spectacle, 177
center, right to, 157–63

center, symphonies of the. *See*
symphonies of the center
Central Park, 181–82
Chronopoulos, Themis, 163–64
Cinema 16, 11, 20, 93–95, 111, 150,
151–52, 171–72, 226, 249nn50–
51
Cinema II, 199
cinematic technologies, and regional
planning at World's Fair, 35–45
cinéma vérité, 187
Circle Line, 180, 185–86
Citizen Jane, 234–35
citizen voices, in *The City*, 64–65
City, The, 34, 42–45
juxtaposition of *Weegee's New York*
and, 94–95
New York and incongruous present
in, 61–71
as progenitor of New York city
symphonies, 71–72
reception of, 45–53
rhythmanalysis of, 44, 52, 53–61
viewer addressed in, 246n66
city symphonies, 2–6, 10–12,
13–26. *See also* New York city
symphonies; symphonies of
the center; symphonies of the
margins
appropriated by 1964–1965 World's
Fair, 200–207
Cinema 16 and, 94–95
contrastive schema in programming,
95
criticism of, 23–24
defined, 18–19
films depicting marginal areas as, 114
first cycle of, 14–15
heterogeneous nature of, 19–20
importance of, to Cinema 16, 11, 20
independent and genre films'
relationship to, 20–23
Naked City's borrowings from,
91–92

political function and reception
context of, 23
postwar, 71–72
potential and limitations of, 24–25
second cycle of, 15–17
techniques used in, 74–75
transformation of, cycle, 200
twenty-four-hour structure of, 52
utopian function of, 237
Weegee's New York and reinvention
of, 92–109
civil rights, 226–27
Clarke, Shirley, 16, 22, 93, 163, 179–
90, 191, 198, 226. See also *Cool
World, The* (1963–1964 film)
cognitive mapping, 159–60, 164, 170–
71, 180, 185, 191, 192, 235
colonial era, depicted in *The City*,
54–56
Columbia University, 142
Commissioners' Plan of 1811, 163
Committee on Slum Clearance, 115
commuting, in *Weegee's New York*,
97–98, 99
conceptual space, 50–52, 78, 87, 91
Coney Island
in *The Cool World*, 221–23
in *Little Fugitive*, 143–50
in *Weegee's New York*, 102–9
*Coney Island, 22nd of July 1940, 4
o'clock in the afternoon*, 102
Cool World, The (1963–1964 film), 22,
26, 197–200
borders in, 225–29
and new rhythmanalysis, 212–25
and nostalgia for modernity, 208–10
Cool World, The (Miller), 197–98, 215
Copeland, Aaron, 57, 65
CORE protests, 193, 197, 207,
258n12
crime film, 22, 198, 200, 219–20
Crowd, The, 104
Crowther, Bosley, 20, 138
Culture of Cities, The, 45

Dassin, Jules, *Naked City*, 22–23, 72–
78, 79, 85–92, 97, 109, 202
Debord, Guy, 68, 162, 182, 255n22
De Brug (*The Bridge*), 114
de Certeau, Michel, 7, 49–50
decisive moments, 113, 114
deindustrialization, 9, 30, 208, 221–22
Deleuze, Gilles, 11, 210–11
Demme, Jonathan, 7
Democracity, 34, 35–36, 37–40, 49
detective fiction, 87, 92. See also
Naked City; *Weegee's New York*
Dimendberg, Edward, 16, 84, 102
Donald, James, 24, 92
dressage, 120–21, 128, 135, 141,
143–50, 228
Dreyfus, Henry, *Democracity*, 34,
35–36, 37–40, 49
Dümpelmann, Sonja, 39, 73–74

East Harlem, 121–31
East Side, West Side, 87
electricity, 14, 104
El train, 168–74
Empire State Building, 99–100
encounter, and right to the city, 12–13
Engel, Morris, 114, 122, 150–51
eurhythmia, 5, 10, 61, 67, 70, 99
eutopias, 36–37, 44–46, 49, 51, 54,
67, 70–71
exchange value, 12, 144, 147, 157
experiential space, 50–52, 78, 87, 91,
95–96

false narration, 210–11, 215, 220
Farmer, James, 197, 198, 226–27
Federal Housing Act (1949), 15,
79–80
Fellig, Arthur. See *Weegee's New York*
Ferrara, Abel, 233
festive play
in *In the Street*, 123–24, 125–27,
128–30
in symphonies of the margins, 121

Field, Edward, 205
Film-Maker's Cooperative, 93
Filmmakers' Distribution Co-op, 93
film noir, 74, 89, 91–92. See also
    Naked City
Forrell, Gene, 176, 179
Fort George, 176–77
Friedberg, Anne, 38–39
Fulton's Landing, 131–36
Futurama, 34, 35–36, 39–42, 49, 81
Futurama II, 193–94

gangster film, 22, 210, 220. See also
    Cool World, The (1963–1964 film)
Gans, Herbert, 116
garden cities, 35, 36–37, 42–45, 46,
    51
Gartenberg, Jon, 18, 21–22
gender difference and expression, 65,
    70, 108
genre films, city symphonies'
    relationship to, 20–23
Go! Go! Go!, 1–3, 16–17
Goodman, Paul, 78
Goodman, Percival, 78
Gordon, Eric, 161
Graf, Alexander, 24
Gray, Spalding, 7, 8
Greenbelt, Maryland, 43–44, 45–53,
    54, 60, 66–70
Greenwich Village, 93, 150, 151–52
Greer, Scott, 116
Grierson, John, 18, 23–24, 44, 46–49,
    60
Gunning, Tom, 89, 124, 130

Hammid, Alexander, 203
handshakes, 182
Harlem, 208–9, 210, 213–22, 224–25,
    227, 253n80. See also *Cool World,*
    The (1963–1964 film)
Harvey, David, 12
Haze and Fog, 17
Hellinger, Mark, 74, 75, 89

"Here Is New York" (White), 136–37
Hielscher, Eva, 16, 20
historic preservation, 156–57, 160,
    180
Holmes, Nathan, 22, 200
Horak, Jan-Christopher, 123, 124,
    128, 143, 251n35

Image of the City, The (Lynch), 159, 162
immobility, in *The Cool World*, 209–10
incompossible, 215–16, 223, 224
independent films, city symphonies'
    relationship to, 20–23
industrial era, transition to, depicted
    in *The City*, 56–60
In the Street, 113–14, 117, 121–31,
    143, 150, 151, 251n35
islanding, 7–9, 67
Ivens, Joris, 114

Jackson, Kenneth, 9, 27
Jacobs, Jane, 16, 20, 159, 160–61, 170,
    191–92, 231–32, 234, 255n15
Jacobs, Steve, 16, 20
Jameson, Fredric, 7, 8, 159, 235
Javits, Jacob, 8
Jazz of Lights, 155, 162, 163–68, 184,
    185
Johnson Wax Pavilion, 203, 207. See
    also *To Be Alive!*
Joosse, Angela, 155

Kaltenborn, H. V., 37–38
King of New York, 233
Kinik, Anthony, 16, 20, 203
Koelinga, Jan, 75
Kofman, Eleonore, 153
Kozloff, Max, 102
Kracauer, Siegfried, 18, 130–31, 140

labor
    in *The City*, 56, 69–70
    and commuting in *Weegee's New*
        York, 97–98

regional planning and exploitation of, 61
in *In the Street*, 127–28
late modernity, 16, 30–31
Lebas, Elizabeth, 153
Lefebvre, Henri
  on architecture and production of bodies, 153
  on center, 157, 254n7
  on dressage, 120
  on encounter and right to the city, 12–13
  on greenbelt towns, 45–46
  on New York city symphonies, 5
  on production of space, 50
  on regional planning, 35, 51
  on rhythmanalysis, 4, 6, 227–28, 260n57
  on right to city, 12–13, 237
  on ways of knowing, 66, 247n71
LeRoy, Mervyn, 87
Levitas, Ruth, 7, 25
Levitt, Helen, 113–14, 123–24, 143, 151, 182–83, 253n82. See also *In the Street*
  "N.Y.C. (Button to Secret Passage)," 124–25
light, in *Naked City* and *Weegee's New York*, 75–77
Lincoln Center, 231–32
Little Fugitive, 20, 21–22, 114, 117, 143–50, 151
Loeb, Janice, 113
Lu, Andong, 19
Lynch, Kevin, 159–61, 162, 170, 171

MacDonald, Scott, 18, 94, 107, 114, 135, 176, 249n59
Manhatta, 16
Manhattan Bridge, 131
Man Who Has a Camera, 75
Man with a Movie Camera, 24
Marcus, Laura, 14, 236
Margaret, 18

marginal areas, 113–17. See also symphonies of the margins
Marin, Louis, 7, 8, 24, 92, 128, 223, 228
Massood, Paula, 122, 123, 210, 215, 226
mediation, potential of city as, 237
Mekas, Jonas, 93, 144, 151, 249n50, 251n35
Melting Pot, 181–82
Menken, Marie, *Go! Go! Go!*, 1–3, 16–17
Mercaro, Teo, 184, 188, 190
Metropolitan Council on Housing, 158
Metropolitan Life Insurance, 80–81
Miller, Warren, *The Cool World*, 197–98, 215
miniature-gigantic, 78
  blight and, 119
  and narration of space in *Naked City*, 87–91
  and postwar planning policies, 79–85
  subverted in *Weegee's New York*, 96, 98–102, 110
mobile gaze, 36, 38–39
mobility. See also motion
  in *To Be Alive!*, 206
  in *The Cool World*, 209–10
  and urban redevelopment, 10
modernity, 16
  amusement parks as loci of, 104
  nostalgia for, 200, 207–12, 219, 224, 233–35
monumental spaces, in *The City*, 61–62, 66–67
Moondog, 164, 166–68
Morin, Edgar, 187
Morshed, Adnan, 40
Moses, Robert
  and Committee on Slum Clearance, 115–16
  grants Clarke access to filming locations, 181

Moses, Robert (*continued*)
    and late modern New York as
        nostalgic utopia, 234–35
    and 1964–1965 World's Fair, 194–95
    and Panorama of the City of New
        York, 200–201, 202–3
    redevelopment under, 26–27, 132,
        158, 160
    reputation of, 243n76
    and Stuyvesant Town, 80
Motherless Brooklyn, 234–35
motion. *See also* mobility
    in *To Be Alive!*, 206
    and connection of time and space,
        211
    success of city tied to, 207
Mumford, Lewis, 36, 41–44, 45, 78,
    81, 156, 245n37
Museum of Modern Art, 150, 189,
    232
mylar, used in *N.Y., N.Y.*, 177
"My Manhattan" (Mercaro), 190

Naked City, 22–23, 72–78, 79, 85–92,
    97, 109, 202
Na'ou, Liu, 75
national day, 28, 43, 46, 52–57, 61,
    63, 65–68, 71, 245n37
neorealism, 138, 139–40
New American Cinema, 11, 151–52,
    210, 226
New York City. See also *Naked City*;
    Weegee's New York
    de Certeau on, 49–50
    as reduced to image, 235–36
    urban planning in, 26–27
    urban renewal and visual culture in,
        79–85
    as utopian, 7–9
New York City Housing Authority
    (NYCHA), 119–20, 122
New York city symphonies, 11–13.
    See also *Naked City*; *Weegee's New
    York*

and alternative history of the urban,
    236
The City as progenitor of, 71–72
and cohabitation of public spaces
    and residential areas, 232
context of cycle of, 9, 11
The Cool World as end of, 227–28
criticism of, 23–24
cycle of 1939–1964 of, 3–4, 8–12
failures of, as utopia, 232–36
fate of, after *Skyscraper*, 191
and late modernity as period of
    stasis, 30–31
new ways of thinking about, 236
popularity of, 20
as produced by and against late
    modernity, 16
race and slum clearance in, 138–39
and rhythmanalysis, 4–6, 11–12,
    236, 237
treatment of race in, 25–26, 233
New York Photo League, 122–23,
    150–51
New York Public Library, 98–99, 219,
    231
    lion statues, 98–99
New York Times, 169–70
New York World's Fair (1939–1940),
    27
    and New York World's Fair of
        1964–1965, 193–94
    regional planning and cinematic
        technologies at, 35–45
    regional planning concepts
        influencing, 34
    White's experience at, 33–34
New York World's Fair (1964–1965),
    27, 193–207
Nin, Anaïs, 164, 166, 168, 185
noir, 74, 89, 91–92. See also *Naked City*
Norton, Edward, 234–35
nostalgia
    for modernity, 200, 207–12, 219,
        224, 233–35

and questioning of spatial relations
    in *The Cool World*, 216, 219
Nothing Personal photo essay, 228–29
N.Y., N.Y.: A Day in New York, 11,
    153–55, 156, 163, 174–79, 203–5

oeuvre, 13
O'Neill, Pat, 17
On the Bowery, 19, 21–22, 114, 117,
    136–43, 150, 151
Orkin, Ruth, 114

Panorama of the City of New York,
    200–203, 259n19
partition, 175
Paterson, 18
Pavsek, Christopher, 11–12, 232
Penn Station, 156–57, 205
Pennsylvania Railroad, 156
Penz, François, 18, 19
phatic, 139, 182
Pittsburgh, Pennsylvania, in *The City*,
    57–60
play
    spatial, 128
    in *In the Street*, 123–24, 125–27,
        128–30
    in symphonies of the margins, 121
polyrhythmia, 5, 172
poor neighborhoods. *See* marginal
    areas
possessive spectatorship, 161–63
postwar city symphonies, 71–72
postwar planning, 77, 78, 79–85
Practice of Everyday Life, The (de
    Certeau), 49–50
present
    in *The City*, 61–71
    in urban renewal, 85
preservation policies, 156–57, 160,
    180
Pritchett, Wendell, 118–19

Rabinovitz, Lauren, 11, 150, 226

race
    abyss linked to, in *The Cool World*,
        225
    and borders in *The Cool World*,
        225–28
    in *On the Bowery*, 138–39
    in Clarke's commissioned films,
        182–83
    and *Little Fugitive*, 149–50
    in New York city symphonies, 25–26
    and regional planning, 35
    in *Skyscraper*, 187–88
    and social upheaval in East Harlem,
        122
    in *In the Street*, 126–28
    and suburbanization, 197–98
    in symphonies of the margins,
        150–51
    in *Weegee's New York*, 103–4
racial difference
    in Greenbelt section of *The City*,
        67–68, 69–70
    in New York section of *The City*,
        65, 71
    in symphonies of the margins,
        150–51
racial oppression
    in *The Cool World*, 199
    and criminalization of people of
        color, 192
    regional planning as dependent on,
        61
Ranciere, Jacques, 175
Red Hook, 131–32
redlining policies, and creation of
    slums, 116
regional planning, 34–35
    aerial photography and, 36, 39–40,
        43, 53, 66–67, 84
    and cinematic technologies at
        World's Fair, 35–45
    and incongruous present in *The
        City*, 61–71
    opposition to, 158–60

regional planning *(continued)*
  and reception of *The City*, 45–53
  versus urban renewal, 82
  and utopian uses of rhythmanalysis
    in *The City*, 53–61
rhetoric, 139
rhythmanalysis
  in *To Be Alive!*, 205, 207
  of *The City*, 44, 52, 53–61
  city symphony as, 19
  in *The Cool World*, 200, 211, 212–25
  Lefebvre on, 4–6, 227–28, 260n57
  and New York city symphonies,
    11–12, 236, 237
  and nostalgia for modernity, 207
  overview of, 4–5
  of symphonies of the margins, 120,
    232
  and understanding city symphony, 6
  in *Weegee's New York*, 92, 111
  of *Wonder Ring*, 168–74
rhythm(s)
  in *The City*, 55–56, 61, 65, 68–69
  in city symphonies, 3, 6
  in *In the Street*, 125, 128
  in *Little Fugitive*, 146–47
  in *N.Y., N.Y.*, 176–78
  in *On the Bowery*, 137, 140
  slum clearance and, 121
  in symphonies of the center, 155–
    56, 157
  in symphonies of the margins, 120
  in *To Be Alive!*, 205
  in *Under Brooklyn Bridge*, 132–33
  in *Weegee's New York*, 95, 99, 100,
    106–7
  in *Wonder Ring*, 172
right to the city, 12–13, 22, 25, 44,
  50, 79, 155, 157, 200, 228, 235
Riis, Jacob, 58
Rogosin, Lionel, 19, 93, 114, 138,
  142, 151
Rouch, Jean, 187
Rustin, Bayard, 197, 198, 226–27

Ruttmann, Walter, *Berlin: Symphony of
  a Great City*, 6, 14–15, 23–24, 47,
  80, 95, 101

Samuel, Lawrence, 194
Sanders, James, 85
San Juan Hill, 231–32
Scorsese, Martin, 233
secret passage(s), 124–25, 130, 150–52
segregation, 25, 28, 60–61, 64, 80
Selz, Thalia, 144
sexuality, in *Weegee's New York*, 106–8
Shiel, Mark, 200
Shirley, Massachusetts, 54–55, 56–57,
  60
Singapore GaGa, 17
single-room occupancy (SRO)
  flophouses, 140–41, 142
skin, Lefebvre on rhythmanalysis and,
  227–28
Skyscraper, 11, 155, 186–91
Slaughterhouse District, 82–83
slums and slum clearance, 115–17
  blight and, 117–21
  and *On the Bowery*, 136–43
  and *Under Brooklyn Bridge*, 131–36
  and *Little Fugitive*, 143–50
  opposition to, 152, 158–61
  and *In the Street*, 121–31
  and urban crisis, 207
space
  conceptual, 50–52, 78, 87, 91
  erasure of, 51
  experiential, 50–52, 78, 87, 91,
    95–97
  irrational, in *The Cool World*, 220,
    222–25
  knowing, 66, 247n71
  and miniature-gigantic, 79
  Naked City and narration of, 85–92
  and narrative in *On the Bowery*,
    139–40
  in New York section of *The City*,
    61–62, 65–67, 70–71

production of, 50–53
in *In the Street*, 123–25
and urban renewal, 78
in *Weegee's New York*, 92, 95–96, 99, 109–10
in *Wonder Ring*, 171–74
spatial play, 128
spectacle, 161–66, 175, 177–79, 180, 185, 190, 192, 218, 255n22
Spengler, Oswald, 43
stasis, 199, 210–11, 212
Steiner, Ralph, 42
Stewart, Susan, 79
Story of Utopias, The, 45
Strathausen, Carsten, 24
Streeter, Edward, 170
Stuyvesant Town, 80–85
suburbanization, 9–10, 158–59, 197–98
suburbs. *See also* Greenbelt, Maryland
history as disbursed by, 68
importance of, to economic life, 195–96
and New York World's Fair of 1964–1965, 196–97
Swimming to Cambodia (Demme), 7
symphonies of the center, 153–63, 190–92. See also *Bridges-Go-Round*; *Go! Go! Go!*; *Jazz of Lights*; *N.Y., N.Y.: A Day in New York*; *Skyscraper*; *Wonder Ring*
symphonies of the margins, 114–15, 117–21, 150–52, 232. See also *Cool World, The* (1963–1964 film); *In the Street*; *Little Fugitive*; marginal areas; *On the Bowery*; *Under Brooklyn Bridge*

Tan Pin Pin, 2, 17
Taxi Driver, 233
Taylor, John, 48–49
Third Avenue El train, 168–74
Thompson, Francis, 153–54, 156, 174–79, 203. See also *N.Y., N.Y.: A Day in New York*

Thompson, Howard, 20, 174–75
time-image, 210–11
time-lapse
in *To Be Alive!*, 204
in *Go! Go! Go!*, 155
in *Weegee's New York*, 74, 99, 100–101
Times Square, 100–102, 163–68
Tishman Building, 186–90
To Be Alive!, 203–7, 259n23
Tschumi, Bernard, 172
Tugwell, Rexford, 60
Turtle Bay neighborhood, 82–83
turtles, 101, 249n65
twenty-four-hour structure, 43, 52, 71, 202
Tyrnauer, Matt, 234–35

"Uncanny City" tradition, 92
Under Brooklyn Bridge, 16, 114, 117, 131–36, 143, 150, 188
Unfinished Business exhibit, 181
United Nations campus, 77, 80–85
urban (re)development, 8–10
urban crisis
and borders in *The Cool World*, 225–29
and branding campaign built around city, 255n20
dawning of, 193–200
and new rhythmanalysis in *The Cool World*, 212–25
and nostalgia for modernity, 207–12
and World's Fair of 1964–1965's appropriation of city symphony aesthetics, 200–207
urban planning. *See also* postwar planning
films critiquing or condemning, 234–35
in *Naked City* and *Weegee's New York*, 74
in New York City, 26–27
postwar, 77, 78

urban planning *(continued)*
  slums and, 115–17, 130
  and urban crisis, 207
urban renewal, 77–78
  decline in popularity of, 109
  fall of, 191–92
  in Harlem, 214–15
  New York city symphonies and, 233
  opposition to, 152, 158–61
  and visual culture in New York,
    79–85
  in *Weegee's New York*, 93
urban space, dual nature of, 45–53
urban vocabulary, city symphonies'
  influence on, 17–18
utopia, 7–9, 25
  The Cool World as end of New
    York city symphonies as utopian
    critique, 227–28
  and Debord on spectacle, 255n22
  as diametrically opposed to
    advocacy planning, 161
  emptiness of, 191
  failures of New York city
    symphonies as, 232–36
  and federal redevelopment
    programs, 30
  liminality of, 63, 136, 139, 145, 175,
    212, 220–22
  and narrative of spaces, 92
  New York city symphonies and,
    11–12, 30
  and nostalgia for modernity, 233–35
  and symphonies of the margins, 150
  utopian function of city symphonies,
    237
utopian fiction, 24–25

Van Dyke, Willard, 42, 180, 181, 186,
    257n73

Vidor, King, 104
ville radieuse, 194
virtual gaze, 38–39
visual culture, and urban renewal
    in *Naked City* and *Weegee's New
      York*, 79–85
vocabulary, city symphonies' influence
    on urban, 17–18
Vogel, Amos, 94, 249n50. See also
    Weegee's New York
voiceover
    in *The City*, 43, 54, 56–60, 64–65,
      67
    in *The Cool World*, 217–18
    in *Naked City*, 74, 85, 90, 91
Von Hoffman, Alexander, 41

Wagner, Robert, 171, 195
Wall Street, 219–20
Water and Power, 17
Weegee's New York, 72–78, 109–11
    influence on *N.Y., N.Y.*, 174
    and reinvention of city symphony,
      92–109
    soundtrack of, 249n59
    urban renewal and visual culture in,
      79, 85
West Side Story, 87
White, E. B., 33–34, 40–41, 72, 83,
    136–37
Wise, Robert, 87
Wojcik, Pamela Robertson, 209–10
Wonder Ring, 155, 162–63, 168–74,
    184
World Beyond War, The, 48
Wright, Basil, 48

Young, Iris Marion, 110, 139, 182

Zipp, Samuel, 8, 77, 80

THE SUNY SERIES

HORIZONS of CINEMA

MURRAY POMERANCE | EDITOR

Also in the series

William Rothman, editor, *Cavell on Film*

J. David Slocum, editor, *Rebel Without a Cause*

Joe McElhaney, *The Death of Classical Cinema*

Kirsten Moana Thompson, *Apocalyptic Dread*

Frances Gateward, editor, *Seoul Searching*

Michael Atkinson, editor, *Exile Cinema*

Paul S. Moore, *Now Playing*

Robin L. Murray and Joseph K. Heumann, *Ecology and Popular Film*

William Rothman, editor, *Three Documentary Filmmakers*

Sean Griffin, editor, *Hetero*

Jean-Michel Frodon, editor, *Cinema and the Shoah*

Carolyn Jess-Cooke and Constantine Verevis, editors, *Second Takes*

Matthew Solomon, editor, *Fantastic Voyages of the Cinematic Imagination*

R. Barton Palmer and David Boyd, editors, *Hitchcock at the Source*

William Rothman, *Hitchcock: The Murderous Gaze*, Second Edition

Joanna Hearne, *Native Recognition*

Marc Raymond, *Hollywood's New Yorker*

Steven Rybin and Will Scheibel, editors, *Lonely Places, Dangerous Ground*

Claire Perkins and Constantine Verevis, editors, *B Is for Bad Cinema*

Dominic Lennard, *Bad Seeds and Holy Terrors*

Rosie Thomas, *Bombay before Bollywood*

Scott M. MacDonald, *Binghamton Babylon*

Sudhir Mahadevan, *A Very Old Machine*

David Greven, *Ghost Faces*

James S. Williams, *Encounters with Godard*

William H. Epstein and R. Barton Palmer, editors, *Invented Lives, Imagined Communities*

Lee Carruthers, *Doing Time*

Rebecca Meyers, William Rothman, and Charles Warren, editors, *Looking with Robert Gardner*

Belinda Smaill, *Regarding Life*

Douglas McFarland and Wesley King, editors, *John Huston as Adaptor*

R. Barton Palmer, Homer B. Pettey, and Steven M. Sanders, editors, *Hitchcock's Moral Gaze*

Nenad Jovanovic, *Brechtian Cinemas*

Will Scheibel, *American Stranger*

Amy Rust, *Passionate Detachments*

Steven Rybin, *Gestures of Love*

Seth Friedman, *Are You Watching Closely?*

Roger Rawlings, *Ripping England!*

Michael DeAngelis, *Rx Hollywood*

Ricardo E. Zulueta, *Queer Art Camp Superstar*

John Caruana and Mark Cauchi, editors, *Immanent Frames*

Nathan Holmes, *Welcome to Fear City*

Homer B. Pettey and R. Barton Palmer, editors, *Rule, Britannia!*

Milo Sweedler, *Rumble and Crash*

Ken Windrum, *From El Dorado to Lost Horizons*

Matthew Lau, *Sounds Like Helicopters*

Dominic Lennard, *Brute Force*

William Rothman, *Tuitions and Intuitions*

Michael Hammond, *The Great War in Hollywood Memory, 1918–1939*

Burke Hilsabeck, *The Slapstick Camera*

Niels Niessen, *Miraculous Realism*

Alex Clayton, *Funny How?*

Bill Krohn, *Letters from Hollywood*

Alexia Kannas, *Giallo!*

Homer B. Pettey, editor, *Mind Reeling*

Matthew Leggatt, editor, *Was It Yesterday?*

Merrill Schleier, editor, *Race and the Suburbs in American Film*

Neil Badmington, *Perpetual Movement*

George Toles, *Curtains of Light*

CPSIA information can be obtained
at www.ICGtesting.com
Printed in the USA
LVHW101736120123
736947LV00003B/308